— THE —
McGRAW-HILL
36-Hour Course

PROJECT
MANAGEMENT

SECOND EDITION

Other books in The McGraw-Hill 36-Hour Course series:

THE ——

McGRAW-HILL
36-Hour Course

PROJECT
MANAGEMENT

SECOND EDITION

Helen S. Cooke and Karen Tate

New York Chicago San Francisco Lisbon London Madrid Mexico City
Milan New Delhi San Juan Seoul Singapore Sydney Toronto

To Richard and Andy, the wind beneath our wings

4 5 6 7 8 9 10 11 12 13 14 15   QFR/QFR   1 9 8 7 6 5 4

ISBN   978-0-07-173827-9
MHID   0-07-173827-4

This publication is designed to provide accurate and authoritative information in regard to the subject matter covered. It is sold with the understanding that neither the author nor the publisher is engaged in rendering legal, accounting, securities trading, or other professional services. If legal advice or other expert assistance is required, the services of a competent professional person should be sought.
          —*From a Declaration of Principles Jointly Adopted by a Committee of the*
          American Bar Association and a Committee of Publishers and Associations

Library of Congress Cataloging-in-Publication Data

Cooke, Helen, 1946–
        The McGraw-Hill 36-hour course : project management / by Helen S. Cooke,
    Karen Tate. — 2nd ed.
            p.   cm.
        Rev. ed. of: The McGraw-Hill 36-hour project management course. 2005.
        Includes bibliographical references and index.
        ISBN: 0-07-173827-4 (alk. paper)
        1. Project management.   I. Tate, Karen.   II. Coke, Helen, 1946–   McGraw-
    Hill 36-hour project management course.   III. Title.   IV. Title: Project
    management.

        HD69.P75C663   2011
        658.4'04—dc22   2010033506

McGraw-Hill books are available at special quantity discounts to use as premiums and sales promotions or for use in corporate training programs. To contact a representative, please e-mail us at bulksales@mcgraw-hill.com.

This book is printed on acid-free paper.

CONTENTS

1

PROJECT MANAGEMENT

OVERVIEW AND GOALS

This chapter provides a general overview of the broad field of project management and its role in the work world. It describes how an age-old process became formalized in the late twentieth century, shows how professional project management evolved to where it is today, and distinguishes thousands of people in the occupation of project management from the new project management professional. It explains why organizations undertake projects, clarifies terms, and provides examples of different types of projects. Its goal is to distinguish project management from other functions.

WHAT IS PROJECT MANAGEMENT?

Many sectors of the economy are identifying *project management* as a new key business process. As project management gains recognition as a distinct way of managing change, differences exist in how it is applied and understood across industries, corporations, governments, and academia. The term *project management* is used freely throughout profit-oriented companies, not-for-profit organizations, and government agencies, but people do not always mean the same thing by it. Some organizations use the term *project management* to describe the task of managing work. Others use it to define the field of work focused on the delivery of project results. Still others mean the profession of project management, encompassing not only project managers but also other project-related specialists. Some use the term to describe traditional management practices or technical management practices, simply transferring those practices from organizational operations to projects. Because this field is emerging into the mainstream, definitions abound. During the course of describing project management practices and concepts, this book will help to distinguish what is unique to this field from what it has in common with general management and the management elements of technical disciplines. It also will identify many of the misleading assumptions about project management that obscure the value of this new field of professionalism.

Project Management Evolves

Projects have been managed since prehistory. Strategies for project management can be found in records of the Chinese warlords (Sun Tzu), Machiavelli, and other, more obscure writers (see Chapter 2). Large projects such as the 1893 World's Fair in Chicago clearly used it. As projects became more complex and more difficult to execute in a context where profit, time lines, and resource consumption competed with defined objectives, twentieth-century managers began to codify the practices needed to plan, execute, and control projects. The government led the way in developing the techniques and practices of project management, primarily in the military.

> It is popular to ask, "Why can't they run government the way I run my business?" In the case of project management, however, business and other organizations learned from government, not the other way around. A lion's share of the credit for the development of the techniques and practices of project management belongs to the military, which faced a series of major tasks that simply were not achievable by traditional organizations operating in traditional ways. The United States Navy's Polaris program, NASA's Apollo space program, and more recently, the space shuttle and the strategic defense initiative ("star wars") programs are instances of the application of these specially developed management approaches to extraordinarily complex projects. Following such examples, nonmilitary government sectors, private industry, public service agencies, and volunteer organizations have all used project management to increase their effectiveness.[1]

Thus, for modern-day project management, the Polaris submarine program and later the Apollo space program launched the systematic application of knowledge, tools, methods, and techniques to the planning, execution, and completion of projects. While these techniques have proliferated broadly among other government programs since the 1960s and 1970s and through research and demonstration programs among other branches of government as well as their contractor organizations, the construction industry was a key beneficiary of these improvements. Large, complex projects, such as the construction of Hoover Dam and the carving of the faces of American presidents into stone at Mount Rushmore in South Dakota, applied these improvements. Since then, project management methods have been implemented in information management and movement, pharmaceuticals, information systems, the entertainment and service sectors, and a variety of global projects. Project management's value continues to grow.

For a clearer idea of what the term *project management* means, compare it with the term *medicine* in a health context. Each term can have many meanings. The all-inclusive view of project management—just as in medicine—will address the practice, as well as the role, the field, the occupation, and the profession. The variations of meaning will also expand depending on which view is taken. Project management in a professional context means applying knowledge, skills, processes, methods, tools, and techniques to get desired results.

Like the word *medicine*, the term *project management* can take on a broad definition or a narrow one. A doctor practices *medicine* (broad). A patient takes a dose of *medicine* (narrow). Athletic discipline is said to be good *medicine*—an ambiguous definition that combines both. The term *medicine* takes on a different meaning depending on the context in which it is used, yet the term is always associated with certain values and goals: medicine supports health; it does not compromise it. Medicine therefore implies a commitment of individuals to the goal of preserving or restoring health. Similarly, although one definition of *project management* may not fit all uses, there are common elements inherent in all meanings ascribed to it. These common elements bind together the individuals and the practices within project management. Together they create a common understanding of what project management is and help us come to grips with why project management is getting such visibility today and why we need to know about it. This book will define a context for project management and put its various roles and uses in perspective for both individuals and organizations.

Definition of the Project Management Profession

A *project* is a temporary endeavor undertaken to create a unique product, service, or result. Because projects create something for the first time, there is a fundamental uniqueness to project work that makes it different from the operational work of the organization: the uncertainties of a project, its lack of existing procedures, and the need to make trade-offs among variables necessitate more dedicated planning and a unique body of knowledge, skill, and capability.

In the late 1960s, several project management professionals from the construction and pharmaceutical industries believed that project management had moved beyond being simply a job or an occupation.[2] Together they undertook the task of defining *professional* project management and created a professional association to put the elements of professional support in place. They called it the Project Management Institute (PMI). They expected PMI to have as many as 1,000 members someday, and they ran initial operations out of the dining room of one of the members in Drexel Hill, Pennsylvania. These visionary leaders considered project management to be an international profession; early members were from not only the United States but also from Canada, South Africa, Europe, and Australia. By the mid-1970s, the goal of 1,000 members had already been reached. PMI chapters had been formed in five countries, and discussions of professional standards were under way at the association's 1976 annual meeting in Montreal, Canada. By 1983, the discussions included topics such as ethics, standards, and accreditation. University programs were being developed (see Chapter 12), a formal examination was created, and by 1984 professionals began to be designated as *project management professionals* (PMPs). Over the following decades, that effort would spread to countries all over the globe, with PMI offices today located not only in Newtown Square, Pennsylvania, the more recent location for the Global Operations Center in the United States,[3] but also in Singapore, Brussels, Mumbai, and Beijing, and their efforts are certifying almost 400,000 credential holders across 385 countries—more certifications than all of PMI's active membership worldwide. There are certified professionals active in the project management profession all around the globe.

Definition of Project Management Standards
The creation of a professional association allowed hundreds of professionals from the field of project management to collaborate in developing an acceptable definition of what *project management* means. The original founders of the Project Management Institute, together with colleagues from business, government, and academia, assembled the professional writings on project management into a massive book-length document called the *Project Management Body of Knowledge*. It started by focusing on the project itself, but by 1986 a framework had been added to incorporate the relationship between the project and its external environment and between project management and general management.

Almost 10 years later, the standards committee published a new version of the document that described the processes used to manage projects, aligning it with the common knowledge and practices across industries, adding knowledge areas, and reducing the original document's construction emphasis.[4] More than 10,000 people in almost 40 countries received the document for review, and the "standard" truly began to proliferate around the world. In a few years 300,000 copies were in circulation. There was common agreement that project management involves balancing competing demands among:

- Scope, time, cost, risk, and quality
- Stakeholders with differing needs, identified requirements, and expectations

A *project* was defined as distinct from operations in that operations are ongoing and repetitive, whereas projects are temporary and unique. Further, it clarified terms: "*Temporary* means that every project has a definite beginning and a definite end. *Unique* means that the product or service is different in some distinguishing way from all similar products or services."[5]

An Evolving Professional Standard

The purpose of PMI's *A Guide to the Project Management Body of Knowledge* (*PMBOK Guide*) was to identify and describe that subset of the project management body of knowledge that is generally accepted, or "applicable to most projects most of the time." With so many professionals contributing to the definitions and processes, and given its proliferation around the world, *A Guide to the Project Management Body of Knowledge* was becoming a de facto professional standard. While everyone seemed to agree, however, that the environment in which a project operates is important, they could not agree on what it should consist of. Different levels of organizational project management maturity across industries prevented building a consensus on the organizational context for project management. For this reason, parts of the original *Project Management Body of Knowledge* (1986) that related to organizational responsibilities were left out of the published standard. It was 10 years before those concepts were accepted broadly enough that the scope could be extended to include *programs* and *portfolios* as organizational contexts for housing and strategically managing multiple projects within a single organization.

Projects are now linked explicitly to achieving strategic objectives, and organizational planning is considered part of the human resources management function. Processes and process groups are also now more fully defined.[6] Some work was done in various countries around the world on professional competencies and credentialing, but these cannot yet be defined as a "standard" because the business context differs so much from one country to the next.[7] As the profession advances, these areas also may merge into one common definition, providing significant benefits to organizations that operate globally.

A New Core Competency for Organizations

Awareness grew that project management, far from being an adjunct activity associated with nonstandard production, actually was the means by which organizations implemented their strategic objectives. The consensus also grew that project management has become part of the core competency of organizations. The definition captured in the 2000 *Guide to the Project Management Body of Knowledge* reflects this growing awareness:

> Project management is the application of knowledge, skills, tools, and techniques to project activities to meet project requirements. Project management is accomplished through the use of the processes such as: initiating, planning, executing, controlling, and closing. The project team manages the work of the projects, and the work typically involves:
> - Competing demands for: scope, time, cost, risk, and quality.
> - Stakeholders with differing needs and expectations.
> - Identified requirements.[8]

This change reflected a shift from seeing project management not only as a profession but also as an organizational function with defined processes addressing both the needs and the expectations of people with a stake in the project's outcome, as well as the functional requirements of the product or service to be produced. It also set as a standard the understanding that the organization has explicit responsibility for the success of its projects. An organization's management is responsible not only for establishing an environment that allows and enables project success but also for approving and authorizing the requirements that the project is to meet. The project team uses those approved requirements to embark on their work.

The shift to an organizational context meant that the project manager was no longer an independent practitioner within the organization, making projects successful despite contrary forces. He now had a defined job title, function, and place on the organizational chart. Just as an attorney works within the organization's legal function, the project management professional works within the organization's project management function. Formalizing the occupation into jobs and career tracks creates a space in which the professional can operate legitimately (see Chapters 3 and 12).

New Groups Embrace Project Management

Organizations and industries tend to embrace project management when they stand to gain significantly by doing so or to lose by not doing so. Many historical projects left a visible legacy behind them, but those in prior centuries left little in the way of a project record. In the twentieth century, the navy and NASA projects mentioned earlier could not have been achieved without project management. The construction industry and other government contractors that won major contracts began to embrace the same project management practices as their sponsoring government agency did. Other industries, such as the pharmaceutical industry, made significant gains in quality and mitigated complexity by using project management. The examples could go on and on.

During the past several decades, most large organizations were integrating computer technology, first into streamlined operations and then into their strategic business systems. This evolving technology was generating hundreds of projects. The shift to an organizational context in project management therefore coincided with an influx of professionals from information systems, information technology, and information management functions into project management. They joined the professional associations in record numbers. Previously, professional practitioners were from the construction industry, streamlined as it was by project management methods and tools from government. The motto of the Project Management Institute's marketing thrust during the early 1990s was "Associate with Winners."

In contrast, information systems and information technology projects were getting media coverage citing 200 percent budget overruns and schedule delays.[9] Low project success rates unheard of in the quality environment were routine.

As these groups shifted their attention from software engineering to project management, they brought the attention of management with them. All were aware of the wasted resources and the opportunity costs of not managing projects well. The idea resonated with senior management that projects simply were not "nonstandard operations" but rather a core business process for implementing strategic initiatives. Senior management was ready to begin managing projects more systematically. Project management became the topic for executive forums, and some executive groups began to review all projects biannually to determine the best use of the organization's strategic resources (see Chapter 12).

The response of the marketplace to recognition of the project manager and the project management function caused interest to skyrocket. Membership in the professional association grew quickly, swelling in a single decade from just under 10,000 members in 1992 to 100,000 by 2002, then to 150,000 by 2005, and 300,000 by 2009.[10] There were more certified personnel than there were PMI members. An increasing contingent of practitioners working on projects around the globe continued to apply for certification without joining PMI. Project management was the subject of articles in business newspapers and corporate journals.[11] Research began to show that organizations with mature project management environments derive more value from project management than those beginning to implement it.[12]

The government had funded a means by which software engineering professionals could judge the maturity of their software development environments,[13] but no parallel instrument existed for assessing the maturity of project management environments. By 1999, professionals from all over the world were collaborating to create an "Organization Project Management Maturity Model" (OPM3), released in 2003 (PMI).[14] Various maturity models were developed in leading business schools (e.g., Stanford University and the University of California at Berkeley), as well as by vendors, and these models were applied to products serving the maturing project management marketplace (see Chapter 12). Like people weaving different corners of the same tapestry,[15] the detail and richness of the profession are emerging from the combined cooperative efforts of many professional bodies and are being advanced by their common application of standards and training in the agreed-on and "generally accepted" project management process. While there is still a good deal of work to be done before these separate fronts merge into one picture, movement toward that end is steady and positive.

Recognition of professionalism in project management remains uneven across industries. In 1986, at the same time the corporate sector was beginning to implement project management fundamentals, the government sector already was moving forward to implement earned-value measurement and performance management. Information systems (IS) and information technology (IT) were expanding into strategic business initiatives, but they were too new to have both product development methodology and project management methodology in place (see Chapter 12). It will be a while before these different parts of the marketplace all speak the same language.

The Role of Project Management in Organizations

When an organization undertakes to develop something "new" and sets out to have it delivered within a specific time frame with the consumption of time, energy, and resources, the effort eventually generates a result. The result typically is turned over for use to those with a stake in the project and its outcomes. Then the team is disbanded.

The role of project management in the world of work generates certain expectations. This is as it should be. People want results, and they look to project management to deliver those results. Ambiguity in the use of the term, however, jeopardizes fulfillment of those expectations. By examining some examples of the application of modern project management, as well as situations where misuse of the term *project management* creates unrealistic expectations, individuals can learn to:

- Distinguish modern project management from look-alikes to gain a clearer understanding of what today's professionals mean when they use the term
- Explain the role project management plays in organizations today
- Clarify some ways to tell what qualifies as a project and what does not
- Clarify the distinctions among the project management work of the professional (leadership), the project tasks (estimating, scheduling, tracking, reporting, and managing quality and risk), and the product development tasks (designing, developing, building, and testing)

Some organizations use the term *project management* to describe the task of managing work that includes projects (see Figure 1-1). This is defined more accurately as managing portfolios or managing programs if it is a higher-level initiative or a cluster of related projects, not constrained as a project is with specified resources, specified time frames, or performance requirements. Some organizations manage all their work using a project approach. Management consulting firms, think tanks, consulting engineers, and custom developers (furniture, houses, medicines, or products) run their businesses project by project. These are "projectized" organizations, and the *PMBOK Guide* refers to this as "managing by projects."[16] Project management would have a central role in these organizations because they rely on projects to generate their revenue and profits. One would expect to see more mature practices and knowledgeable professionals in these types of organizations. The roles of individuals in the projects themselves are the subject of Chapter 3.

The Field of Work Focused on Projects

Often the term *project management* is used to define the entire field of work that is focused on the delivery of project results. Others use it to describe

FIGURE 1-1   Role of project management in organizations. The authority, role, resources, and title given to project management vary by type of organizational structure. (*PMBOK Guide 2004*)

Project Management Areas/ Structure of the Organization	Organized by Functional Areas	Weak Matrix	Balanced Matrix	Strong Matrix	"Projectized"
Amount of authority of the project manager	Almost none	Limited	Low to moderate	Moderate to high	High to almost total
Amount of staff working full-time on projects	None	Up to 1/4	Between 1/6 and 2/3	At least 1/2 up to 90%	Almost all
Amount of project manager's time spent on projects	Some	Some	All	All	All
Common titles for project manager's role	Project leader or coordinator	Project leader or coordinator	Project officer or manager	Program manager or project manager	Program manager or project manager
Administrative staff supporting projects	Part-time or none	Part-time or none	Part-time	Full-time	Full-time

traditional management practices or technical management practices, simply transferring those practices from organizational operations to projects. The field of project management encompasses the planning and execution of all sorts of projects, whether they are construction planning and execution, events planning and execution, design planning and execution, development of new products, creation or design of complex tools, mitigation of negative effects such as radiation cleanup or oil spills, or the exploration and production of new resources. Large and small projects alike are included in the field, as are simple projects, sophisticated projects, and complex projects. Complex projects are easy to identify as legitimate projects, but there is a gray area where it is more difficult to determine whether we are addressing a project or simply a refinement of "operations." Why would we want to know? The rules are different, and the roles are different.

Here are a few examples to aid in making the distinction between projects and operations.

Research and Development

Some projects develop entirely new products or services; this is often called *research and development*. Examples of terms for these types of activities are:

- *Design*
- *Synthesis*
- *Prototypes*
- *New development*
- *Product creation*

Because the new product or service is "different in some distinguishing way from all similar products or services," these efforts qualify as projects. Another term, called *research and demonstration* in government circles, applies development from one context in a completely different context that varies widely in environmental, legal, or social elements. While the product may not be significantly different, the context in which it is applied makes it different; it therefore qualifies as a project (e.g., nuclear power plants transferred from the United States to developing countries such as South Korea or Brazil).

Revisions and Enhancements

Other groups undertake major revisions to existing products and services, and these may or may not be projects, according to the generally accepted definition. Sometimes these are referred to as:

- *New releases*
- *Updates*
- *Enhancements*
- *Redesign*

A familiar process or software tool released on a completely different technological platform may seem the same but may require a major design effort to create.[17] If the work is temporary, if the group disbands after completing it, and if the work is turned over to someone else to operate, then it is probably a project. In cases of evolving technology, the uncertainties and complexities of an enhancement or redesign may qualify the work as a project.

Refinements

In contrast, some organizations produce versions of a similar product or service repeatedly. This is more commonly referred to as *production*. Other terms for this type of activity are:

- *Capacity increases*
- *Remodeling or modernization*
- *Renewal*
- *Release maintenance*
- *Refurbishment*

To be classified legitimately as a project, each distinct effort must meet the criteria of "every project has a definite beginning and a definite end" and of product or service uniqueness, meaning that "the product or service is different in some distinguishing way from all similar products or services." For example:

- A developer of residential housing may be executing a "production" by building multiple houses of the same design or configurations of houses that are repeated over and over. This is not a project, because it is a repetitive fabrication, except for the first development or when a repeat of the development is done on significantly different terrain.
- A custom developer creating homes of different sizes, styles, and materials for separate customers is managing a series of projects. In this example of a "projectized" organization, the developer is using a new design and new contractors each time.
- A person designing and building her own home, alone or using professional contractors, is definitely implementing a temporary endeavor creating a unique product.

WHY MAKE A DISTINCTION BETWEEN PROJECTS AND OPERATIONS?

It is important to make a distinction between *projects* and *operations* for several reasons, the first of which is that there are major differences in:

- The decision-making process
- The delegation of authority to make changes
- The rules and methods for managing risk
- The role expectations and skill sets
- The value sets
- The expectations of executive management for results
- Reporting relationships and reward systems

Project scope or complexity can vary, so size can cause a project to fall within the generally accepted definition of a project. A subgroup enterprise unit may initiate its own products or services using projects, complete them autonomously with a single person in charge, and then turn them over to another group to operate. Designating this accurately as a project depends on its temporary nature and reassignment of the staff member after completing the unique product or service (contrasted with just moving on to another job assignment).

The Decision-Making Process

The decision-making process relies on delegation of authority to the project manager and team to make changes as needed to respond to project demands. A hierarchy of management is simply not flexible enough to deliver project results on time and on budget. The detailed planning carried out before the project is begun provides structure and logic to what is to come, and trust is fundamental to the process. The project manager uses the skills and judgment of the team to carry out the work of the project, but the decision authority must rest with the project manager. The PMI standard for program management explicitly requires this delegation of authority. Whether the project is large or small, simple or complex, managed by a temporary assignment of staff from other groups (matrix structure) or with full-time team assignments, the delegation of authority is fundamental to the project manager's ability to perform the job.[18]

Projects with a strong link to the organization's strategic objectives are most likely to be defined by executive management and managed at a broader level, with higher degrees of involvement and participation from multiple affected departments. Depending on organizational level, the project manager's involvement in establishing strategic linkages for the project with the organization's mission will be more or less evident. Some larger organizations use a process of objective *alignment* to ensure that projects complement other efforts and advance top management's objectives.[19] Projects at higher levels in the organization probably will state the link with the organization's mission in their business case and charter documents. Projects at a lower level will need to clarify that link with management to ensure that they are proceeding in a way that supports the organization's mission. Many organizations formalize the process and use portfolio management to monitor project and resources priorities (see Chapter 12).

It is unlikely that a project linked directly with the organization's current strategic initiatives would be implemented by a single person;[20] a team would be assigned to implement it. The project manager has delegated authority to make decisions, refine or change the project plan, and reallocate resources. The team conducts the work of the project. The team reports to the project manager on the project job assignment. In non-"projectized" organizations, team members might have a line-manager relationship for reporting as well. Line managers have little authority to change the project in any substantial way; their suggestions are managed by the project manager—along with other stakeholders. (Line managers do, however, control promotions and salary of "temporary" project team members.)

A subgroup project generally has more input from local management, has less coordination with other departments, and generates less risk for the organization should it fail to deliver. It might be coordinated by an individual working with a limited number of other people for a few weeks or months, until completion of the deliverable. In many large organizations, only larger projects of a specific minimum duration or budget are formally designated as projects and required to use the organization's standard project management process.

Role Expectations and Skill Sets

Whereas a few people can accomplish small projects, larger projects—especially those critical to an organization—tend to be cross-functional. Participation by individuals from several disciplines provides the multiple viewpoints needed to ensure value across groups. An important high-level project will be more likely to involve people representing various groups across multiple organizational functions; it may even be interdisciplinary in nature. The varied input of a cross-functional team tends to mitigate the risk of any one group not supporting the result. Interdisciplinary participation also helps to ensure quality because each team member will view other team members' work from a different perspective, spotting inconsistencies and omissions early in the process. Regardless of whether the effort is large or small, the authority to manage risk is part of the project manager's role.

Basic project management knowledge and understanding are required for the individual project manager to complete smaller projects on time and on budget. However, professional-level skill, knowledge, and experience are necessary to execute larger, more complex or strategic projects. The project manager leads, orchestrates, and integrates the work and functions of the project team in implementing the plan. The challenges of managing teams with different values and backgrounds require excellent skills in establishing effective human relations as well as excellent communication skills and team management skills. Honesty and integrity are also critical in managing teams that cross cultural lines.

The project manager of a small project may carry the dual role of managing the project team and performing technical work on the project. The project manager of a large, strategic, complex project will be performing the technical work of project management, but the team will be doing the technical work necessary to deliver the product or service. Often a larger project will have a team or technical leader as well and possibly an assistant project manager or deputy. Small projects are a natural place for beginning project managers to gain experience. The senior project manager will be unlikely to take on small projects because the challenges and the pay are not in line with the senior project manager's level of experience. An exception, of course, would be a small, critical, strategic project for top management, although if it is very small, it too could be considered simply "duties as assigned."

People who work in project management will have varying levels of skill and knowledge, but they all will be focused on the delivery of project results. Their background and experience will reflect the functional specialties within their industry group, as well as the size of projects they work on. The diversity of projects is so broad that some people working in the field may not even recognize a kinship or commonality with others in the same field. They may use different vocabularies, exhibit diverse behaviors, and perform very different types of work to different standards of quality and with differing customs and behaviors.

The project management maturity of the organization hosting the project also will cause the organization to place value on different types of skills and experience. A more mature project environment will choose professional discipline over the ability to manage crises. A less mature organization or a small project may value someone who can do it all, including both technical and management roles, in developing the product and running the project.

It stands to reason, then, that hiring a project manager from a different setting or different type or size of project may create dissonance when roles, authority, and alignment with organizational strategy are involved. Selection of the right project manager for different projects is the subject of Chapter 3.

The Occupation of Managing Projects

The field of project management includes not only project managers but also specialists associated with various functions that may or may not be unique to projects. Those who identify themselves with the occupation of "managing projects" implement projects across many types of settings. They are familiar with the basics in project management and know how projects are run. They may take on different roles within a project setting or the same role on different types of projects. But they always work on projects. Specialists exist in a type of work associated with projects, such as a project scheduler, a project cost engineer, or a project control specialist. Others will specialize in the use of a particular software tool, knowing all the features and capabilities of that tool, even targeting a particular industry (see Chapter 12). Some specialists perform a sophisticated project function, such as an estimator on energy-development sites (a specific setting) or a project recruiter (a specific function). Still others specialize in implementing a unique type of project, such as hotel construction, transportation networks, large-scale training programs, or new mainframe software development.

Some of the individuals associated with projects may have entered the field by happenstance, perhaps through a special assignment or a promotion from a technical role in a project. What distinguishes those in the project management occupation from those in the technical occupation of that project is that they choose to tie their future and their development to project management, expanding their knowledge and skills in areas that support the management of a project rather than the technical aspects of creating, marketing, or developing the product or service resulting from the project. There are thousands of people engaged in the occupation of project management, most of them highly skilled and many of them extremely knowledgeable about what it takes to plan, execute, and control a project.

Emphasis on the Profession of Project Management

A growing number of people recognize the emerging profession of project management. The profession encompasses not only project managers but also other project-related specialists taking a professional approach to the development, planning, execution, control, and improvement of projects. The profession is getting broader because of a number of factors in business today:

• *The increased rate of change in the business environment and the economy.* It used to be OK to say, "If it ain't broke, don't fix it." Today, if you don't fix it before it breaks, the window of opportunity may already be closed.

• *External factors.* Technological changes, market changes, competitive changes—these all influence projects, as well as changing expectations of those who use or receive the products, services, or benefits of the project. Some may change without the project organization's participation or knowledge. Government regulations are an example of an external change, as are legal decisions in the courts. Understanding project management is necessary to integrate these changes into the organization's products and services.

• *Internal factors.* Some organizations have to release new documents, products, or services to stay in business. Whether it is a software company creating "not so necessary" releases or a government organization refining aviation maps or making policy changes, the changes may be generated internally. Project managers are needed to manage these revenue-generators.

Different industries are driven by varying motives to implement projects:

• Revenue generation
• Technology
• Changes in the environment
• Changes in markets or competition

The project management profession draws from those in the occupation, but it targets individuals who consciously address the more sophisticated and complex parts of project management—building knowledge, skills, and ability over time.

THE RELATIONSHIP OF PROJECT MANAGEMENT TO IMPLEMENTING DESIRED CHANGE

Traditionally, project management has been how organizations manage anything new. Organizations always have used projects to manage initiatives that found "normal operations" inadequate for the task. Normal operations are designed to accomplish a certain function, but they lack flexibility. Managing a project to implement any truly new venture is fraught with ambiguities, risks, unknowns, and uncertainties associated with new activity.

Change is often a by-product of projects. Creating a project that operates differently simply adds to the chaos. "Why don't we just do it the old way?" people ask. They usually are referring to the tried-and-true methods of operations that had the benefit of continuous improvement; in other words, the inconsistencies had already been worked out of them by repetition. When change is needed, in most cases someone has already tried getting the desired change using operations processes and found that the "old way" failed to produce results. Given the discomfort of change, there is usually a compelling business reason for organizations and their management to undertake it voluntarily. Usually, the reason is that change is a necessity. In most cases, someone in a leadership role has determined that the results of the project (the product or service and even the change) are desirable and that the outcomes of making that change have value. In other cases, the dangers inherent in not creating a project and making the change simply are too risky to tolerate.

Once the outcome of a project has been established as beneficial, and the organization is willing to undertake a project, the project manager and team are engaged. Seldom is the project manager brought in at the earliest concept development stages, although early involvement of the project manager occurs most frequently in organizations where projects are linked to the main line of business. The people who are engaged in the project—as project manager or team member—are not involved voluntarily in creating change. "My boss told me to" is a more common reason for becoming involved in a project.

Why Organizations and Teams Undertake Projects

People embrace change when they believe the value of change is worth the pain. Based on this belief, a project is formed. The assumption is that if a project is formed, the value of the results will be achieved and the pain everyone goes through will be worth the effort. Implicit in project management is the concept of commitment to change and the delivery of results. It is not always a good assumption that the people on the project team favor the change or even support it. They may get their project assignment under the paragraph called "duties as assigned" in their job description. The project manager takes on the role of leader of the people assigned to her project. She then shapes the commitment and motivation of the individual team members to deliver the intended results. If the assumptions made about the project and its ability to deliver are not realistic and achievable, it is the project manager's responsibility to validate or change those assumptions before embarking on the project. Part of the value set of a professional is not to take on work that is beyond one's means to deliver. It is not uncommon for sales and management to "sell" a concept because of its appeal, without a full understanding of the challenges involved in achieving those results. After all, nothing is impossible to those who do not have to do it.

If you happen to be the individual selected to implement change, it feels a lot better if the change is desirable and people support the effort. But having support at the beginning of a project does not guarantee acceptance later, when the discomfort of change sets in. And popular support seldom delivers the value of change over time. If change were that easy, someone already would have done it. People usually support the comfort and familiarity of the "old way" of doing things before the project came along. In some cases the project changes things that people rely on, alters their familiar data, or replaces their old product or service with a new one. Engaging and managing the risk of human attachments to their familiar methods is one task of the project management professional. It takes conscious, dedicated effort on the part of the project's sponsors, project managers, and project teams to deliver change that meets expectations. Increasing the chances of a successful outcome is one element that can get a team working together on project management activities, methods, and practices. Delivering on the project's commitment to results that have value in a challenging modern context is what gets people inside and outside the project to work together toward success. Delivering project benefits is satisfying work.

Benefits of Managing Organizational Initiatives Systematically

Why do organizations need project management? When initiatives with high risk and change are undertaken, a systematic process for managing *known unknowns* frees time, energy, and resources for managing *unknown unknowns*. This sort of "risk triage" increases the chances that the project will deliver successfully on its commitments using the committed resources. There are a lot of elements to manage. Figure 1-2 shows some of the benefits of managing them more systematically using project management disciplines and practices.

• *Visibility into the problem.* The analysis that goes into systematic management reveals a lot of hidden issues, overlaps, and trends that were not visible before. If management is to resolve organizational challenges, it must first make them visible. A precept of project management, attributed to the project manager for the construction of the tunnel under the English Channel, is "to make the invisible visible so that it can be managed."[21] Management consultants consider the biggest challenges in working with organizations to be less the identified problems than the unspoken ones.

• *Leveraging scarce resources.* The money, time, and effort to undertake organizational initiatives are finite. To get the most leverage out of them, resources should be made available only when they are needed, and

FIGURE 1-2 Benefits of managing organizational initiatives systematically. When initiatives are planned systematically, the results are more effective and efficient and the organization benefits from the professional development of the project team.

Element	Check
Visibility into the problem	✔
Leveraging scarce resources	✔
Building a skill base	✔
Planning for easy changes in the future	✔

they should be transferred to more pressing needs when a particular initiative is over. Unless management knows what exists and its status in terms of completion, scarce resources can be scattered and not used effectively.

• *Building a skill base.* Most of the key functions present in organizations are also present in projects, but they are abbreviated, condensed, or applied in unique ways. For individuals in project management, learning the fundamentals of most organizational functions, as well as those unique to project management, comprises the basics. Mastery of the basics takes commitment and dedication over a number of years. As staff members learn project management, they also learn the fundamentals of organization functions so that they make more informed decisions in their work for the organization.

• *Planning for easy changes in the future.* Managing organizational initiatives systematically preserves the overall quality of the outcomes for stakeholders and the organization as a whole. Quality deliverables are easier to maintain over time.

As an analogy, consider a person building a house with only a general plan and no architectural drawings. By means of routine decisions, myriad minor compromises occur during the building process, without any overall intent to compromise: The number and placement of electrical outlets can affect the use of appliances and limit future work capacity; unplanned placement of vents and piping can affect future comfort and ability to manage temperature. Placement of load-bearing walls can affect remodeling or later modification. Use of different standards for different parts of the construction can prevent later consolidation of separate systems.

Seemingly minor compromises can erode the overall quality of life for the occupants and limit what can be done with the house in the future. Many such ad hoc houses are in fact demolished and replaced because it is cheaper to rebuild than to remodel, particularly if new standards must be taken into account.

Similarly, taking a more comprehensive view of an initiative—and systematically planning its development, deployment, and resourcing—can provide benefits to the organization as a whole by leveraging its common potential and protecting quality.

Comparing Project Management with Problem Solving

The phases of a project are basically the same as an individual's method of problem solving, but when the project's outcome is bigger or more challenging, the system breaks down. People in separate functional departments see the problem differently. Agreed-on approaches get interpreted differently by specialists with diverse values and training. Actions influence other actions, sometimes undercutting each other or slowing implementation. Somehow, small problems can evolve into myriad complexities, dependencies, and challenges. Priorities become difficult to sort out.

Projects require a process just as in problem solving (see Figure 1-3). The first phase, usually called *initiation,* is when the idea is worked out and described, its scope and success criteria defined, its sponsors identified, its resources estimated, and its authority formalized. Then the project manager and team decide how it can be achieved practically, plan it out, and allocate the resources and risks by task and phase. Its effort and time frames are quantified and approved. Finally, the project manager and team put the plan into action during project execution. Project management professionals counter the complexity just described by formalizing the process. They then orchestrate it with teams, managing task interfaces, reducing or mitigating risk, and solving the remaining implementation problems within resource and time constraints. Once they have the experience behind them, they assess whether it turned out the way it was expected to, explain why or why not, and define what can be done better next time. The group applies the learning to sequential projects and makes best-practice examples available to other projects in the organization. The phases of a project closely resemble the stages of problem solving: *initiation/concept development* (analyze the problem), *high-level/detailed planning* (identify options/select one), execution/control (implement an option/see if it works), and *closure and lessons learned* (refine for next cycle of analysis).

FIGURE 1-3 Comparing project management with problem-solving cycle. Both project management and problem solving require a process to be effective. Project management uses more systematic analysis up front to reduce the risk of trial and error.

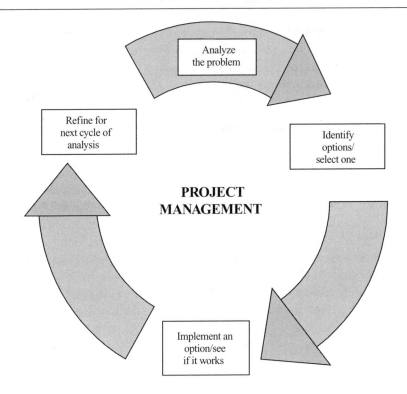

Long-Term Value of Project Outcomes

Major undertakings produce outcomes that are believed to deliver great value to their users. It is difficult to know whether the value of a major project will be short-lived or will endure over time. As necessary as they may be when begun, some projects deliver important results for only a short period of time and then are replaced by new methods or new technology. Others persist.

The Panama Canal connected two great oceans, and the reversal of the Chicago River—an engineering marvel—linked the East Coast shipping trade with the great Mississippi transportation corridor. Pony Express riders delivered the mail over land. But railroads swiftly replaced shipping as a low-cost method of moving people and goods over long distances. The railroad projects across the northern states became the primary link between those two great oceans. Northern railroad builders adopted a standard gauge so that railbed segments could be connected into a vast transportation network. But the southern states adopted a narrower gauge and had to reset their tracks to benefit from this vast network.

There are intangible benefits to project outcomes as well. The Eiffel Tower in Paris and the Space Needle in Seattle—both engineered to draw attention to a big event—put those cities on the map for tourism and marked them with emblems of innovation that have endured. The astronomical wonder of Stonehenge in England, huge stone statues in Africa and Asia, South America's "lost cities" in the Andes, and the cathedrals of Europe inspired the people of the past, and they continue to inspire us today (see Figure 1-4).

Viewing the results of massive projects in history reminds us that our advanced technology, learning, and project methods have shortened the time frames needed to get project results. Cathedrals sometimes took 200 years to complete; the World Trade Center was built in 20 years. But a still longer view is needed to address the really big challenges facing modern societies. The United States has begun to address the upgrade of its vast network of interstate highways, which were built after World War II. But using piece-meal projects over a series of years is not an adequate approach to complete such a large undertaking. Many of the government planning agencies were

FIGURE 1-4 Long-term value of project outcomes. Project deliverables or outcomes have value beyond the immediate benefit, and part of the value is intangible.

Project	Outcome	Value
Panama Canal	Connected Atlantic and Pacific	Reduced time for sea transport
Chicago River	Reversed flow	Linked eastern shipping with great Mississippi transportation corridor
Railroad	Connected rail systems	Enabled coast-to-coast rail shipments
Eiffel Tower in Paris, Space Needle in Seattle	Public awareness of engineering marvels	Attracted tourists, put cities on the map
Stonehenge	Astronomy	Inspired people, enabled agriculture

found in the late 1980s to have no plan for raising funds to maintain society's infrastructure.[22] The federal government that built the highways did so under strategic initiatives of national protection. But the states have not systematically maintained them. Television coverage of a bridge collapse in Minnesota, together with stimulus money from the American Reinvestment and Recovery Act, have spurred efforts to tackle the worst parts of the network, but a larger project may be warranted. Given the competition for scarce government dollars, a national system is needed to align project priorities. The nation is saddled with debt. Health care costs are rising. The responsibility for solutions is clearly federal, but who is responsible for funding the projects and delivering the results? The authority remains an open question. Putting an infrastructure in place to manage benefits across projects is not an easy thing to do. It requires sponsorship, resources, and a link to overall strategy. It requires leadership and vision and courage.

Not only our individual enterprises but also our society as a whole needs the infrastructure in place to initiate, fund, plan, and execute major projects. Currently, many separate agencies are responsible for different parts of these massive projects. Running nationwide projects without a central project authority in government is much like running projects separately within a large organization. A realistic supportive environment is important if we want to ensure project success and keep costs down. Where is this project management initiative to come from?

In Capetown, South Africa, a large segment of freeway stands above town along the waterfront, built by government officials without consideration for the funding required to link it with other transportation systems. Local project managers say that the city leaves it there as a reminder to think long range in their planning.[23]

Professional ethics address the professional project manager's responsibility to society and the future. While it is easy to say that a project is responsible only for the outcome defined for that project over the period of time it is in existence, we know that outcomes have a life cycle, and quality and value are assessed over the entire life cycle of a product or service until it is eliminated, demolished, or removed from service. Considering how it will endure over time or be maintained is part of management's responsibility, but the project manager has the opportunity to build such considerations into the plan.

Cooperation Builds the Future
Fortunately, professional societies in the field of project management have begun working with government agencies in a number of different countries to integrate project management with the school systems and the policies governing public projects. More on these topics will be addressed in later

chapters.[24] In Chapter 12 we address how mature project environments man-age the interdependent elements of projects and also describe some of the methods used to align projects across boundaries, establish priorities, allocate resources, and ensure that the benefits of a single project are linked properly with others and delivered to the organization as a whole.

Failed Projects Spur Improvement

Thanks to modern communications technology, failed projects also have staked out a space in human history. We may not consider them projects or even know why they failed, but they sit as examples in our minds as we contemplate a new undertaking. We see images of ancient cities in the Middle East covered by desert sands, victims of environmental degradation. The steamship *Titanic* rests on the ocean floor, an engineering marvel that fell prey to its own self-confidence. Other less visible project failures are in our conscious minds through the news media. The Alaskan and Gulf of Mexico oil spills, the release of nuclear pollution onto the Russian plain, attempts to stem the AIDS epidemic's relentless march—all are common project examples in our news media and our history books. All share the legacy and challenges of project management.

In some cases, the use of professional project management might have prevented the failures. In others, the combined effects of minor errors in judg-ment were enough to spell their doom. The bureaucratic failure of Hurricane Katrina in New Orleans was examined for months—retaining walls that were designed for only "mid-sized" hurricanes failed as they had been predicted to do when a stonger hurricane materialized; the unsuccessful merging of a project-based emergency management agency with a functional bureaucracy that did not know how to manage across projects. Seafront development after the Indonesian tsunami destroyed the local economy. Scrambled attempts to give aid to Haiti had no capstone project to replace local coordinating agencies destroyed in the earthquake. In other cases, the long-term effects of projects are often clearly overlooked. New financial products like credit default swaps in 2001 were released from insurance safeguards and then pro-liferated as toxic assets swamping banks and investment firms seven years later. Ambitious projects continue to be conceived, planned, executed, and completed—with varying degrees of "success." Sometimes teams study these examples to capture learning and improve our project track record in the future. Sometimes we have no answers, just the reminder of risk unmanaged or faulty assumptions. Pointing the finger of blame seems futile in the face of such massive losses. But project management is designed to tackle just these types of challenges. We would be remiss not to apply it better in the years to come.

Projects typically are carried out in a defined context by a specific group of people. They are undertaken to achieve a specific purpose for innovators, sponsors, and users. But project delivery of something new is also judged in a broader context of value. Projects are not judged at a single point in time but over the life cycle of the project's product or outcome. Managing complex project interdependencies as well as the future effects of the project is part of the professional challenge. It is the profession of project management that is devoted to increasing the value and success of projects and ensuring that what is delivered meets the expectations of not just immediate users but also a broader set of stakeholders. This broader definition of project success is another element driving project management toward the status of profession.

How Different Organizations Define the Value of Projects

The value produced by the practice of project management is not the same in every sector of the economy (see Figure 1-5). With the risk of oversimplifying:

- Corporate projects need to make money, and projects are judged by their contribution to increasing revenue or cutting unnecessary cost.
- Not-for-profit organizations are charged with providing benefits to a broader society, and projects considered successful have broad or conspicuous contributions.
- Government projects must provide needed services or benefits to groups defined by law. Projects that provide those services or benefits to the stakeholders of public programs and services, and do so within the regulations, are considered successful.
- Academia organizes knowledge into curricula and courses of study, and projects that push knowledge into new areas or advance human understanding are recognized as valuable. Project management must be sufficiently challenging intellectually to warrant attention from leading scholarly institutions.

THE VALUE-ADDED PROPOSITION: DECLARING AND REVALIDATING PROJECT VALUE

Usually the selection of a project for funding and authorization includes a careful analysis of the value it is to provide its intended audiences. However, changes occur in the environment, regulations, social interests, and

FIGURE 1-5   Benefits of adopting project management approaches. Different sectors derive significant value from project management by achieving strategic goals.

Type of Organization	Value
Corporations	Increase profits
Not for Profit	Provide more benefits to society
Government	Improve services
Academia	Advance human learning and understanding

market opportunities while a project is under way. Sometimes the outcome of another project, or even reorganization, can make the outcome of a current project obsolete. It is important not only to communicate the value of a project at its inception but also to revalidate the effort and expenditure at key intervals, especially for lengthy projects.

It would be ideal if a project's value could be established in practical terms so that the project's management, sponsor, customers, and users could agree that it had delivered on its promises. Some of the ways to gain agreement on objective measures are addressed in Chapters 6 and 12. Those familiar with the benefits of project management do not need "objective" reasons; they feel that the reduced ambiguity, managed risk, shortened time frames, and product existence are benefits enough.

William Ibbs and Justin Reginato, in their research study entitled *Quantifying the Value of Project Management*,[25] cited a number of dimensions where organizations reaped tangible benefits. But some sectors discount project management's contributions or diminish its overall scope. Most of these are low on the scale of organizational project management maturity because the higher the maturity level, the greater are the realized benefits. Companies with more mature project management practices have better project performance.[26]

Spending a little time defining the different benefits of project management according to the primary values of its own economic sector will help an organization clarify how value can be delivered by a project in its own context. Some sectors will benefit from a focus on resource leverage or efficiency; others from a focus on maturity. After such an analysis is complete, the strategic objectives of the organization and its management, customers, and user groups need to be considered. Building success criteria into the plan ensures that all know what the goals of the project entail.

BENEFITS OF ADOPTING PROJECT MANAGEMENT APPROACHES

Recent research and publications help in quantifying the benefits of project management, including executive surveys of what they consider to be its benefits.[27] However, continuous improvement should be the norm; good performance "on average" is not sufficient (see Figure 1-6).

The negative impact of not practicing effective methods of project management includes the escalating costs of high-profile projects. The risk is that the sponsoring organization does not achieve its desired goals despite its investment in the project. Some analysts have suggested that a company's stock price can drop if a failed project becomes public news.[28]

Taking a systematic approach to managing projects creates a number of benefits, regardless of the host organization's particular emphasis on outcomes. These benefits are:

- *Quicker completion.* Quicker time-to-market delivery of rapid development can make all the difference in the profitability of a commercial product. It is said that one-third of the market goes to the first entrant when a breakthrough product is introduced. In some sectors, delays enact penalties.
- *More effective execution.* When projects are formed to create a desired product first, the project that delivers results on schedule simultaneously may deliver large profits to the host company. Other projects must meet exact requirements.
- *More reliable cost and schedule estimates.* Making adequate resources available when they are needed increases the likelihood that a project will deliver benefits or services within budget and resource constraints. Resources can be leveraged.
- *Reduced risk.* For highly visible projects, such as shuttle launches and space exploration, the potential loss of life is an unacceptable political downside to a project that does not deliver. In not-for-profit organizations, the losses associated with a failed project may consume the resource contingencies of the whole organization or make its reputation unacceptable to its member customers. The organization's actual existence—continuation of a whole organization—can be at risk if losses exceed the organization's capital reserve.

FIGURE 1-6   Benefits of adopting project management approaches. Adopting project management raises awareness of costs, risks, complexities, and benefits, thereby making it easier to respond to these issues.

Benefit	Effect
Quicker completion	Increase market share Financial benefits realized earlier Problems solved faster
More effective execution	Less rework More adherence to the project plan
More reliable cost and schedule estimates	Resources are available when needed Benefits and services delivered within budget
Reduced risk	Reduction in loss of life Reduction in wasted resources Increased reputation and confidence
Reduced cost	Leveraging resources Reduction in wasted resources

- *Reduced cost.* Maximizing schedules, linking dependent tasks, and leveraging resources ultimately reduces waste, including wasted time and effort on the part of the project team's highly skilled and trained staff.

A major benefit of adopting project management is that it raises awareness of costs, complexities, risks, and benefits early in the process of development, enabling sponsors to know where they stand in proceeding with a given commitment and allowing action to reduce negative influences so that the investment pays dividends and delivers on its promises. The end result is that society gets benefits with the expenditure of fewer resources.

What is ultimately needed is an environment where systems and processes work together with knowledgeable and skilled professionals to deliver on the promises of project management. While mature integration has not yet been achieved, this new direction is well on its way.

SUMMARY

The term *project management* means different things depending on how it is used. As the emerging profession distinguishes those projects that demand professional skills from the myriad projects at all levels in society, more clarity and agreement on the terminology and concepts will evolve. Chapter 2 presents some of those concepts, including how to determine what qualifies as a project, natural phases within projects, and how project management is applied in different settings.

REVIEW QUESTIONS

1. The term *project management* does not always mean the same thing when people use it.
   a. true
   b. false
2. Project management balances competing demands of:
   a. scope, time, cost, quality, processes, and requirements
   b. stakeholders, requirements, unidentified requirements, quality, scope, and benefits
   c. quality, stakeholder needs, time, cost, risk, scope, requirements, identified requirements, and expectations
   d. requirements, unidentified requirements, time, cost, scope, stakeholders, and owners
3. What is the primary difference between projects and operations?
   a. operations are ongoing and repetitive, whereas projects are ongoing and different
   b. projects are ongoing and repetitive, whereas operations are temporary and unique
   c. operations have yearly planning cycles, whereas projects do not require yearly planning
   d. operations are ongoing and repetitive, whereas projects are temporary and unique
4. Which of the following is the most important reason for a project in an organization?
   a. it is an adjunct activity associated with nonstandard production
   b. it is the means by which organizations implement their strategic objectives
   c. it means extra duties for some people in addition to their regular jobs
   d. it is the easiest way to get things done
5. Organizations that take a systematic approach to managing projects realize financial benefits earlier.
   a. true
   b. false

6. Research shows that:
    a. organizations with immature project management environments derive more value from project management than those that formalize project management
    b. organizations with mature project management environments derive more value from project management than those newly implementing it
    c. organizations with immature project management environments derive less value from project management than those that do not use it
    d. none of the above

7. Organizations that manage all their work by projects and run their business project by project are called:
    a. project-managed
    b. managed by projects
    c. project-based
    d. projectile
    e. "projectized"

8. What are the benefits of cross-functional projects?
    a. participation by several disciplines provides multiple viewpoints
    b. the varied input of a cross-functional team tends to mitigate the risk of any one group not supporting the result
    c. cross-functional participation helps to ensure quality because the team can identify inconsistencies and omissions early in the process
    d. all of the above
    e. none of the above

9. Some projects develop entirely new products or services; this is often called *research and development.* Examples of terms for these types of activities are:
    a. design
    b. synthesis
    c. prototypes
    d. new development
    e. product creation
    f. all of the above
    g. *a* and *c* only
    h. none of the above
    i. *a, c, d,* and *e*

10. It is not necessary for the project manager to have decision authority to perform the job.
    a. true
    b. false

PROJECT MANAGEMENT CONCEPTS

OVERVIEW AND GOALS

This chapter provides a general overview of the role projects have played in the world, identifying the fundamental elements shared by projects throughout history. It defines the project life cycle, the product life cycle, and the process of project design that integrates and aligns the two into one or more projects.

The *triple constraint* is introduced as important in defining and managing projects. How project management evolved helps to explain how it is applied in different settings today and why those differences developed. And while the standard life cycle for projects applies uniformly across industries, the levels and types of detail that must be developed on projects varies by industry and by the size and complexity of the individual project. This chapter proposes that general project management approaches be tailored based on the types of projects being managed.

WHAT IS A PROJECT?

In Chapter 1 we distinguished projects, which are temporary and unique, from operations, which are ongoing and repetitive. Projects have little, if any, precedent for what they are creating, the project work is new, and workers are unfamiliar with expectations. In contrast, operations are repetitive, routine business activities. They follow an organization's existing procedures, are familiar, and are typically documented. They have benefited by improvements over time, and worker expectations are written into job descriptions.

Projects can be applied to different ends. They are used to implement strategic initiatives, meet identified needs, or step up to new opportunities. Their flexibility makes them valuable for getting business results. A project can create a product that can be either a component of another item or an end item in itself. It can create a capability to perform a service (such as a business function that supports production or distribution). It can also create a result such as an outcome or document. (For example, the findings of a research project may develop knowledge that can be used to determine whether a trend is present or even to develop a new process that will benefit society.)[1] Thousands of project management professionals have agreed that a project has a clear beginning and a clear end, as well as a resulting product or service that is different in some significant way from those created before. The unique product or service in a project management setting is often called a *deliverable*, a generic term that allows discussion about the result without getting specific about its characteristics. The project's deliverable may be the ultimate product or service, or it may be a clearer definition needed for the next consecutive project, such as a design or a plan. In some cases it may be just one part of the final deliverable, consisting of outputs of multiple projects managed by different organizations.[2]

The distinction that projects have "a clear beginning, a clear end, and a unique product or service" is important because the "rules" for managing projects are different from the "rules" for managing operations. The roles of the people in relation to the project are different as well. To better understand the distinction, we can compare it with how the rules and roles differ in sports.

General Rules for Project Management

In sports, whether one is participating or simply watching the game, one needs to understand not just the sport itself but also the rules associated with it. There are different rules and roles in team sports such as baseball, soccer/football, and cricket. Automobile racing has different rules and roles from horse racing and ski racing. Applying experience and knowledge associated with one sport while watching a different sport would lead to frustration, discouragement, and eventually lack of interest in continuing to watch the match. Similarly, applying rules that apply to routine business operations in a project context would lead to frustration, discouragement, and lack of interest in continuing involvement in the project. As obvious as this concept seems, operations management concepts are applied to projects regularly, on a daily basis. In many organizations, both the project team and the sponsoring management share this negative experience but do not realize why it is occurring.

What makes a project temporary and unique also makes it unsuited to the rules and roles of operations management.

Roles in project management are different from those in operations. In operations, a manager in finance will have a different job from a manager in human resources or product development, but a project manager will have a very similar job whether the project is a finance project, a human resources project, or a product development project. While a line manager can push a problem "upstairs" to a higher-level manager, or even delay its resolution, the project manager is expected to manage the risks, problems, and resolutions within the project itself, with the help of the team, the sponsor, or the customer, to keep the project moving forward.

Project manager is clearly a role; the project manager is the person responsible for the management and results of the project. Each project has only one project manager. Some organizations with established project management functions (such as a project management office) will have a job description and position classification for project manager, and some even deploy project managers to other divisions when that expertise and role are needed. But the position is not just a manager role with a different title on it. The performance expectations are as different from each other as offensive or defensive positions on a sports team. Project management roles are always "offensive" (see Chapter 3).

In another sports analogy, if the sponsor of a project is like the owner of a sports team, the project manager is like the coach. The team's owner provides resources to the coach and team but delegates to the coach the decision authority to win the game. Any expectations or requirements the owner may have are negotiated up front. The owner then delegates to the coach responsibility and authority for winning. He holds the coach accountable for managing the resources (team members and time) in whatever way will best win the game. The complex variables needed to win are best understood by the coach and his team, and owner interference is generally accepted as counterproductive. Even sports commentators can only guess at the variables considered in pursuing one winning strategy over another.

In an operations context, the professional project manager does not function like a team leader or a line supervisor. The project manager reports to her manager much as a senior manager reports to an executive. An executive provides direction, strategic goals, and authority to a senior manager and communicates any major constraints but does not interfere with the senior manager's decisions—or supersede her authority—except in dire circumstances. Whether the project manager reports to the executive level or to a midlevel program manager, the executive or program manager must delegate decision authority to the project manager and simply hold her accountable for results. The trade-offs and variables at play in a fast moving project are best known within the team. Support and guidance are welcome, but overt interference is most often counterproductive.

Project Management's Underlying Assumptions

There are a few fundamental concepts that, once accepted, make many of the unique practices and processes in project management more logical.

- *Risk.* Organizations need to believe the risks inherent in a project to provide adequate management backing and support, and the team needs accurate and timely risk information. When doing something for the first time, many unknowns have the potential to affect the project in some way, positive or negative. One goal is to "flush out" as many of those unknowns as possible—like a bird dog flushes birds out of the bushes—so that they may be managed and the project's energy can be redirected to managing the surprises that inevitably arise when the work is unfamiliar.
- *Authority.* Because the project has a start and an end and specified resources, there is a need to balance the competing requirements of time, cost, and performance. The authority to balance these competing requirements—and the decisions associated with balancing them—is delegated to the project manager and the team.
- *Autonomy.* The risks associated with the project must be managed so that they do not obstruct progress. As risks mature into real issues or problems, the project manager and team need autonomy and flexibility to resolve some and ignore others based on their potential to hurt the project.
- *Project control.* To anticipate and predict needed change, the project manager and team need ways to determine where they are in relation to the projected time, cost, and performance goals. They use this status information to make needed adjustments to the plan and to refine its execution strategy.
- *Sponsorship.* The project manager and team need the backing of management, or a sponsor and champion, to ensure that the project is aligned properly with executive goals, to protect against external interference, and to provide resource backing (see Chapters 3 and 12).

Examples of Projects in History

One way to gain perspective on projects of today is to compare them with projects of the past. In some ways projects remain the same as they have always been, and in some ways project management has evolved over the ages. Let us review a few projects from history where enough evidence has been gained through research and historical records to make some project management comparisons.

Project: Building the Egyptian Great Pyramid at Giza

One of the first major undertakings that project managers clearly identify as a project is the construction of the Great Pyramid at Giza. There is some historical evidence—we could call it *project history*—that gives us insight into its scope and effort.

Project records exist in the writings of Greek philosophers, Egyptian hieroglyphics, and archaeological findings. High-level estimates of time and effort "in the press" during that period were apparently inaccurate. Herodotus wrote that the pyramid took 100,000 people 30 years to complete. Archaeological research and records pare those estimates to 20,000 people and 20 years to complete. Hieroglyphics in the tombs reveal some of the methods (technical approaches and tools) used to construct the pyramid: Stone blocks were carved from a quarry by hand using stone hammers and chisels. Then the stones were slid on pallets of wood over wet sand, and workers used wooden beams as levers to heft them into the desired position.

If Herodotus's estimates had been accurate, the team would have been made up of approximately 10 percent of the entire population of Egypt—and the work would have taken more than 3 million effort-years. It was more likely 20,000 people, 2,000 of whom were in continuous service (the core team) and 18,000 of whom were tracked by DNA evidence in bones on the site to villages all over Egypt. If we were to translate their structure into a modern context, this would correspond to a core team (the ancient group of continuous service) with various team members assigned temporarily as resources from the departments (the ancient villages) in the sponsor's organization (the ancient dynasty). The work shift was long in those days; the team rotation was about 12 weeks. At that point the workers on loan to the project went home and were replaced by new workers.

The power of the project sponsor was very helpful in getting such a huge project done. The project sponsor was executive management (the pharaoh also was viewed as "god"—making it easier to get permission to leave the family and village job to work on the assignment). The work was hard, there were occupational hazards (bone damage), and the pay was low (including fresh onions for lunch). People who died on the project were buried on the project site (hence the DNA evidence to trace their villages).[3]

Program: Building the Railroad System in the United States

A program of the U.S. government implemented by government contracts, the railroad system in the United States was "one of the greatest technological achievements of the age."[4] It was a series of projects, some large and spectacular and some small. The most famous was the joining of the eastern half of the railroads with isolated western states—with rail that had to be newly constructed. The U.S. Congress funded two major corporations to complete the connection, the Union Pacific Railroad (working westward toward the Rocky Mountains from Missouri) and the Central Pacific Railroad (working eastward from California). Each managed a project. The two projects spanned the period from 1865 to 1869. To finance the work, resources were earned by each corporation as work progressed, until the goal was achieved.

No meeting point was defined, but funding and critical success factors were defined; the two railroads had to join each other's track. The corporation that laid the most railroad track toward the connection point got more revenue. Government funds were supplemented with land grants. Here is a list of some of the projects' parameters:

• The scope covered delivery and construction of 1,775 miles of track, budgeted at $16,000 per mile on the flatland and $48,000 per mile in the mountains. On flatland, progress was 2 to 3 miles of track laid per day, using 10,000 laborers. In the mountains, progress slowed to 15 inches per day through solid rock, using 11,000 laborers.

• Logistics included shipping rail to the end and transferring it by wagon to the work site. Each rail weighed 700 pounds. Blasting in the mountains required 500 kegs of explosives per day. Shifts were "around the clock," rain or snow. Some snowstorms lasted two weeks.

• Schedule risk in the mountains was due primarily to worker turnover (desertion to the gold fields was common, as was loss of whole teams to snow slides). The risk response of project management was to hire Chinese workers, who had "built the great Wall of China." One concession, however, had to be made. All bodies of Chinese workers who were killed on the job had to be returned to their ancestral homes for burial.

• Schedule risk also existed in the flatlands. One derailment was caused by "Indian raids." Risk response of project management was to engage military defense. Deceased workers could be buried on site.

- Closure of the projects was announced publicly by a ceremony. The two coastal railway systems were joined with a "golden spike" (actually, two gold, one silver, and one a blend of both). The hammering of the spike was photographed, but the hammer missed. The error was ignored; a message, "Done," was telegraphed manually, triggering New York ceremonies and ringing of the Liberty Bell in Philadelphia.

Not everything worked perfectly in the creation of this new railway system. Some rework was required, and this was handled at the program level. Since the northern states and the South had different standards (standard gauge versus narrow gauge), the South had to undertake a new project of widening its tracks to standard gauge to link all the railroads throughout the United States. The product (the rail system) is still used today, although sections have been retired.

When each project was finished, the railroads were turned over to corporations to manage and maintain. Many railroads, and the towns they supported, have disappeared because of new competition from the trucking industry, lack of maintenance funds, and shifts in economic climates. In many other areas, the products are still in service, including a few narrow-gauge railroads in Silverton, Colorado, and elsewhere.

Railroads continue to provide valuable service to society, and their status rises and falls with shifts in the economy. As the U.S. interstate highway system peaked in the last half of the twentieth century, rails and equipment fell into disrepair. However, with more recent increases in fuel costs, even trucking companies ship their trailers long distance by train and use a rig for short hauls. In cities, commuters use the rails instead of automobiles to escape traffic congestion. Railroad tickets appear even cheaper as supply and demand pushes the cost of gasoline ever upward.

Some of the lessons learned from railroad projects are useful for the future. For large public undertakings, standards and a central authority are crucial to preventing the need for massive rework.

Humans continue today to create wondrous constructions, from skyscrapers and dams to spectacular homes. We believe that our technology and our knowledge have shortened the project cycle and made it easier to implement quality outcomes within time and resource constraints. However, many challenges common to projects in ancient history remain challenges to projects today (see Figure 2-1). Consider the project that built the Great Pyramid of Khufu. Even though a pharaoh could do whatever he wanted, unlike modern-day sponsors, there were still issues of managing teams, continued access to needed skills, resource availability, task interdependencies,

FIGURE 2-1   Projects from history. When you examine projects from history, note the similarities of projects, even those 2,300 years apart!

Project name	Great Pyramid of Khufu	Linking the U.S. Railroad System
Location	Giza, Egypt	U.S.A.
Time frame	20 years duration 2500 B.C.	1865–1869
Deliverable	Pyramid	Rail system
Acceptance criteria	Tomb for the Pharaoh Khufu	Golden spike joining the eastern and western railroads
Challenges	Injuries, transporting materials	Transporting 700 lb per rail, blasting rock, different gauges, weather, Indian attacks
Size/effort hours	400,000 effort-years	1,775 miles of track
Costs	2.3 million stones, etc.	$16,000 per mile (flat) $48,000 per mile (mountains)
Sponsor	Pharaoh Khufu	U.S. Government, Congress

and risks. All are still hurdles in project management. Our technology has given us better tools, but the challenges remain.

Advances in Civilization Affect Project Management

It is not uncommon for the purpose and goals of a project to evolve if it endures for some time. The world around us changes, and those changes affect not only the project itself but also the way the project's results will be received and used when it is complete. Some deliverables are obsolete before completion.

Projects typically are undertaken in a specific context by a select group of people to achieve a defined purpose for sponsors, customers, and users. But project deliverables are also judged in a broader context of value. Projects are not judged at a single point in time but at closure over the life cycle of the project's product or outcome. A deepwater oil well, for example, drilled and constructed as an operating platform for a major oil company, is put in place as a project, meeting revenue expectations and deadlines as they are defined in that project at that time. Common overt risks are managed at the highest level. But after an explosion on the platform destroys the manual shutoff controls, single decisions to forego a remote trigger shutoff valve and save a quarter million dollars, perhaps leave a nonfunctioning pipe element in place, or cut short a gas pressure test that should have run for 12 hours seem shortsighted. The project's legacy is judged by its outcome, years afterward.[5]

Managing internal project interdependencies as well as the external effects of a changing social and environmental context is part of the professional challenge. Professional project management is devoted to ensuring the long-term value and success of projects so that what is delivered meets the expectations of immediate users, in addition to a broader set of stakeholders over time. Managing the effect of external changes in the business climate and technology to ensure project success is another element driving project management toward a profession.

The field of project management is advancing and is influenced by changing trends in the business management environment. There is evidence of progress in how projects use time, technology, resources, and human effort, as well as new definitions of social value. Efficiencies are evident on many fronts.

- *Delivery.* What used to take several lifetimes to build by hand is now accomplished in a decade or two using sophisticated planning techniques and scheduling tools, coupled with technology. Society expects results faster.
- *Resource standards.* What used to be acceptable as a standard of resource consumption and environmental degradation is now considered inadequate. The resources of the project and its environment are managed more carefully and at a higher level. Society expects better resource stewardship as the finite limits of resources generally are acknowledged.
- *Overall effort.* What used to take many iterations and false starts to accomplish can be put in place swiftly by a small team using experience from prior projects.
- *Stakeholder satisfaction.* Projects spend more effort on predicting how the outcome of the project will be received and defining requirements. What used to be judged successful by a single group of users can now be declared a failure by the population at large based on its effects on outside groups. An example might be the settlement of the West at the expense of Native American cultures.

Project management success continues to be judged as much by the process it follows as by the results it achieves. An educated population knows more about effective processes and is more aware of what to expect in the future. Participative democracy has trained whole populations to expect involvement in the products or services that affect their lives and to have a voice. Advances in science, education, communications, technology, and the educational level of the human population not only have accelerated the progress of projects but also have increased the general expectations of those judging their outcomes. Maturity in organizational project management requires that these differences be managed as well.

NATURAL PHASES OF PROJECTS

All projects have natural phases, and they represent "gates" of definition and certainty through which the project evolves. They are not arbitrary. They are natural. If a phase does not move toward its close, the next phase cannot begin. These phases are a common element of communication in project management. People often discuss them by diagramming the phases on paper and talk about the progress from phase to phase.

The examples of projects from history can be diagrammed on a chart showing their initiation phase, planning phase, execution phase, and closeout

FIGURE 2-2   Project life cycle and resource usage. A project life-cycle diagram is presented here that shows resource use by phase. During the initiation and planning phases, resource expenditures are relatively low. During the execution phase, resource expenditures are typically at their highest and peak before the closeout phase, when expenditures go to zero.

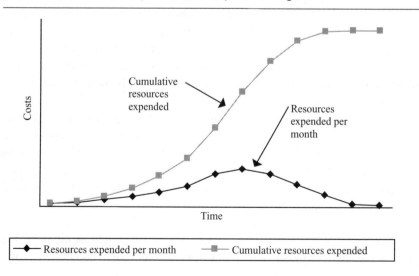

phase. The common way to illustrate this series of phases is called a *project life-cycle diagram* (see Figure 2-2).

While the project life cycle will be presented again in Chapter 4, this figure shows the typical pattern of how projects use resources as they move through consecutive phases. The life-cycle diagram here starts on the axis with a dark line, signifying zero or no resources being expended at the beginning, and escalates during planning because planning takes effort (a resource). The resource expenditure (per unit of time) curves up during execution because the main part of the project's work consumes the most resources. Finally, after peaking toward the end of execution, it curves downward to signify the reduction of staff and activity as it moves toward closeout. The end of a project shows zero resources being expended because the project site is closed and the people have moved on. A project life-cycle diagram is a high-level means of communicating the phases a project goes through on its way to closure and of anticipating the points in the project that will demand the most resources.

When a high-level diagram is used, one assumes that the details of the project are still to come or are on file elsewhere. Some projects spend more resources in the planning stages than they do in the execution phases. Most expend their resources during execution.[6]

Top-Down, Bottom-Up Integration

The process of initiating and creating a project is similar to the planning process in organizations. Top-down planning represents management's executive leadership and direction that provides the expectations and boundaries within which work is carried out. Bottom-up planning represents the more detailed or knowledgeable planning of the actual work that can be carried out only by the people who are trained and qualified to do that work. The point where the top-down "general" plan and the bottom-up "detailed" plan are integrated is the end of a phase, the planning phase. When the integration is complete and both management and workers can agree on what is needed, the work can begin.

In a project, the initiation phase represents the "management" view of the project: The goals, outcomes, results, and performance expectations of the project are defined, and the time and resource boundaries are sketched out. Any caveats or constraints are also voiced and recorded. The resources are approved by management to proceed with development of a detailed plan. End of phase.

The planning phase takes the box (boundaries) and begins to decide what goes into it. Another analogy is that the team takes the definition of the game (playing field, stripes on the ground, and equipment and people provided, with all their unique roles and talents) and begins to create the game strategy for that particular game for that particular team's challenges. When the game plan is complete and each team member has a defined role, the team declares itself ready to play. End of phase.

The execution phase is when you "play ball." Once the actual project begins, there is a lot of simultaneous activity going on, sometimes complementary and sometimes conflicting. A certain amount of it is pure distraction. Because the sponsor (owners), the project manager (coach), and the team members (players) all know the rules and the roles, they can each keep track of what is important and what is just "noise." There are key points for status reporting where the points are tallied and people rally to begin again (innings). When the time for action has elapsed or the delivery date arrives (clock runs down or the cycle of play concludes, which differs by type of sport), the project execution (game) is declared over. End of phase. A few projects (and a few games) go into overtime.

The closeout phase is when everyone congratulates each other, mourns lost opportunities, tells family and friends what happened, and grants press interviews (and in sports, sends the uniforms to the laundry). Everyone goes home (the players, the coach, and the fans). It's done. End of phase. In some projects, just as in some games, you do an analysis of what went right and what went wrong right then and there, at the end of the action (postgame interviews). Others schedule a debriefing session later to review in greater detail what should change before the next project (coach's game debriefing). The learning is distributed to the individuals (the team), the project manager (coach), and sometimes the sponsor (management) or customers (fans).

An analogy such as this one (sports) makes familiar sense to all of us. So do projects.

How Much Definition Is Enough?

You cannot manage what you cannot control, and you cannot control what you have not planned. Without planning and control, the only options are ad hoc activity, damage control, or quick fixes.

How much definition is enough? Adequate definition is needed for each of the first two phases, initiation (top down) and planning (top down and bottom up), before a team can move forward with confidence.

• A detailed definition of a plan's management view and technical view is needed before a plan can be considered adequate, primarily because the lack of clear decisions and detailed knowledge often is what keeps the project manager and team from moving ahead. Things just seem to bog down, grind to a halt. Planning is complete when everyone agrees that the plan is specific, manageable, achievable, realistic, and timely—and that the consensus is objective.

- The deliverable (product or service or result) needs to be described in adequate detail to estimate the time and resources to create it, and those estimates are needed to schedule work and resources.

- The plan needs to be described in adequate detail to be declared "realistic and achievable" by management (go/no-go decision). Approved!

- The team needs management's sign-off, as well as detail and resource approval, in the plan before it can execute the plan with confidence. Finally, the deliverable needs to be defined in complete enough detail (product acceptance criteria with project success criteria) to determine when it is in fact "done."

- The product or service must be defined as it will be when it is "complete" to know when it is ready to hand it off to another person or group. Only then can the project be closed out and the resources reassigned.

Project Life Cycle

Regardless of whether you have planned a project out in detail or simply started into it, there will be natural phases of definition that the project will progress through as it moves toward completion. Initiating a project (high-level planning), detailed planning, project execution, and project closeout are the commonly agreed-on terms to describe how projects progress in their definition (phases). However, a project also has a *life cycle*, opening when an idea for the project is first articulated and closing when the outcome of the project—as defined—has been completed to the satisfaction of the project's sponsor and customer and the product or service is moved into operation (or production) or, in some cases, the result is handed over to another project. The project is over, and the team disbands (see Figure 2-3).

There are names to describe the "output" for each phase. While organizations occasionally craft their own names for them, outputs have common names to describe them in project management: project charter, project plan, project deliverable, and project closeout report. Each output is the project's internal deliverable, which becomes the "input" for beginning the next phase of the project's life cycle. Each output provides information and authorization the project manager and team need to move confidently forward until the effort is complete and the project finally is closed.

FIGURE 2-3   Note: All projects must go through these phases, whether or not they are acknowledged and planned.

Project Phase	Input	Output
Initiation	Business need	Project charter
Planning	Project charter	Project plan
Execution	Project plan	Project deliverable(s)
Closeout	Project deliverable(s)	Project closeout report

CONTRASTING PROJECT LIFE CYCLE AND PRODUCT LIFE CYCLE

There is an important distinction between a project life cycle and a product life cycle that is often blurred to someone who is accustomed to creating a project to produce a product.

• A *product life cycle* typically is defined from the earliest stage when the product is conceived (concept development) to the point where it is retired from service or scrapped.
• A *project life cycle* typically is defined from the earliest stage when the effort is recognized as a project and not normal operations to the point at which the team can be sent home and the office cleared out to be used by another project, with the deliverable turned over to the operational owner.

Many people assume that a project life cycle and a product life cycle overlie. Actually, it is unlikely that a project life cycle will neatly overlie a product life cycle because it is assumed that for some portion of the product's existence the product will be "producing" value in an operations environment, subject to maintenance, refinements, and, eventually, retirement. A given product or service may be the subject of more than one project over its life cycle if, for instance, it is converted to another technology or subsumed in a larger project system. Some may even be subject to environmental remediation after retirement (see Figure 2-4).

How to Tell Whether Your Phase Is Complete

Again, projects have natural phases, and they are reasonably easy to define. It is a good general rule that if you cannot describe the final deliverable on

FIGURE 2-4 Product life-cycle stage chart. Products/deliverables go through stages of development. The number and type of stages differ widely based on the type of product being created. Whole projects can be created to develop only one stage if not enough is known to plan a project covering several stages. For such consecutive projects, the stage deliverables are handed off to the next project.

Stage	Stage of Development	Stage Activities	Stage Deliverable(s)
1	Concept or definition	Define the end-customer need Define the characteristics or features of the product, service, or process that will be designed	Description of the deliverable Customer needs and requirements document
2	Design	Design the product service or process Review the design Validate or test the product, service, or process design	Design plan(s) for creating the deliverable
3	Develop, construct, install	Pilot and verify design Train people Install equipment and/or build a facility	Constructed deliverable
4a	Start-up, initial production	Implement the design Produce and deliver initial product to the end customer Provide initial service to the end customer Initial process runs	Verified, tested deliverable
4b	Production, operations, and maintenance	Operate process at production levels for the end customer. (Usually not part of the project unless the project deliverable is a service)	Deliverable performing or producing at expected levels
5	Retire	Return resources (people, equipment, and/or materials) to the organization Dismantle equipment Dispose, recycle, or reuse materials	Deliverable removed from service

a project in substantial detail, you will have great difficulty estimating the cost to produce it or the time frame in which you can deliver.[7]

If you cannot describe the work in adequate detail to estimate how much time it will take and assess the resources, it is too early to enter the work tasks into a project scheduling and tracking system (such as Microsoft Project, P3, or online software). And if you have no project target date for delivery, you will not have a basis for reevaluating the process to refine it.

If you do not have reasonably accurate estimates against which to track the project, you will be going through a bureaucratic exercise to report on its status, because the plan will not be reliable enough to use for decision purposes or the decisions made on the basis of those status reports will be unfounded.

If you do not have a clear definition of project success, you will not be able to develop critical success factors, identify risks, or select risk countermeasures.

If you do not have clearly defined product requirements and project critical success factors from management, the user, and the customer, then you will have a hard time deciding whether the product or outcome of the project is really "done." And if you did not have those requirements and critical success factors defined in adequate detail before you began to plan and staff the project, you will find it extremely difficult to "redesign" the outcome to meet the satisfaction of the stakeholders.

If you cannot obtain acceptance of the product, service, or outcome of the project from the operations group, you are not "done" and will not be able to close out the project and send team members back to their regular jobs (or their next project).

Finally, if you have no mechanism for capturing the "lessons learned" from the project and feeding them into the systems and processes of the next project, the next project may not be any more successful than this one was. Even if you are fortunate enough to get the same talent on your next team, often the same mistakes are repeated.

The mechanisms and methods for accomplishing these phases are addressed in Chapter 4.

Project Design

How project phases overlie the product's development stages is at the heart of project design. Many people overlook this important element of project planning. A common view of a project is that an outcome (product or service or result) is first developed as a concept, then a project is created to make it happen, and finally the project terminates when the product or service or result is complete.

This is a perfectly logical view, but there is an element of complexity to it. For many projects, the information and decisions needed to complete a product or service at the same time as the project simply are not available. There are many reasons why the information and decisions may not be adequate to proceed.

• Sometimes a similar product or service does not exist, so there is no precedent to look to. Estimates are really "guesstimates."
• In other cases the technology, resources, and requirements are not defined adequately, so unanswered questions remain unanswered.
• In some cases the people who will use the product or service are either not yet identified or simply not available, so only general knowledge exists as to just what is to be created.

In each case the missing information must be documented and management signatures obtained to confirm its understanding of the associated risks.

Ambiguity and lack of information are nothing new. Products have been created without a market, and markets have been created without a product. The key point to remember is that the "deliverable" must be defined in adequate detail to make a realistic estimate of the time and resources necessary to complete it. If the performance requirements are vague, the chances are greater that the time and resources needed to create the product or service will be higher than expected rather than lower. A good rule of thumb is that the project manager, team, sponsor, and customer need to be reasonably comfortable that the outcome can be achieved within the time and resource estimates. Estimates are estimates. There is really no "final" number until the project is over. Some say that all estimates are wrong; some are just better than others.

Create a Project Plan to Reflect What You Can Deliver

The neat overlay of product stages and project phases is not always possible. A certain amount of vagueness or uncertainty is part of doing something for the first time. If the individual(s) who conceived of the idea for the project expect(s) the result to be obtained at the end of the project, the project manager needs to address whether that result is indeed achievable.[8] One means to determine whether it is achievable is by planning. The activity detail and increased visibility of risks and resource needs that result from planning provide information to determine the feasibility of the outcome of a single project. This is why the go/no-go decision follows planning.

What is often not clear to people discussing projects is that the outcome conceived as the initial idea for the project need not be the outcome of the first project. A particularly vague or uncertain undertaking can be implemented using a series of consecutive projects. A project might be created, and the outcome (or deliverable) may end up being a plan rather than a product or service. If a plan is all you can deliver, then the deliverable outcome of the project should be a plan. A plan may spawn a new project or several projects. Another project may create a design, not a product. The results of an initial project may generate a change in the organization or business, without a second project formed at all. A project is created around what can be reasonably planned and achieved. A goal of project management is to make the invisible visible so that it can be managed.

Ideally, very early in the process the project manager and team should be able to determine whether or not only a plan is to be created. Normally, professionals do not undertake tasks beyond their capability to deliver. With an inexperienced team and a new venture, however, a project can be embarked on, and in the course of concept definition it may be discovered that the project is too vague or too "undefined" to execute as a project at all. Typically the planning process generates an adequate definition to allow the decision to proceed or not proceed with a project. If the planning process itself is problematic, then a whole project can be defined just to create the plan.

On the other hand, just because the early stages of a project reveal that the initial project idea is vague or undefined does not mean that the project cannot occur. Many projects cannot be defined fully at the onset owing to legitimate constraints. The scope of the deliverable and the approach to the project can be redefined and confirmed as the project proceeds and more information becomes available. This point of redefinition is a great opportunity for replanning. Many people, however, avoid the term *replanning*. In some organizations, doing something again implies that someone goofed and consequently no one is willing to take on the stigma. On the other hand, plans are always subject to revision. Major revisions of a plan logically can be called *replanning.*[9]

As a general rule, whenever vagueness persists, define what you can. Seek agreement that proceeding under ambiguity is acceptable. If the product or service is expressed in a plan that seems realistic to the sponsor, achievable to the team, and possible to accomplish to the stakeholders within the specified time frame and resource limits, then the project can move forward. Everyone simply can agree that the plan may change as it progresses.

Defining the scope of the project is important but often challenging. *Scope* is a boundary that defines what is to be done in a project and what is outside the project's territory. Discovering early on that a project's scope is too broad is considered good. If the scope must be narrowed, the change can be made early, before problems develop, thereby saving time and resources and preventing disappointment. Sometimes the best (or only) way to uncover problems with a project's definition of scope is to begin to document it. This documentation process—and the communication that goes with it—will expose disagreement early, triggering compromise that can prevent problems later.

Once the scope of a project is refined so it can be executed, and the deliverable is defined with adequate detail to proceed, a key area of ambiguity is removed. At this point you at least know what is to be produced—a plan. It stands to reason then that the methods to produce a plan are planning methods, not building methods. There is an end to the confusion, and the project proceeds with confidence. The approach, the work plan, and the tasks can be defined, estimated, and assigned to people knowledgeable in how to generate and produce a good plan. The deliverable—that is, the plan—needs to be defined in adequate detail so that it can be refined and executed on a subsequent project.

The plan could be refined by the same group or by a completely different group. If another group is to implement the plan, it needs to own and revise it. The group responsible for executing the plan needs to do the task of replanning so that it reflects their knowledge, their skills, and their understanding. The new group will need to ensure that the elements are still in place to allow success, so they also will refine the project's critical success factors. The project (under the leadership of a new team and using a "new" plan) then gets approval from the sponsor to proceed.

How Many Projects, One or Many?

People often confuse the project management phases of a project with the product development stages of creating the product, service, or other result of the project (the deliverable). However, even when the project is not ambiguous, do not assume that carrying out a project means full implementation of the final deliverable. The end of a project need not coincide with the production of the product or service it is designed to create. When there are many unknowns and different expertise is required to resolve those unknowns, it is common for multiple projects to be carried out, and even after multiple projects the outcome may be no further along in product development stages than design. When different teams and/or different organizations possess the needed expertise, each is given a piece of the product life cycle to implement. Each is created as a project, and the deliverable from the prior project becomes the input material for the next project.

If there are multiple projects that are expected to contribute to a final result, the requirements and specifications for each portion of that result must be explicit and integrated across projects, often at the program level. The success of the subordinate projects is determined by their conformance to specifications. Each project is reviewed for conformance to specifications both at the beginning (requirements planning) and at the end of execution (key deliverable) before sign-off can be obtained to finish the phase. Large federal government projects often operate at this level of complexity. The end product is the result of several projects, each of which enables the subsequent or final project's work. Project success is measured by conformance to specifications; procurement processes and contracting specialists play a key role in making sure the project results conform.

For example, during the 1970s a nuclear power plant was identified as needed to generate power for a community through the controlled production of nuclear reactions. At the early stages of this developing technology, it was unlikely that the specific requirements for final construction of a nuclear power plant could be known in the planning phase of the project. A research project may have been the first project to be launched. The deliverable from the first project was factual information and parameters necessary before realistic planning could begin.

Because research skills and construction skills are so different, a different project manager and team would create the research than would construct the large physical plant. Therefore, the first project would be a research project, delivering its report to a planning project.

Complex planning and design of a nuclear power plant require different skills from either research or construction. Therefore, the second project to create the plan would have a different project manager and team from either the researchers or the team to construct the physical plant. The second team would turn over an architectural design with technical specifications to a construction project.

The final project would develop a detailed plan to construct the plant; then the team would construct it; and then the team would turn it over to operations and disband. After a series of projects, construction of the nuclear power plant would be complete.

Years later, after the plant was decommissioned, another project could be formed to restore the land to its natural state so that a residential community could be built there. Again, the skills and expertise of health physics would be required to decommission a nuclear plant and restore the land—

different skills and knowledge from those needed to construct it—so a new organization and a new team would be involved.

If instead of a complex nuclear power plant a single-family home were being constructed, and both the technology and the normal requirements of a family home were familiar, then the whole concept-to-plan-to-construction process might be a single project, with experts (such as an architect) hired during the early planning and architectural design phases rather than a completely different team. Multiple projects are unnecessary when the variations across phases can be resolved with expertise on the project and when no intermediate financial or market decisions are required.

Integrating Consecutive Projects
Projects are formed to meet a need, create a result, or take advantage of an opportunity that management has defined as important. Projects are carried out by people. Project management is the application of their knowledge, skills, tools, and techniques to project activities to meet the project requirements. Whether a product or service is developed as a result of a single project or many projects, the sequence of development for that product or service follows an iterative process—gathering available information, planning that stage based on available information, developing the deliverable using the planned approach, monitoring and controlling the work so the deliverable meets requirements for completion, and then closing out that specific effort, handing off the deliverable of that stage of development to the next team or project activity. While the cycle is similar, the approach or work plan differs based on what is being developed. The approach used to develop an architectural design is different from the approach used to construct a large facility. The approach used to develop software is different from the approach used to implement it on a large system or a handheld device.

First, consider the development of a large project. A project has a life cycle that includes the phases to initiate, plan, execute, and close the project. Throughout the project's life cycle there are parallel efforts within each phase to cycle through the processes. Each phase has within it project activities designed to initiate, plan, execute, control, and close the process in that phase (see Appendix A). These activities add detail and update the specificity of the plan so that the project is completed on time, on budget, and having produced its end result to specified requirements. The deliverables from each phase are turned over to the next phase for others to use as they proceed with the project. There are deliverables associated with initiating a project (a charter and business case, with supporting documentation of meetings, agreements, approvals, preliminary estimates, delivery date projections, constraints, assumptions, stakeholders, and desired benefits). There are deliverables associated with planning a project (a high-level plan and a detailed plan, with supporting documentation of the budget, technical approach, management strategy, work breakdown structure [WBS], tasks, activities, milestones, effort estimates, resource lists, risk plans, staffing charts, communication plans, and baseline schedules). There are deliverables associated with executing, monitoring, and controlling a project (status reports, meeting minutes, updated plans, change requests, risk lists, quality data). There are deliverables associated with closing a project (reports, acceptance documents, check sheets, legal releases, reassignment papers, cost data, equipment inventories, and closure forms). The type of deliverables and their names can differ by size and type of organization, industry, level of project management maturity, and type of project.

At each phase—as the plan is updated and made more accurate—the schedule is corrected to reflect real progress, the risks are refined to eliminate or add risks, the communications plan is advanced to the needs of the next phase, the data are updated, and the initial assumptions are refined or revised. At times, approvals are requested for major changes. (Sometimes this procedure is documented for use on various projects and called a *project management methodology.*)

A product or service has a similar life cycle that extends from its inception to its retirement. Typically, the life cycles of products or services involve the stages necessary to conceive, design, develop, build, install, operate, maintain, and, finally, retire the product or service (see Figure 2-4). Projects can be used at various points in a product's life cycle to create the product and put it into service, change it or adapt it for different purposes or users, or replace it with a more appropriate or timely product or service when it is "retired." The cycle is similar whether it is applied to creating a high-speed rail service, a physics textbook, or a Tesla roadster.

To integrate multiple projects, the handoff of one project phase to another and from one project to another must include the handoff of detailed requirements for the product or service and may even create the same functions in the next utilization. To lump together as a single project all the stages of a product's or service's development—from the time it was conceived to the time it is retired from service—is not necessary from a project management point of view. All that needs to be in the first project is enough clarity and definition to proceed through the normal project phases. You plan and execute what you can reasonably accomplish.

Sophisticated planning methodologies have been created to plan large, complex initiatives prior to detailed planning. Saying "We could not plan because we did not know how things were going to turn out" is no longer a viable statement.[10]

Fitting the product development stages to the project phases—and the handoff of quality deliverables from one phase or project to the next—is necessary for successful multiproject integration. Specific measures of quality and success are needed.

The Triple Constraint Plus Risk

The need for clear definition at the beginning of a project is not simply a preference; it is a necessity. As much as the project team may wish a project to move to the next phase, it cannot do so until there is adequate definition to move ahead. How much is enough?

The project can progress or proceed when the amount of clarity and definition is sufficient to convince the team, sponsor, and customer that the outcome can be achieved within the allowable and estimated bounds of time, resources, and quality of performance agreed to before the project starts. When the point of convincing the stakeholders is reached, the project manager and team can proceed with the plan. Typically, signatures of approval are gathered. The team then applies project management methods and techniques to create a project plan, then executes the plan, and finally delivers what it said it would within the time period, resources, and performance expectations defined for the project. (Of course, in real life it is not quite so smooth! There are risks, unknowns.)

Project management professionals refer to the *triple constraint*. The triple constraint is a balance of time (schedule), resources (cost), and performance (scope/quality)—the usual fixed parameters that a project inherits as it is approved. If one of these three must change, then at least one of the remaining two also must change (see Figure 2-5).

One would assume that an expert is needed at this point because things can become uncertain rather quickly when embarking on something quite new. However, even a novice can run a project once it is planned and documented. The trade-off is risk. The risk that the outcome cannot be achieved on time and on budget increases if a novice is running the project.[11] The decisions regarding risk—what is risked and whether it is acceptable risk—are part of the responsibility of management, those sponsoring and funding the project. The amount of risk the whole organization is willing to assume is the domain of executive management. One responsibility of the project manager is to quantify risks for management. The selection of an appropriate professional to run the project is management's responsibility (see Chapters 3 and 12).

FIGURE 2-5   The triple constraint. Once a project has completed detailed planning and the schedule, cost, and scope/quality are approved, changing any one of these three requires a change to one or both of the other two, because project commitments are based on the resources available, etc. An exception to this may be the introduction of an innovation or a new way to do something. The triple constraint is visible during project execution because a change in scope will impact the expected outcomes, deadlines, and budget.

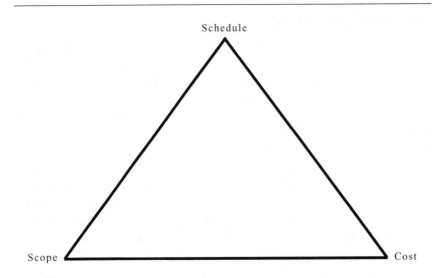

The triple constraint is often described as a triangle, with time, cost, and scope (performance/quality) diagrammed as the three constraints placed on the project's execution. Lengthening or shortening one side of the triangle has a simultaneous effect on the other two sides. If you shorten the time frame, the performance/quality side and the cost side are affected. If you want to reduce cost, you may need to reduce performance requirements or do less within this project (reduce the scope). If you decide to increase performance, you may find yourself faced with corresponding increases in cost and time unless innovation or technical improvements define a new, different way of accomplishing the same objective.

Many project management professionals will diagram the triple constraint together with sponsors and customers to communicate the impact of changes on the project. Discussing the priorities helps establish project critical success factors. Getting management's view of what can be changed and what should be kept the same also helps the project team when faced with later decisions.

TYPES OF PROJECTS

Whole projects can be focused on just one product stage—designing, developing, or retiring a product or service—and the methods used within that stage mirror the critical success factors for that stage. People who know a product or service can describe the criteria for successful concept development, planning, design, building, and removal or retirement. Not only are the methods different from one stage to the next, but the style of project management also is different. What project management professionals see as aberrations in the applications of project management by other professionals often are just the differences in style from one type of project dominant in that industry. It puts a new twist on the term *diversity*. Project management professionals and their applied methods come from many different contexts, yet they are all part of the same profession and field of work. The next few pages present some examples.

Projects Focused on Concept Development

There are a number of projects whose sole purpose is to generate ideas. Examples include some of the projects that attempted to create totally new solutions to problems that telephone companies were experiencing with vandalized phone booths. A technique for generating creative ideas without fear of being too impractical was created; the creators named it *goal wishing*. The rules of the project removed the barriers to creativity and broadened the options. They finally came up with a solution that was feasible: the stainless-steel hanging brackets for wall phones now seen on external walls of public buildings or the metal phone cubes in conference centers, malls, and airports that shelter pay phones or buffer noise during cell phone conversations. When creating totally new solutions, there are many facilitating techniques for generating ideas, sorting them, and enlarging on concepts that apply well to these types of projects.

Projects Focused on Planning

Some projects are generated with the sole intent of creating sophisticated, complex plans. Master planning projects are long-term undertakings. Many projects initially incorporated under a master plan may be implemented under a new plan, different from the one in effect when they were initiated. The master plan is refined as it moves forward. An example is the planning of the entire transportation system for Yellowstone National Park and the entire park service. A planning tool created at the Illinois Institute of Technology

School of Design was applied, managing the efforts of planners and eventually generating a planning document that, when printed, wrapped around three sides of a room. The plan was applied to renewing the whole travel, parking, and tourist management strategy in our national parks today.[12]

Projects Focused on Design

Architectural firms are famous for generating projects focused on design. The integration of human ergonomics, aesthetics, practical construction, cost-efficiency, and community acceptance into the renewal of a decaying urban area is a sophisticated example of a design. For example, Buckminster Fuller—most famous for his "geodesic dome"—designed the concept of the modular molded-surface bathroom decades ago that is being installed in modern homes at low cost today. The input from various technical specialists is important in design; it can be assisted by automation, but design needs a strong human component to be successful. Design implies customization, and the group affected by the design needs to be actively involved in the project to ensure that it reflects the needs of that group. For example, technical people who will implement the design would provide insight into technical needs; users would provide input into the users' needs. A trend seen in this age of electronic devices and global communication is to enrich our spaces with the pleasure and comfort of good art and design.[13]

Projects Focused on Building

Construction firms do a huge number of projects focused on building. These firms build dams, skyscrapers, planned communities, airports, towers, and even monuments. The emphasis on these types of projects is on following specifications and maintaining control; if the project is not carefully controlled, it may collapse, it may generate unacceptable risks in the future, or it may not meet the project plan's scope, time, or cost parameters. Often, in a commercial environment, meeting the target date for use will generate money (revenue from customers), whereas delays will result in losing money (lost earnings as well as contract penalties).[14]

Projects Focused on Tearing Down or Retirement of a Structure

After something is declared to be obsolete, it is decommissioned or demolished. Programs are completed, closed, and often replaced completely. Whole projects can be centered on efficient, risk-tolerant approaches to removing things without lasting damage either to the environment in which the things existed or to the people in the community. Removing old nuclear sites requires complex soil measurement and decontamination procedures, whole teams trained in reducing exposures, and compliance with complex government regulations to ensure completion. Controlled explosions are used to collapse old buildings efficiently, managing air emissions of fiberglass and asbestos so that others are not damaged by the blast. The end result of these projects is a clear site. When programs are retired or replaced, those depending on the programs are relocated and services transferred before removal is complete. When a software application or a system is retired, needed functions are transferred to another system or replaced by a different type of service or technology, and those relying on the data from that system or software are directed to the new source of comparable data. Sometimes the old and new systems run parallel during the final transition stage of the product.

HOW PROJECT MANAGEMENT IS APPLIED IN DIFFERENT SETTINGS

When we look at the varied environments in which project management is applied, we find that each has evolved to suit the type of projects most common to that setting—or perhaps simply those that evolved first. Project management tools, methods, and processes are developed to manage the most challenging tasks in the project's environment. Many of today's well-known project management tools were created for use on government contracts or construction projects and then adapted to modern users in different industries. Different tools have different strengths. In military and defense or pharmaceuticals, the critical success factors in that sector will drive the emphasis placed on different aspects of project management. Tools designed to manage those projects may not perform well when applied to projects with significantly different critical success factors.

Taking on methods and tools designed with other project types in mind may introduce unnecessary complexity into project management. Similarly, adopting a project management methodology designed for a different work environment can be unwieldy. What may be an important consideration in one setting is not in another. For example, the definition of success for a given project may depend on what phase of the product life cycle is going on when a project is initiated. That in turn affects what tasks are carried out in detail while others are dropped. Consider the flexibility of tools in the face of technological shifts. Some of the online tools tailored to coordinating projects for knowledge workers may not adapt as well to physically intensive projects, even if those tools are easily accessible geographically and convenient to field managers. On the other hand, sophisticated collaboration tools linking every office of a global consulting firm may not be as useful if workers are not spending much time at their offices.

Before adopting a methodology or approach developed in a different industry, ask: Is the purpose of projects in one industry to work through a new concept until a deliverable can be fully defined (a new medical product)? Then the emphasis of the project will probably be on the planning phases. On the other hand, does the product already exist and its application is from a familiar setting to one less understood (installing heating and cooling systems in modern skyscrapers)? Then the emphasis of the project will be on control. Developing new concepts is a significantly different process from adapting an existing product to a new setting. The tools and methods for managing these projects will also be significantly different.

To determine similarities or differences in project methods and approach, first ask questions. What are the differences in how these projects are conceived, researched, planned, documented, estimated, refined, staffed, and budgeted? What skills are needed? Where will the bulk of the resources be spent? In planning or in execution? Will the team on one type of project be tasked with using completely different methods, tools, and support systems than the team on the other, vastly different project? Is size—project or product size—a factor? What type of project manager is best for this particular type of project?

These questions were a looming challenge when project management professionals got together to create a common standard for project management, one that might apply to all projects. They finally agreed that it is possible to create a single standard for all types of projects. The standard simply needs to be adapted—tailored—to accommodate the differences.[15]

The Standard Approach Tailored to Different Styles of Project Management

As evidenced by the existence of a project management standard that was reviewed and approved by professionals around the world, project management can be *standardized*. However, the way the project management process is implemented varies according to where it is used. Many major sectors of the economy, or industry sectors, have evolved different styles of project management, with echoes of the different types of projects reviewed earlier. Their management context is different, and the critical success factors for managing projects are different. Some industries will have created elaborate quality planning and control systems, and others will have sophisticated methods and tools for getting the most out of every moment of time. Still others will have broad involvement in planning the project and will apply participative methods to their teams and activities to get their customers involved and supportive up front.

These differences will be reflected in what each type of project needs to do to be considered a success. A quick review of the different sectors and their objectives highlights the differences in their project management approaches.

- Projects in business need to make money or maintain and control the corporation to be considered successful. Some are required to do so by law (Sarbanes-Oxley Act). Many must renew their product portfolio and innovate continuously to stay abreast of competition. Since most revenue is generated on the upswing of a marketing curve, each maturing product with a flat revenue stream must be replaced by another entering the upswing. In capital-intensive competitive industries such as transportation, simply automating services such as airline ticketing and toll collecting reduced costs by reducing payrolls. Some clothing industries are sensitive to swings of fashion; the ability to transmit custom data direct to line managers allows them to refine their processes even in the course of production. Projects with high revenue potential in fast-changing industries will utilize cutting-edge technology and labor-saving approaches.

- Projects sponsored by government must provide services within the regulations, but more is expected from government each year without the benefit of added resources. Some government projects are not specifically required by law but are initiated to improve service to taxpayers to leverage existing resources more effectively. Internal Revenue Service (IRS) tax collection projects cut costs while improving the image of the IRS through online filing. Some projects are begun just to maintain existing services to an ever-increasing population, such as overhaul of the U.S. Social Security system's database structure.

- Public service (not-for-profit) organizations provide benefits to a broader society in exchange for favorable tax treatment. Their projects often benefit specific groups of citizens. In the United States, to shift resources to more critical functions, some hospitals are adopting digital communications and roving computer stations. Instead of staff returning to desks or nursing stations for information and communications, the information goes where the staff members are. Thousands of hours of free time are made available for better patient care. Automated processes also reduce human error where life-and-death consequences hang in the balance. Cross-checks of drug prescriptions to the medical condition can reveal errors or prevent adverse drug interactions. Projects to install case management systems in human services can help to protect children in foster care or the dependent elderly from harm or neglect, especially when staff caseloads get too high. Given the severe shortage of nursing personnel in the workforce, automation pays off.

• Projects in academia push knowledge into new areas or advance human understanding. Research projects that apply methods or technology from one field of study to a completely different field often generate new insights or challenge existing paradigms. An example might be the application of mathematical models to the study of social phenomena or logarithmic patterns to data on human body functions across large populations.

Evolution of Different Project Management Approaches

Just as the management and technical practices in each of these major economic sectors differ, largely due to the different missions and critical success factors they must address, their project management practices differ somewhat as well. They share the "generally accepted" practices defined in the project management standard, but they also have "common" or "generally accepted" practices unique to projects in that particular operating environment. These practices have been tailored over the years to address the elements necessary for success in those types of projects. Many of these differences can be attributed to the following:

• *Function.* The types of functional departments in their organizations and their relative importance in doing business shape project management. Some organizations rely on their legal department, government affairs department, public relations department, marketing department, personnel department, or purchasing department for services important to the business. Government does not have a marketing, public relations, or government affairs department. Those functions are not needed, but related functions exist in smaller areas under less obvious names, such as consumer rights or intergovernment liaison office.

• *Industry.* Some industry groups, such as manufacturing, financial services, medical products, and education, have tailored project management standards to the unique needs of their projects. An industry such as automobile manufacturing may have requirements for project practices that would not be relevant in education or the public utility industry.

• *Specializations.* Worker specializations exist within the management environment of various industries, allowing management to delegate mastery of the nuances of a particular discipline to a department or function so that its expertise is available to the organization in proportion to its importance to doing business. Regulatory expertise would be a major specialization in the pharmaceutical industry or new product development environment. Government contracting would be a specialization in organizations with substantial revenue from government sources.

- *Competitive culture of the organization.* Organizations that strongly compete with similar organizations or vie for larger markets will have specializations that research, refine, and verify company position or changing demand.

Because of these differences, individuals with experience in a particular sector of the economy (e.g., military, civilian government, construction, automotive, and health care products) will be strong in the areas required for successful projects in that industry sector but perhaps weak in the areas required for another. However, many critical success factors and typical problems of projects are very similar. Project management fundamental approaches and techniques are applicable to all projects. It is possible to engage experienced project management talent from another sector if a trusted technical lead can bridge the gap on specialization or cultural nuances (see Chapter 3).

SUMMARY

The similarities among projects over time show us how the natural phases of a project move through progressive elaboration of the outcome using one or many projects to implement a single concept or need. What makes projects unique and temporary also makes them unsuited to standard methods of operating management. They require autonomy and flexibility to manage all the unknowns and clear definitions and direction to produce a result that not only has immediate value to customers and users but also has enduring value to society.

In previous years, broadening the use of projects meant outsourcing to organizations experienced at delivering results through successful projects. Today the proliferation of internal small projects or even internal large projects has blended and obscured the boundaries between projects and operations. While they may appear to be the same, they are distinct.

The project management concepts in this chapter are useful for people who are engaged in implementing projects, as well as those who only interact with them from the outside. The chapters to come will focus on professional practices, the roles, and the rules of project management. They are as valuable to the project team member or project customer as they are to the project manager or other professional in the field.

When everyone understands what makes projects "temporary and unique" and the roles and rules needed for them to operate effectively, every employee or staff member who interacts with a project can work more smoothly with the differences, and all will benefit.

REVIEW QUESTIONS

1. The best description for a unique product or service in a project management setting is a:
   a. design
   b. product or service or result
   c. deliverable
   d. plan
2. A line manager can push a problem "upstairs" to a higher-level manager, but a project manager is expected to resolve the issues and the problems of the project within the project to keep the project moving forward.
   a. true
   b. false
3. Which of the following is *not* the role of the sponsor?
   a. support the project manager and team
   b. ensure that the project is aligned properly with executive goals
   c. provide resource backing for the project
   d. provide detailed plans for the project manager
4. When a project is declared "done," the deliverables normally are turned over to the process owner to manage and maintain them.
   a. true
   b. false
5. In a project, the initiation phase represents the management view of the project—the goals, outcomes, results, and performance expectations of the project are defined and documented in the charter.
   a. true
   b. false

6. For the project to move forward, the deliverable (product or service) needs to be described in adequate detail to estimate the _____ and _____ to create it. Which is the best answer?
   a. time, resources
   b. subjective, achievable costs
   c. realistic, accurate outcomes
   d. specific, easily met dates
7. Which of the following project phases or process groups is optional?
   a. initiation
   b. planning
   c. execution
   d. closeout
   e. controlling
   f. none of the above
8. The six life-cycle stages of a deliverable include:
   a. concept/definition, design, and start-up
   b. operations, retirement, and prototype
   c. construct, operations, and retirement
   d. execution, planning, and operations
   e. *a* and *b*
   f. *b* and *d*
   g. *a* and *c*
9. Consecutive projects make sense because the project manager or team that has skills applicable to some product life-cycle stages may not also possess skills for other product life-cycle stages.
   a. true
   b. false
10. The triple constraint helps to explain the balance of scope/quality, cost, and time. If scope changes, what must happen?
   a. cost must change
   b. time must change
   c. cost and time must change
   d. all of the above

3

THE PROJECT MANAGEMENT LEADER

OVERVIEW AND GOALS

This chapter provides insight into the role of the leader of projects. The role of leader is not restricted to the project manager. There are other roles of leadership on a project. In fact, leadership may be a fundamental building block of project management, and the leadership building blocks are needed on technical as well as managerial tasks within the project.

However, leadership is only one of the fundamental areas of project management competency. Project managers also are expected to have specific knowledge, skills, and abilities, as well as experience with the other roles that exist within a team. The design of a project will determine what knowledge, skills, and abilities will be needed by the project manager as well as those that might be allocated among the sponsor, team, and customer.

This chapter also will address the other roles on the project team, with an emphasis on large projects (where the greatest number of roles is found). As with any sports team, each role has a specific part to play on the team. Deciding on these essential roles—who will perform them and how they work together—is a key responsibility of the project manager working with the team when planning a project.

In addition to project management roles, there are product or service development roles that focus on creation of the project deliverable. The configurations of these product- or service-related roles vary by type of project and by industry sector. These will not be addressed here. While the project needs technical specialties related to creation of the project outcome, only the roles related to project management are addressed in this chapter, with general examples given as illustrations. However, the integration of these roles—both project management and technical—is part of project management.

This chapter also introduces the importance that individual values such as integrity play in managing projects. Values are important in getting and keeping the support of the team, as well as in exercising necessary authority and autonomy for effective project management. Professional ethics, moving into the spotlight after years of business scandals, is a hallmark of the project management professional and is part of the project management professional (PMP) certification examination.

THE PROJECT LEADER'S INTEGRATED SKILL SET

There is an inherent synergy and tension in successful projects because the functions to be performed so as to deliver project outcomes are as diverse as functions within the organization itself. Business discussions frequently point to the contrasts between different functions, such as engineering as a discipline or marketing as a discipline. Acknowledging those inherent differences helps us appreciate the effective project manager as simultaneously engineer and marketer. A project manager is expected to analyze and manage project detail while simultaneously aligning the "big picture" of the project with the "big picture" priorities of the work environment, the sponsoring organization's goals, and the customer's priorities.

Often, technical knowledge and competence are taken for granted in the project manager role. Technical knowledge and competence are only one pillar in the structure of project planning and execution. To recognize the balanced view of the project manager's repertoire—including knowledge, skills, and abilities—we need to acknowledge the value of the diversity of thinking styles—analytical and technical, strategic and integrative, interpersonal, and organized—that may exist on the team in addition to the skills the project management leader should possess (see Figure 3-1).

One of the reasons a project manager's "reach" needs to be so broad is that many different approaches can be taken to diagnosing and resolving project challenges. An effective project manager will apply different

FIGURE 3-1 Diversity of thinking style (quadrants). The best solutions come from a balance of diverse thinking styles. The project manager must be able to value, understand, and integrate these diverse points of view to explore possible innovative solutions and at the same time stay on track, focused, and on plan.

Logical **Analytical** **Fact-Based** **Quantitative**	**Holistic** **Integratng** **Intuitive** **Synthesizing**
Sequential **Organized** **Detailed** **Planned**	**Kinesthetic** **Interpersonal** **Feeling-Based** **Emotional**

approaches as adeptly as a carpenter uses a tool, for they are all part of the project manager toolkit. Beyond knowledge and skill, there are elements of personal character and values that are critical success factors in effective project management. We need to distinguish the "captain of the ship" within a project from the "king on the mountain" concept of the general manager in a routine operating environment. There is less slack to pass off responsibility to someone else when both your procedures and your strategy are daily elements of project survival.

Finally, the project leader or manager does not deliver results alone. Necessary support from the organization enables application of new knowledge, best practices, and effective resource control as the project progresses. The processes and guidelines set up to run the project balance the diagnostic and strategic planning functions within the project with the external controls and management strategy of the larger organization. The project manager simultaneously adds structure while estimating, planning, and tracking the work within the triple constraints of time, cost, and performance. A leader can shape project results in the larger organizational context while managing the details of teamwork and product quality.

ESSENTIAL CHARACTERISTICS OF THE PROJECT MANAGEMENT LEADER

Leadership is the bedrock of the project management role. The importance of the leader gets the spotlight right up front in any review of project management. Whether leadership is held at the top or delegated freely within the team varies by industry or corporate culture. Nevertheless, leadership is crucial to successful projects. It is even more important in work environments where the project manager must use influence instead of delegated power to get the work done.[1]

Projects are how organizations manage something new. The ambiguities and changes that are by-products of newness create confusion and indecision. Leaders are needed to bring order to the chaos and to insert confidence into the mix. Trust is also fundamental, based on confidence, as are honesty and integrity.[2]

There are different styles of project leadership as management is applied in different settings. Why these differences developed becomes obvious when you examine the predominant types of projects in different industry sectors. In Chapter 2 we examined the way some projects emphasize the initiating and concept-development stage of a product's life cycle. Others emphasize the design or development stage, and still others the operation/maintenance stage of a product's life cycle. Why are these different styles of project leadership significant to the success of projects in different industries? Because leadership must be appropriate to the organization's culture to be accepted.

Leadership Requirements by Project Phase

To explain the combination of the project manager and team in terms of general project management approaches requires us to look again at the types of projects being managed.

Planning a project is an exercise in leadership because it is at the planning stage that the vision, objectives, outcomes, value, and approach are negotiated among the sponsor, team, and customers/users. Gaining agreement is a subtle balancing of technical detail, conceptual acceptability, and accepted definitions of performance, quality, and value. Many of these elements are abstract and quite dependent on the culture of the environment in which the product or service will be developed and deployed.

A quick review of the natural phases of projects and the development stages of products can provide insight into what kind of leadership is needed to bring closure to each phase. First, review the life-cycle phases of a project:

- Someone's idea of a project needs to be translated into a more detailed definition (management view and technical view) before a plan can be considered adequate—primarily because the lack of clear decisions and detailed knowledge is often what keeps the project manager and team from moving ahead.
- The need or problem must be defined and boundaries placed around what is to be accomplished so that the project manager and team can manage scope.
- The deliverable (product or service or result) needs to be described in adequate detail to estimate the time and resources needed to create it, and those estimates are needed to schedule work and resources.
- The plan needs to be described adequately to be declared realistic and achievable by management (for the go/no-go decision).
- The team needs management's sign-off (permission and authority) as well as work activity detail and resource approval (a plan) before it can execute the project tasks with confidence.
- Tasks need to be defined in adequate detail for resources to be assigned, for work activities to begin, and for the project control function to track and measure progress.
- Finally, the deliverable needs to be defined in complete enough detail (product acceptance criteria) to be accepted by the customer, and project quality and performance requirements met, so that the team knows that the project is in fact "done" (project success criteria).
- The team executes the plan, creates the deliverable, turns it over to operations (or another project), closes out the project, captures lessons learned, and disbands.

In almost every one of these areas, leadership is required to create and negotiate acceptance of the definitions, the criteria, and the plan. Planning is complete when everyone agrees that the plan is specific, measurable, achievable, realistic, and timely. Accuracy is not the issue in these early stages; agreement is the issue. Getting agreement and keeping it are leadership tasks.

Leadership Requirements by Product Stage

Next, we can review the life-cycle stages of a product to see how leadership plays a critical role (see Figure 3-2 and Appendix E). Essential characteristics of a project leader buttress each of the life-cycle stages in creating the project's or series of projects' ultimate deliverable. The life-cycle stages of the product or service are the stages necessary to conceive, design, develop, build, install, start-up, operate, maintain, and, finally, retire the product or

FIGURE 3-2   Leadership requirements by product life-cycle stage. As this chart shows, leadership requirements and leaders may change at each life-cycle stage.

Stage	Stage of Development	Leadership Requirements
1	Concept or definition	Creativity and integration
2	Design	Design standards and integration
3	Develop, build, construct, install	Organizing Creative problem solving, discipline, and order
4a	Start-up, initial production	Customer-focused Value to the customer
4b	Production, operations, and maintenance or service delivery	Consistency Problem-solving
5	Retire	Meeting expectations

service. For each stage certain behaviors will become critical success factors for leadership in a project focused on that life-cycle stage. They involve creative thinking, integration of diverse ideas, application of standards, thorough and timely communication, organization and discipline, customer focus, problem solving, and consistency. At various points in the product life cycle, crisis management is useful, as are sales and closing. A single project that is focused on a particular stage of a product or service life cycle will require leadership that is strong in that area. To illustrate these one at a time, consider what happens in these separate stages:

• *Concept stage creativity.* In conceptual development, creative thinking, "thinking outside the box," and the integration of disparate points of view are critical to the success of new ideas. At this point diverse ideas are welcome because they round out the viewpoints of the end product and help to identify potential risks. Creativity and integration are necessary characteristics of the project leader in concept development. (A field that emphasizes this stage is research.)

• *Design standards and integration.* As the concept progresses to the design stage, not only creativity but also rules of design need to be considered. Quality must be defined adequately and at a level of detail to ensure not only product value but also acceptance by the project's customer. Specialists provide depth and rigor, both of which are incorporated in the design process. In other words, knowledge of standards, integration, discipline, and creativity are all characteristics needed in design. (A field that emphasizes this stage is architecture.)

• *Organizing for development.* In development, the ability to distinguish and discriminate among details, organize them, allocate them, link them, and prioritize them is critical. The key word is *detail.* Organizing, managing, and prioritizing detail and balancing conflicting factors into a workable outcome of value are needed during development. (A field that emphasizes this stage is events management.)

• *The discipline of building.* In the building stage, integration and efficient action are a key focus. The ability to follow a plan, get it done right the first time, and keep to the schedule all combine to place leadership foresight, insight, and action on the front burner. Creative problem solving, discipline, and order are needed during the product build stage. (A field that emphasizes this stage is construction.)

• *Customer-focused installation.* In installation, the focus is on plan execution, delivery of the product, and value to the customer. What works best, ease of use, fail-safe methods, integration with the work processes, and the work focus of surrounding areas make the installation leader the king of detailed accuracy and control. (A field that emphasizes this stage is hardware equipment installation.)

• *Operational consistency.* In operations, consistency and efficiency are key. Fine-tune the machine; refine the process. No rocking the boat. Fix it if it needs to be fixed, but focus on reliable, consistent performance. (A field that emphasizes this stage is manufacturing.)

• *Maintenance problem solving.* In maintaining products or services, exceptions and failures are not what people are looking for. The goal is to meet expectations: keep it running and keep it producing. Creative fixes, accuracy, and "heroes of the night" come into play. If (heaven forbid) a crisis should occur, maintenance looks to the low-key delivery of a return to normalcy—as soon as possible. (A field that emphasizes this stage is public utilities.)

• *Meeting expectations at product retirement.* In retiring a product or service, tying up loose ends is a key focus. Every nuance of completion has to be addressed to satisfaction (or overlooked to everyone's satisfaction) because when you are done you are done. Thoroughness, understanding of the requirements of what retirement really means, addressing the transitions, closing the loop on regulatory issues—all point to fastidiousness and persistence to the end. This is not the place for glory. Quiet service reigns. Legal and regulatory compliance also helps. (A field that emphasizes this stage is demolition services.)

There is a role for leadership in every one of these stages. Some leaders are conspicuous and visible; others are quiet and behind the scenes. The style of project leadership is not so important. What matters are the results it generates.

Does it stand to reason that the project manager and team leader would have different values, behaviors, and characteristics in each of these roles? Can all these roles be fulfilled by a single project management professional, or are the roles shared among the team? Will most project leaders selected to lead projects in these separate fields share common traits? These questions are answered differently depending on the *phase bias* of the industry and the culture of the organization.

Leadership Expectations Reflect an Organization's Management Maturity

Just as different industries and fields of work focus on different types of project leaders due to the life-cycle emphasis of products and services, companies within those industries at different levels of *organizational project management maturity* will also focus on different types of project leaders (see Chapter 12). Even with the same knowledge and technical ability, the leader's style will be different in a less mature management environment. In an organization that is *not mature* in its project management processes and practices, high value is placed on the project manager who is able to fix unforeseen problems, push a project through despite roadblocks, and take on the role of hero in saving failed projects. Skills in conflict resolution are expected, as well as good crisis decision making.

In an organization with *mature* project management processes and practices, a disciplined professional has greater value than the "cowboy" who is good at maneuvering around the barriers. In industries such as the military and construction, because they have evolved over many decades toward more mature project processes and methods, the project leader's ability to plan and manage projects using metrics and metric models is taken for granted. Knowledge of best practices is expected, as well as a network of references and colleagues capable of contributing benchmark examples or process insights.

Which is more important to project success, the *maturity* of the project management organization or the *competencies* of the project manager? Several research studies over the past few years have tried to quantify this. They looked at data and dug through corporate histories to determine just what ingredients are needed to produce a project that delivers results on time and on budget.

In his book entitled *Quantifying the Value of Project Management*, William Ibbs declares in Chapter 3's heading that "companies with more mature project management practices have better project performance."[3] In other words, companies with higher project management maturity tend to deliver projects on time and on budget. Ibbs's five-year, two-phase research study of data from nine major organizations clearly linked better project management to more reliable cost and schedule performance, and the project management maturity of the organization to the ability to complete projects on time and leverage resources for competitive advantage and business value (see Chapter 12).

On the other hand, Frank Toney, organizer of the Top 500 Project Management Benchmarking Forum, stressed the fact that a competent project manager is the key to project success. His interviews with executives of leading corporations clearly linked the character traits of the superior project manager to projects that perform well. "Judgment, integrity, and ethical conduct" were observed in the best of the best.[4]

How does one go about reconciling these seemingly conflicting conclusions? Ideally, an organization would have both.

The Project Manager Defines the Starting Point

Establishing the foundation for moving forward by means of a project requires that the project manager establish where the organization stands—its actual status or starting point—before proceeding. This is an act that sounds much easier than it actually works out to be. Individuals—and groups as well—persist in illusions as to their maturity and well-being. They will talk as if everything is solid and reliable. However, it is safe to assume that all is not as it should be, or the change would not be necessary. The project manager has to establish trust in accurately reading the status quo and independently check for facts to support what people are saying. To check facts, the project manager needs the ability to read behavioral cues (a science called *neurolinguistic programming*) as well as to locate physical artifacts of processes to determine whether the status of the organization is what people say it is. But trust is necessary to gain the cooperation of others in moving the work of the project forward. To do so, the trust of employees outside the project is needed so that they "tell things as they really are." The trust of the team is needed so that team members—confident that their work rests on a solid base—point out problems and issues as they see them. As pointed out earlier, the best solutions come from a balance of diverse thinking styles (see Figure 3-1).

Whatever the style of the project management leader, "doing well in a leadership job, regardless of level or formal title, demands an attention to relationships and to issues of cooperation and resistance."[5] The project leader must define what tasks need to be carried out, whose cooperation or compliance is needed to accomplish those tasks, and how differences will be managed between the leader and the people whose help is needed.[6] The leader then must tap sources of credibility from knowledge, track record, reputation, personal characteristics, values, benefits, power, or resources to build a link with the people whose support is needed so that they will provide it.

Furthermore, within the team itself, the project manager is responsible for anticipating and managing the internal competition and tensions that arise when longtime employees work with external hires or the "quick-fix heroes" go head to head with the "workhorse performers." It is important to the success of the project that everyone be able to do his or her job without being sidetracked in territorial squabbles.

Most surveys that attempt to define the perfect project manager tend to emphasize character traits more than professional competencies.

The heavy emphasis on what seem to be character traits more than professional competencies is underscored by research. In the December 2000 issue of the *Project Management Best Practices Report*, we reported on the research findings of Dr. Frank Toney, organizer of the Top 500 Project Management Benchmarking Forum. His work stressed the fact that a competent project manager is the key to project success. But he pinpointed a surprising competency as number one for PMs: Honesty, he said, was the make-or-break factor. [His findings have since been published in the book *The Superior Project Manager* (New York: Marcel Dekker, 2001).][7]

The Project Manager's Leadership Style Needs Support

Some organizations have relatively mature project management processes and support systems. Others do not. Some will prefer the disciplined professional; others the "quick-fix hero." While leaders can be identified in every type of organization, they are not the same style of leader. Each reflects the maturity, culture, and values of the organization that provided most of that leader's training.

If you take one leader out and replace him with another who shares the values, behavior, and emphasis of the organization, things work rather smoothly. Replace that leader with a leader of a totally different style or different values, behavior, and emphasis, and things do not run smoothly at all. It is management's responsibility to distinguish what type of leader is needed for a specific type of project in an organization at that particular level of management maturity and in that particular industry (see Chapter 12).

On the other hand, even a great project manager cannot juggle all the complexities of a new endeavor without a little technical help from the organization itself. The organization's past projects, technical environment, policies, procedures, human resources, and estimating data are all part of the project manager's toolkit. Unless those data and resources are available, the project manager is relying on past personal experience and knowledge that may or may not apply in the organization as it exists today. A mature environment provides support, making the judgments of the project manager more reliable and the possibility of project delivery on time and on budget more likely.

A mature project environment without a good project manager cannot produce a successful project. Both are needed. But a good project manager cannot do it alone either. The key to repeated project performance is to focus on project management practices that lend themselves to improved organizational performance—something organizations with low project management maturity tend not to do. A disciplined professional will use the lessons learned on each project to improve the processes that will support the next project and the next key initiative. A mature project environment will establish ways to capture lessons learned on multiple projects in the organization's portfolio, make them available to project managers, use them to collectively refine the organization's processes, and thereby increase future projects' likelihood of success. An efficient project environment will have those improvements and refined processes on an enterprise-wide system.

Conceptual Leadership

One of the key functions of leadership is to create and maintain the concept of the project in the minds of team members and project stakeholders. While the project manager is the point person for leading the project and the team, every member of the project team, including the sponsor and the customer, will have leadership qualities to be tapped. Gaining agreement within the team as to what the project is trying to accomplish is a good first step; then each team member should help "sell" that concept to stakeholders, customer representatives, and his or her own line management.

In his book entitled *The Idea of Ideas*, Robert W. Galvin, a chief executive himself at Motorola, wrote:

In the 50s, I wondered why so many problems and questions were bucked up to the top people. The many men and women I knew in lab and office and factory seemed more than able to deal with most of them. I urged certain of our managers to work out some scheme to involve those closest to the subjects in problem solving and initiatives. The management efforts to do so were scattered and more often than not insufficient. The common wisdom of boss over worker was too entrenched. . . .

> The common thread, the uncommon thrust of these refinements of now ordinary ideas, is a reaching out to the leadership qualities that all people possess to a larger degree than traditionally appreciated.
>
> Our appreciation of the existence and potential of these pervasive involvement/ leader qualities came earlier than most. Their full potential is yet to be fully tapped. Of this I feel confident, our people at all levels of responsibility will rarely be found wanting as the appreciation of their qualities are more evidently invited and trusted.[8]

In the work world of the future, the simple rate of change in the workplace will ask each person to step up to leadership. Although a few organizations still cling to the old 1950s "boss over worker" model, employees who previously worked in modern management environments will be less willing to take on employment with them, and change will occur over time.

Integrity as a Building Block

It is a good idea to look carefully at the part that individual integrity plays in managing projects and in getting and keeping the authority and autonomy needed for effective project management. Dr. Frank Toney, who we said before conducted a series of executive forums to study what corporations considered important in managing projects effectively, cites honesty as superior to education, experience, or even intelligence as a desirable quality in project managers.[9] His benchmarking forum indicated that the project manager is key to the success of a project. The best project managers are recognized by stakeholders as the single most important factor in project goal achievement, are truthful in all dealings and relationships, exhibit eagerness to organize and lead groups, exhibit evidence of a strong desire for goal achievement, are even-tempered, have faith that the future will have a positive outcome, and have confidence that their personal performance will result in a positive outcome.[10]

This can-do attitude and the imposition of structure and discipline on a project management environment create a leadership culture that keeps people working and pushes toward positive results.

All management requires trust. It is what sustains the link between authority and performance. What behaviors instill a feeling of trust will vary by industry or work setting. As noted earlier, each stage of the product life cycle will place greater or lesser emphasis on these trust behaviors. Whole industries will place higher value on some than others. Industries that hire cross-culturally will need to place more emphasis on training and team development to create a common value structure. Industries that hire many workers with the same background, education, and values will be able to rely on that consistent platform to align the work behaviors of the team. As we move into a dispersed-worker marketplace, however, the ability to locate workers with similar backgrounds will diminish significantly. And the challenges in managing them will grow.

The biggest increase in employee demand over the past decade has been in the technology and medical fields. Since technology has been interlaced with strategic initiatives and project management, technology-savvy project managers were also in short supply. As a result of the job growth in these left-brain dominated fields, most developed nations—from the United States to the United Kingdom and Japan—have devoted considerable time and treasure to producing left-brained knowledge workers. But this trend is shifting. As we move with digital technology from the information age to the conceptual age, logical, sequential, knowledge-based workers will have to add new capabilities. Daniel H. Pink, in his 2006 *New York Times* and *BusinessWeek* bestseller, *A Whole New Mind: Why Right-Brainers Will Rule the Future,* acknowledges that what he terms *L-Directed Thinking* "still matters of course. But it's no longer enough. Today we're moving into an era in which R-Directed Thinking will increasingly determine who gets ahead."

The reasons for this trend, he reasons, are that as many knowledge worker jobs move to offshore locales to reduce labor costs, the new knowledge workers who manage them will need to do what workers abroad may not be able to do equally well for much less money—use R-Directed abilities. He cites such activities as forging relationships rather than executing transactions, tackling novel challenges instead of solving routine problems, and synthesizing the big picture rather than analyzing a single component.[11]

Doesn't that description of the new knowledge worker seem a lot like our description of the project management professional? That is no coincidence. When the founders of the Project Management Institute set out to create a professional association for project management, they had already acknowledged that both right-brain and left-brain functions were needed to do the job. And when PMI added a second building to its headquarters for reference and assistance to those professionals, one of those founders, James R. Snyder, dubbed the building named in his honor "the PMI Knowledge and Wisdom Center." Just knowledge—a left-brain or L-Directed capability—is not enough for the project management professional. Wisdom is the other half of the equation, and wisdom is right-brained.

In this transition, when logical and sequential transactions are increasingly performed by computers, and dispersed workers must be forged into teams over long distances, the project manager will need to tap all of her skills to create projects that can succeed in this radically new environment.

Because of the short time frames in some projects and the priority placed on success, honesty and integrity are survival skills. But they are more important in some jobs than in others. Honesty and integrity are critical in the project manager role and very important to the leadership team. As a general rule, looking good is nice, but *doing good* is better. Popularity is less important than performance.

Looking good but not delivering is not project management; it's something else entirely. Would a project manager in the entertainment industry have to be very concerned with looking good? You bet. Ask anyone who does the behind-the-scenes work at Disney World. Deliver *and* look good.

KNOWLEDGE, SKILLS, AND ABILITIES OF THE PROJECT MANAGER

Much has been said about the knowledge, skills, and abilities of the project manager. Editors James S. Pennypacker and Jeannette Cabanis-Brewin, in their book *What Makes a Good Project Manager*, list the fundamentals according to many formal sources around the world:

> . . . Technical skill seems to be taken for granted; that's what gets a project manager candidate in the door. After that, the role seems to succeed or fail based on what are variously termed "Organization and People Competencies" (Association for Project Management, U.K.), "Personal Competencies" (PMI), or "High Performance Work Practices" (*Academy of Management Journal*, 1995). PMI's list of project manager roles (from *A Framework for Project Management*, 1999) reads like a soft-skills wish list: Decision-maker, coach, communication channel, encourager, facilitator, behavior model. . . .[12]

It is a safe bet that the successful project manager will need all of them: organization competencies, people competencies, personal competencies, high-performance work practices, and soft skills.

Not every project manager, fortunately, needs to be a superhero (at least not on the surface). Being a hero probably helps, but a realistic project manager will apply methods, techniques, and procedures to fill the gap. The expectations placed on the project manager for personal performance and effective project delivery vary by type of project and the industry sector sponsoring the project. Some industries will place more or less emphasis on technical over personal abilities, leadership over control, mentoring over conflict resolution, and so forth. The management maturity of the organization also will shift the emphasis a bit from crisis manager in organizations of lower management maturity to disciplined process manager in more mature organizations. While a project manager may adjust his or her style to a degree, a good match in the recruiting process is fundamental to a project manager's successful integration into an organization. The project management professional, as well as the organization's recruiting manager, need to assess the fit of individual leadership strengths to each project management position to reduce the risks of a mismatch in leadership style.

Viewpoints on What Makes a Good Project Manager

The viewpoint of the person judging what makes a good project manager also will vary based on the priorities of the person making the judgment. Management may put more emphasis on bringing the project in on time and achieving the benefits anticipated for the project. The team may value the structure, guidance, and discipline that make the daily work achievable. "A key insight from the past decade of project management/human resource research is that perhaps what is good for the team . . . is good for the bottom line."[13]

Here are a few viewpoints, each a synopsis on the fundamentals of what makes a good project manager.

Knowledge

The Project Management Institute's (PMI's) standard, *A Guide to the Project Management Body of Knowledge* (a key reference for the certification examination for the project management professional),[14] lists knowledge areas as "project integration management, project scope management, project time management, project cost management, project quality management, project human resource management, project communications management, project risk management, and project procurement management." Knowledge of project methods, tools, and techniques, as well as knowledge of the organization, industry, and functional area emphasized by a particular project, is also needed, some of which is the responsibility of the project manager and some of which is captured by the team.

Technical and Administrative Credibility

The project manager needs to have a reasonable understanding of the base technologies on which the project rests and must be able to use technology to manage the team, explain project technology to senior management, and interpret the technical needs and wants of the client (and senior management) while guiding the work of the project team. The project manager needs to be administratively credible, performing key administrative responsibilities of the project "with apparent effortless skill."[15] And although it is not necessary for the project manager to know the subtleties of all of the technical areas involved in creating the project's product, service, or result, he should put substantial effort into understanding it well enough to judge a team member's technical prowess or to determine the appropriateness of a proposed alternate solution.

Sensitivity
Successful project managers should be able to sense conflict very early and confront it before it escalates into interdepartmental and intradepartmental warfare. The project manager must be able to "keep the team 'cool' . . . in spite of rivalries, jealousies, friendships and hostilities," encouraging cooperation among the team despite personal feelings and likes and dislikes. The focus on project goals is put above interpersonal conflicts.[16] Sensing when things are being "swept under the rug" is a necessary survival skill, especially important in establishing the real status of the intended change early in the project. Sensitivity to trends and hidden agendas combined with tough business acumen keeps the project manager stable and working effectively even under a project's everyday stressful conditions.

Leadership Behaviors
Positive leadership behaviors are a recurring theme in the literature on project managers, including what the best project managers exhibit: "a love of their work . . . and embracing its challenges, a clear vision . . . and communicating this vision, strong team-building skills . . . and setting positive tones, structure and alignment . . . creating the environment and direction [for the project], strong interpersonal skills . . . listening to and leading their teams, discipline . . . completing each phase of the project properly, and communication skills . . . knowing when and to whom to communicate."[17]

Ability to Engage the Management Culture's Support
In addition to these leadership behaviors in the individual, one must look for the same behaviors in the management culture of the organization if the leadership abilities of the project manager are to be used fully: clear vision of the organization's mission, its purpose, and its goals; a strong team culture; positive expectations for performance and outcomes; willingness to listen to project teams and use the learning gained by listening; discipline and follow-through; kept commitments; and effective communication channels for different types of personnel at different levels of the organization. Without these leadership behaviors in the management culture of the organization, the project manager will be swimming upstream to implement projects successfully. However, even if this is the case, the effective project manager is willing, and

usually able, to engage the management culture's support, even if only by establishing individual alliances to enable the project to thrive. Interpersonal skills in this area are a critical ability for the project manager.

Integrative Problem Solving

The superior project manager is able to use problem-solving skills in multiple arenas: the strategic arena of leadership, vision, and strategy; the "soft" skills of team building, conflict resolution, coaching, mentoring, and forging diverse relationships; the administrative arena of planning, controlling, documenting, and communicating the key work tasks, goals, and risks of the project; and the technical arena of analytical methods, tools, techniques, and business management. Because project problems must be anticipated and managed in advance so that they do not create barriers to progress, the project management professional works hard to become well rounded and to exercise that breadth on behalf of the project and its goals.

What Does a Well-Rounded Leader Look Like?

If we were to look for a good example of a public figure to exemplify the project manager profile, we need look no further than Theodore (Teddy) Roosevelt, 26th president of the United States, in his "project" role as champion of the Panama Canal.

Teddy Roosevelt was well-known for establishing sweeping national programs such as the U.S. National Park System. He is less well-known for being a conspicuous "well-rounded" individual—the 20th-century counterpart to the "renaissance man." His "many ventures in totally different fields of human activity" were to earn him the designation of the "most interesting career of any American."[18] Further, he was called an "astonishingly multifaceted man" and "the most potent influence for good upon the life of his generation."[19]

Roosevelt's Credentials

Theodore Roosevelt certainly had the well-rounded skill set of the project management professional. His public achievements were extremely diverse:

- As a government official (executive manager), he was New York state assemblyman, governor of New York, vice president of the United States, and president of the United States; he also was deputy sheriff of Dakota Territory, police commissioner of New York City, U.S. Civil Service commissioner, assistant secretary of the Navy, and colonel of the "Rough Riders"—all by the age of 42.

- As a public executive (organizer and sponsor), he established the Department of Commerce and Labor.
- As a not-for-profit executive (leader and group founder), he was elected to the American Academy of Arts and Letters, was president of the American Historical Association, founder of the National Collegiate Athletic Association (NCAA), and founder of the Long Island Bird Club, as well as member of the Boone and Crockett Club.
- As a technical specialist, he was a naturalist (scientist/researcher), considered the world's leading authority on large American mammals; he also led scientific expeditions for major museums in both South America and Africa.
- As a family man and homeowner (private life), he ranched in the West, hunted on several continents, and raised a family of six. He was married twice (his first wife died in childbirth).
- As a communicator (documenter and scholar), he wrote well over 150,000 letters to his extraordinary network of friends and contacts, authored more than 35 books, and read a book a day.
- As a liaison to external environments (world leader in foreign affairs), he led the United States into the arena of international power politics, leaving behind American isolationism and striving to bring order, social justice, and fair dealings to American industry and commerce.
- In conflict resolution (mediator and problem solver), he mediated international disputes over Venezuela, the Dominican Republic, and Morocco. He was the first world leader to submit a dispute to the Court of Arbitration at The Hague and the first head of state to call for convening the Second Hague Peace Conference, where he obtained equal status for Latin America and outlawed the use of force in the collection of foreign debts. He negotiated an end to the Russo-Japanese War and won the Nobel Peace Prize.
- As a policy role model (as U.S. president), he established the first prototype of the "modern presidency" in domestic and foreign policy, followed by most of his successors in the White House (with the possible exception of Ronald Reagan). He expanded the powers and responsibilities of the presidential office. Many of his actual policies were adopted by succeeding presidents (Woodrow Wilson and Franklin Roosevelt). His foreign policy emphasized arbitration and world courts over war, the free movement of American goods and capital anywhere in the world, and the linking of a powerful and reliable defense with domestic prosperity (his "New Imperialism").
- As a resource manager (conservationist president), he designated 150 national forests, the first 51 federal bird reservations, 5 national parks, the first 18 national monuments, the first 4 national game preserves, and the first 21 reclamation projects. He provided protection for almost 230 million

acres of land (equivalent of Maine to Florida if laid along the East Coast of the United States).

• As an ethical businessman (human resources advocate), he "busted" trusts, bringing the large corporations under the control of the people, and secured two acts to regulate the railroads. He preached a "Square Deal" for all Americans, enabling millions to earn a living wage. He secured passage of the Meat Inspection Act and the Pure Food and Drug Act for consumer protection and the Federal Employers' Liability Act for Labor. (His values were marred by Victorian elitism in areas of race and gender.)

• As a risk manager and control specialist (military leader), he built up the navy and was a major force for military preparedness entering into World War I.

As a project champion (leader), Teddy Roosevelt began the construction of the Panama Canal, championing it and managing any threats to its construction until its completion in 1914 (see the next section). His role in funding the Panama Canal was one of his proudest—and most controversial—accomplishments.

The Panama Canal Project

A believer in Captain Mahan's theory of sea power, Roosevelt began to revitalize the navy after President McKinley's assassination made him the youngest president of the United States in 1900. Believing as Mahan did that a canal between the two oceans flanking the United States would become a "strategic center of the most vital importance," Teddy Roosevelt took it on full force. "The Canal," Roosevelt said, "was by far the most important action I took in foreign affairs during the time I was President. When nobody could or would exercise efficient authority, I exercised it."[20]

One of Roosevelt's first actions as project champion was to acquire U.S. rights to building and operating a canal in Panama. A French business still held rights to the canal because it was a follow-on initiative to the Suez Canal project. Roosevelt offered $10 million to the French business for the rights and then began to negotiate with Colombia (since at that time Panama was part of Colombia) for a 50-mile strip 10 miles wide across the isthmus. Colombia refused. The chief engineer on the project, under the New Panama Canal Company, organized a local revolt, and the project's cause was supported by a detachment of marines and a battleship sent by Roosevelt. The Colombian rebels accepted the offer, and the Canal Zone was established. Roosevelt then ordered the army engineers to start digging, and thousands of workers "tore up jungles and cut down mountains" in the malarial heat to break through the harsh land of the isthmus.

As project champion, once committed to the canal's completion, Roosevelt took whatever action he felt necessary to ensure that it occurred. He bought land, fought rebels, ordered digging despite insurgents, and eventually quit Congress. People fiercely debated his methods and his right to be there, but, said Roosevelt, "While the debate goes on, the canal does too; and they are welcome to debate me as long as they wish, provided that we can go on with the canal." The Panama Canal was finally completed in 1914.

Roosevelt liked to repeat an old African saying, "Speak softly and carry a big stick. You will go far." He was willing to use the military and pure rugged determination to complete a project once he had begun it. He just stayed focused on results.

If there were an honorary project manager designation—and projects were defined as initiating something new—it would be hard to keep this man out of the running. While all may not share his values or his goals, his diverse skill set, initiative, decisiveness—as well as his attention to the various relationships that enable project success—set him up as a real example of leadership in action. The Panama Canal still plays a key role in linking two oceans, bridging the North American and South American continents.[21]

Styles of Project Leadership

Leadership will continue to be a necessary characteristic for project managers in the future, especially as the workforce becomes increasingly educated and culturally diverse and as change in the business environment creates added layers of complexity. Leadership can exhibit itself in many ways. The overt team facilitator, the directive leader, and the indirect leader who empowers team members all have a "best" application. Perhaps there is even a value to different styles of leadership for each team member so that collectively they encompass the means to capture and engage the cooperation of others in their project efforts. (In some teams, each key team leader is assigned a particular relationship with a stakeholder to ensure that the linkages are forged early for a successful project implementation and monitored as the project progresses.)

We also will find different cultural definitions of what it means to *lead*. In some cultures, decisiveness and direction are considered good leadership (as in western Europe and the Middle East). In others, humility and team empowerment are considered good leadership (as in Scandinavia or Japan).[22] Translate familiar concepts of leadership into a more detailed and "modern" context, and you have a foundation for forging a definition of effective project leadership that is tailored to the needs of the immediate project. The workforce will bring to projects adequate diversity, complexity, and nonstandard cultural behaviors to challenge the modern project manager's leadership. Suffice it to say that a really effective leader will be able not only to deduce the leadership behaviors needed for the project but also to exert personal discipline on his own natural behaviors so as not to impede progress in a new project environment.

Definitions of Success

Project management carries its own definitions of success, primarily in areas of prevention rather than remediation. Delivering desired results is, of course, necessary to project management success. However, other fundamentals also are expected. Maintaining the "wholeness" of a team is a critical success factor. Avoiding fixes when the problem could have been foreseen and prevented is a critical success factor. "No surprises" is another critical success factor, assuming that effective planning and risk analysis should have identified much of what was to come. The rate of change, the strategic importance of successful achievement of project outcomes, and the proliferation of knowledge place the onus for self-learning squarely on the shoulders of the student of project management—and the project manager—to nurture, develop, and apply leadership wisdom.

Styles and effects of various modes of leadership, the value of effective leadership to project completion, and the stewardship of human resources for future projects will continue to be part of the project manager role into the future.

Role of the Leader

An effective project manager makes situational trade-offs daily. Crises demand strong and decisive action. Morale and retention demand team participation. The leader of a project or team must question and challenge the status quo to unearth potential risks and threats so that they can be resolved before they become problems. Balancing these seemingly conflicting roles on a fast-paced project, the leader who can be simultaneously courageous, diplomatic, and self-aware is most able to lead effectively.[23]

Leadership is a critical success factor in overall team effectiveness. As a project management professional advances, there is value in assessing whether the team leadership role needed for a particular phase is her strength or even whether leadership might be delegated. If certain leadership functions could be implemented just as effectively in other support roles— for instance, in the role of technical decision making or development of the project plan—then delegating that leadership provides a developmental opportunity to strengthen a subordinate's leadership abilities. In a lengthy project, a backup leader can be a valuable resource for future challenges on the project.

OTHER LEADERSHIP ROLES ON LARGE PROJECTS

As we compare personal abilities with those of the project manager, the interest value of different project roles increases. Not all students of project management or even certified project management professionals are ready to assume a project manager role, but they might find a place in the field of project management as a technical team lead, scheduling tool specialist, communications coordinator, risk manager, or cost or quality specialist. The added roles of sponsor, customer, program manager, PMO manager, and mentor are introduced to tack down the upper reaches of the project's larger context within organizations. Deputy and liaison roles are also presented as necessary roles on large projects. Individuals who choose the technical role in project management might move on in that technical track as a project engineer or control specialist.

There are various formal and informal roles that team members play in creating successful projects, as well as the potential for a single person to play more than one role simultaneously on smaller projects.

There are methods, tools, and concepts inherent in managing any project, with the potential that any one of them might be a whole area of specialty in large organizational contexts. Many longtime project managers use the roles and functions of a project team to introduce the methods and functions of managing a project, with the potential for a single project manager to learn and use all these functional methods over time.

Part of planning a project team's work is to distinguish among the roles the project manager plays in planning and executing a project life cycle and the functions that can be carried out by others. What might be accomplished easily as a task on a small project or done by a single person using forms, methods, tools, and techniques might require the daily attention of a project specialist on a much larger project.

Compare the functions performed on a project with the functional departments in a large organization:

- *Technical lead or work supervisor.* The technical lead has experience in creating a similar project, product, service, or result and is sufficiently technically grounded to supervise the technical work of other people on the team.

• *Knowledge expert.* The person people go to for answers is a knowledge expert or specialist. This individual can explain what is involved and how things work together, as well as the processes and issues that surround the tasks.

• *Technical developer, worker.* The developer takes pride in getting things done and often works independently on specific technical areas of the project. Some are generalists, and some are specialists in a unique area. Specialties are often hired as external contractors.

• *Communications specialist/technical writer.* This is a skilled individual who knows the functions and purposes of various media and the channels to communicate with various levels of the organization. He develops and even implements the details of the project's communications, including manuals, websites, or public descriptions of the project and its progress for publication. In some international projects, knowledge of the language and communication customs may also be needed in this role.

• *Human resources specialist/trainer/recruiter.* The human resources specialist is familiar with the roles of the project, the skills and knowledge required, and the typical sources of these resources, as well as the procedures and legal requirements for each.

• *Process engineer.* This is the person who can document, refine, and streamline processes and helps to create the project management process or tailor it from a combination of industry best practices and local organizational standards.

• *Project engineer.* This is the person who knows how projects work—their phases, methods, reports, and tools—and is a key resource to the project manager. She keeps the project plan effective and up to date and is a source of ready knowledge for managing the project.

• *Purchasing or contracts specialist.* Timelines, requirements, labor contracts, purchasing sources, and legal or financial requirements are valued in the role of purchasing specialist. Developing contract provisions that are realistic and appropriate for the project can make a big difference to the sponsoring organization's profitability. Proper lead times allow resources to be on site when needed.

• *Technology specialist.* Tools, software, media, and digital technology make up a field of knowledge critical to projects in today's business environment. Global projects and virtual projects rely heavily on these specialists to make sure the team can work together effectively.

• *Analyst/reviewer.* This is the person who knows how things are intended to work, can spot issues or gaps in the program, can break through logjams, and can keep people on track. The analyst also can help with project design and integration tasks under the project manager, working with team elements to be sure they are linked to the overall results.

   • *Audit/control specialist.* The project manager and executive sponsors need to be sure that numbers are accurate, regulations are being honored, and actual progress is reflected properly in reports so that accurate and timely decisions can be made and problems can be averted.

   Remember, if the team does not do it, the project manager gets the duty by default. If there is a function to be performed that is important to the success of the project and no support for that function is provided from either inside or outside the project, the responsibility devolves to the project manager. He can manage the priorities among them, but when it comes to managing the project and the role of the project manager, "the buck stops here." For a project leader to perform effectively, support is needed from the organization and superiors. These are the leader characteristics and the support that enables them:

   • *Leadership vision and communication.* The project manager needs information about the formal vision and mission of the organization, the intended project results, and the executive agenda being implemented by both the host organization and the customer organization if the project results are strategic.
   • *Resource effectiveness.* The project manager needs a thorough understanding of the resource climate—ample or scarce—as well as the measures that determine resource effectiveness. If people are defined as a resource, a resource management system for people will reveal their availability, unit cost, overhead, and time allocations, as well as policies for leave and longevity. Variables for effective financial management fit here.
   • *Leadership in accuracy and realistic expectations.* Conventions for expressing accuracy (e.g., ranges, percentages, and rounded numbers) and systems for collecting historical project data support the project manager in high-level and detailed budget and schedule estimates. Trends in previous project performance also are helpful.
   • *Leadership in team building.* The project manager should get physical appearances of sponsors and champions at key meetings, especially early in the project life cycle, so that the project is received well and gets appropriate support from external departments.
   • *Leadership in motivating and managing the team.* The authority granted to the project manager to assign or promote within the team, as well as options if project team members on loan are called out for other conflicting assignments needs to be clear.

• *Leadership in recognizing team members and groups.* Options for recognizing, rewarding, or acknowledging team or individual performance help to shape the project environment.

• *Leadership in discipline, persistence, and commitment to the plan.* Assuming the estimates are reasonably accurate and the due dates are achievable, the project manager needs the authority to ask team members to "go the extra mile" when needed, with the backing of team members' supervisors and options available to the project such as adding staff or contracting when such approaches are inadequate.

• *Leadership in learning and using the combined knowledge of this and former groups.* Any repositories of project information should be made available to the project manager, including best practices, formulas, historical data, lessons learned, and benchmark data available from similar organizations.

Weak leadership is a little understood factor in project failure, and placing leadership responsibility where it should reside within and beyond the project team is a good foundation for improving project success ratios in years to come. Whether advancing professionals master the nuances of virtual team leadership, situational leadership, technical leadership, political leadership, multicultural leadership, the ability to create a clear vision of what is to be accomplished, communicate it to others, and motivate others always will be key parts of delivering successful results through projects.

SUMMARY

Leadership plays an important role in making sure that projects operate as they are intended to. Many people agree that the project's leader is the most important factor in project success. Leadership is of critical importance in the role of project manager, but other roles on the project have leadership aspects to play as well. There are leadership roles on the project management team, including those that identify trends and act on them, those that prevent problems, and those that maintain the vision and goals of the project within the team and with their counterparts in the customer organization. There are leaders who support the project in ensuring product quality, organizational acceptance, and management support.

In Chapter 4 these roles will be placed in the context of the project environment—the project's initiation, high-level planning, detailed planning, execution, and closeout.

REVIEW QUESTIONS

1. **Which is the most important leadership role of the project manager?**
   a. clearly communicate the vision to the project team
   b. align the project with the priorities of the customer and sponsoring organization
   c. motivate the project team
   d. *a* and *b*
   e. *a* and *c*
   f. none of the above
   g. all of the above
2. **Projects that meet the deliverables acceptance criteria and the expectations of the project customer:**
   a. create confusion in the minds of the management team
   b. increase confidence in the leaders
   c. lead to order and decisiveness
   d. none of the above
3. **In an organization that is not mature in project management, a high value is placed on a project manager who is a disciplined professional instead of the cowboy or hero project manager.**
   a. true
   b. false
4. **Which of the following is *not* necessary for project management success?**
   a. delivering desired results
   b. maintaining the "wholeness" of a team
   c. developing fixes when the problem could have been foreseen and prevented
   d. "no surprises"
   e. stewardship of human resources for future projects
5. **An effective project manager makes situational trade-offs daily.**
   a. true
   b. false
6. **A task on a small project might require the daily attention of a project specialist on a much larger project. As a result, project managers working on smaller projects mean:**
   a. the project spends more money on human resources
   b. customer needs get more attention
   c. future project leaders can learn important skills to be used on larger projects
   d. the project is more successful

7. Considering trends in the jobs and value of knowledge workers, which of the following skills should today's project managers possess for success?
   a. synthesize the big picture, forge relationships, solve unique problems
   b. execute transactions, solve routine problems, analyze details
8. The successful project manager will need:
   a. organization competencies
   b. people competencies
   c. personal competencies
   d. high-performance work practices
   e. soft skills
   f. all of the above
   g. none of the above
   h. *a, b,* and *c* only
9. The final deliverable is the ultimate responsibility of the project manager, who must step in, by default, if the team does not perform.
   a. true
   b. false
10. Leadership roles on the project management team include:
    a. those that identify trends and act on them
    b. those that prevent problems
    c. those that maintain the vision and goals of the project within the team and with their counterparts in the customer organization
    d. all of the above
    e. *a* and *b* only
    f. none of the above

4

THE PROCESS OF MANAGING PROJECTS

OVERVIEW AND GOALS

This chapter describes some of the ways organizations manage projects, sketches out the entire project process of a single project from start to finish, describes the purpose and function of each of the project's phases, and discusses the first phase—initiation. Less attention will be given to the product of the project and its developmental stages because these vary by industry or type of work, except to clarify what is part of the project and not part of the product's development.

While discussing the basics of project phases and deliverable stages, the text also introduces the importance of establishing the support systems (e.g., standards, tools, methods, and approaches) that enable the project professional to produce a successful outcome efficiently and effectively. Details on those supportive elements will be expanded in the next several chapters. The organization's support for projects is expanded in Chapter 12.

People who work in mature project environments as well as those who work in less mature project environments can benefit from a review of the process of managing projects described over the next few chapters. A review can help them analyze and refine existing approaches, adjust the emphasis, or implement new processes so that the next project team can deliver results more efficiently and more reliably. Thinking through a generic model description of the project management process can provide value as well. By comparing processes that are used today in the reader's organization with standard processes that reflect what other organizations are doing around the world helps to unify and refine our understanding of what makes a project successful.

THE BASICS

Discussions that center on unmet needs, opportunities, or problems that need to be resolved often result in a project. Early discussions are usually focused on normal business approaches. When it becomes clear that a resolution cannot be achieved using existing operations processes, and a project is required, project managers usually are brought in to help shape the project and develop some of the parameters necessary for management to make a decision to go ahead with it.

Project managers usually are brought into an active role on larger or more strategic projects after executives, senior managers, and/or sponsors created the concept. Sometimes even the proposed technical approach or collaborative partners have been defined during the early discussions. The project manager and key experts use their professional judgment and experience to validate, refine, or alter the concepts into a plan capable of delivering the intended results. Once the plan is fully developed and considered adequate for resource commitment and control, the project's sponsor and senior management will approve it for execution. Then the emphasis shifts from planning to actually doing the work and creating the final deliverable for the customer.

Smooth project execution makes the intensive planning and infrastructure less visible to the naked eye. A lot of intensive planning goes into a successful project. The project can still succeed whether or not everyone uses the same terms for what is required. Most projects will proceed through a logical, commonsense process regardless of where they are located or who sponsors them or even what they are called. However, one of the benefits to using a standard process and terminology is that they create a common understanding of project management and project phases and product stages. This "common understanding" results in an increased ability of the sponsor, management, and team to communicate effectively about the status of the project and to agree on any actions needed to ensure its ultimate success (see Figure 4-1).

The standard process for managing a project is sequential and therefore has phases. Each phase begins as the prior one is completed. The life cycle starts with initiation and ends with closeout. Each specific project phase has project management tasks and activities associated with it, as well as project

FIGURE 4-1   Product/deliverable life-cycle stages versus project life-cycle phases. Aligning which product life-cycle stages are included in the project defines what sort of project you will have. First, determine the points in the product life cycle where the project begins and ends—that is, the affected stages. Then, during each product/deliverable life-cycle stage, apply project management. To illustrate how they align, hand-diagram the product's life cycle stages, then box out a project's scope to cover only one stage of development, as well as a project's scope that covers multiple stages, using examples such as the ones in Appendix E. Once the stages to be included in the project are defined, the remaining stages are "out of scope" for the project.

Life-Cycle Stages	
1	Concept
2	Design
3	Construct/build/install
4a	Test/verify/startup/launch
4b	Operate/maintain
5	Retire/decommission

Project Phases	
1	Initiation
2	Planning
3	Execution
4	Closeout

management deliverables that are needed to move the project into the next phase. Project phases are the project's life cycle. The phase names identify the purpose of the phase:

1. Initiation
2. Planning
3. Execution
4. Closeout

The final deliverable(s) of the project that enable the project's intended outcome consist of products, services, or processes and sometimes a plan or study. Each deliverable has a life cycle. A generic set of life-cycle stages for that product or service would be:

1. Concept
2. Definition/design
3. Develop/build/install
4a. Test/verify/start-up/launch
4b. Operate/maintain
5. Retire/decommission

The names used to describe the product's development stages differ from product to product and industry to industry. For example, software development's life cycle uses specific terms for these stages: analysis, design, development/coding, testing, implementation, maintenance, and retirement. The portions of the product life cycle that will take place in a particular project will shape the approach, methods, and deliverable that will be produced over the project's life cycle. A project's scope may cover the entire creation and development of a product, service, or other result—such as a plan or research report (life cycles 1–4a). It may cover placing the deliverable into operation (life cycle 4b) or revising it for a completely different use. It may cover just the conceptual definition of that deliverable (life cycle 1), handing it off to a different project whose purpose is to develop it (life cycles 2–3). Some projects exist just to dismantle a complex facility (life cycle 5). (See Appendix E for examples of deliverables' life cycles for products or processes, including Six Sigma.)

The project is defined to cover that period of the product's development life cycle necessary to produce the expected final deliverable and enable the intended business result. If clear definition and clarification of the product's entire development life cycle cannot be quantified and planned, then more than one project may be required to complete the development process.

Project Selection

To make the best use of the organization's resources, executives often prioritize projects based on their contribution to the organization's strategic initiatives. A project's potential financial contributions (cost-benefit, rate of return) are assessed, as well as strategic benefits (market position, entering a new market). The term *project selection* implies that management has chosen the project based on its benefits. Some projects are selected for execution based on profitability or benefits promised over time. Others are selected based on how they contribute other types of benefits to the organization, such as improved infrastructure or better market visibility. Getting a no-go decision does not necessarily carry a negative implication. Some projects are considered worthwhile but discretionary; they may be delayed until some future time if resources are scarce. Others might be planned but not selected for completion based on increased cost of materials in the marketplace, legal issues, or perhaps competitive timing. A competitor's product entry into the marketplace suddenly can undercut potential profits. Organizational changes—new executive leadership, a merger or reorganization—also can make a perfectly sound project suddenly obsolete. Changes in technology can change the assumptions on which the product's value was based, and the project can be stopped because it is not properly aligned with technology's new direction.

What Makes a Good Plan

A project progresses through its own life cycle, independent of the product or service it is creating. Before the project itself has been fully defined (initiation), it is described in general terms without much detail and perhaps some target dates or desired results. Once it is planned (planning), the project documentation has adequate specificity that time, cost, and quality performance can be defined and the project team has what it needs to manage the project. When the project is at its peak (execution), its plan and its team are performing effectively, both in developing the deliverable(s) and in managing the project. When the project is done (closeout), the product, service, or result is complete and delivered; the project plan is closed, and its records and processes are turned over to others for reference by future projects or by process improvement teams.

When developed fully, the plan itself will specify not only the project management deliverables from each of the project's phases (initiation, planning, execution, and closeout) that enable the team to move to the next phase, but also the documented approaches the project manager and team will take to create the customer's or user's deliverables and address each of the most significant management elements of the project (balancing competing project constraints such as scope, quality, schedule, budget, resources, and risk).[1]

The Project's Planning Environment

In more mature project environments, the executive management of the organization relies on project management professionals to initiate, plan, execute, and complete key projects, working in conjunction with other managers and specialists in the organization. The organization usually will have a defined process for managing projects, a policy on what qualifies as a project, how projects are to be selected, acceptance criteria, standards for judging a good project and a good product, and project management training so that everyone inside and outside the project can have a reasonable understanding of what to expect. Most organizations also will have a limited set of standard software and project management tools particularly suited to their projects, as well as a repository of best practices, providing training and guidance to project professionals on when and how to use them.

The job of the project manager is to take the expectations and information about the project—together with its desired outcomes—describe them, get agreement on scope, clarify the deliverable, then analyze the resources, methods, time frames, and actions needed to deliver results. The project manager and team will work together to create reasonable estimates and a plan suited to making work assignments and tracking progress, revising the estimates as needed until the project is closed.

In many organizations, project management professionals are rare, and the process of managing projects is not well defined. As a result, the organization underestimates the complexity of projects and relies on technical staff to produce an outcome that meets the intent of the project. The knowledge needed to implement the project is conveyed to inexperienced project team members via their tools, methodologies, and processes, and errors or inefficiencies are corrected after the fact. Operations staff may attempt to implement projects using the methods employed to manage other types of operations, usually with limited success and much rework. Some even employ project management tools to control the project team, as if they were operations staff. As discussed in earlier chapters, project management was formalized because operations processes usually are inadequate to the task.

People can manage the project management processes. If documented processes do not exist, they should be developed and made available to project teams. When followed, they can assist in ensuring that the work is done properly. A process document describes the information and artifacts needed to conduct the process, describes in simple terms what is done during that process, and specifies the resulting information or documents that should be generated as a result of the process (see Appendix A). If the process of managing projects, capturing lessons learned, and making process improvements is intact and generates continuous improvements over time, even these less mature environments will increase their success rate gradually. In most circumstances, more experience equates to more project management maturity if lessons learned are used for continuous improvement. The higher the maturity level, the greater are the realized benefits.

As the project is executed against the approved plan, the project's stakeholders, the sponsor, and the owners of the product all have an opportunity to capture learning, refine what exists, and add quality to the overall project management environment. Part of the professional's responsibility is to put that learning process in place. With each completion, results become more predictable and the risks inherent in managing projects are somewhat reduced.

Organizational Alignment

Many organizations have a standard process in place for creating, reviewing, and tracking projects within a portfolio—groups of similar projects managed the same—or across the enterprise. In larger organizations, the person who oversees these groups of projects is called a *portfolio manager.* Others who often oversee projects hold the title of *program manager* or *director.* Some organizations have formal portfolio management systems and a portfolio manager who uses the systems to quantify and prioritize the projects by resources, risk, strategic importance, or other established management criteria (see Chapter 12). Others use the term *account manager* to describe the portfolio manager for specific groups of projects that align with large customer accounts or revenue-producing products. Locating the proposed project's position within that hierarchy and determining who needs to be monitoring and reviewing it for the appropriate level of management is an initial task of high-level planning. Obviously, if the project is initiated at the highest level of the organization, it will undergo some type of executive scrutiny and require support from the management of more than one division. However, if the project is not enterprise-wide or highly important to the company's overall strategic initiatives, it may be relegated to a lower level of the organization.

How the project is positioned by management when it is initiated can affect the project manager's ability to shape its success. The project manager of a project that is not categorized as critical to the organization's success can have trouble competing for resources and might not get appropriate management support to succeed. If a project is critical to the organization's success but positioned at too low a level, a strategy may need to be put in place for building and keeping management support at every phase.

There is a general rule for selecting the level of management that will provide oversight and sponsorship to the project. The project sponsor should have enough authority to resolve all issues that arise within the project across any groups involved in its delivery. The project manager will utilize that sponsor to remove barriers and advance the project to its conclusion. For projects that may cause controversy or create turf issues across departments, it is even more important to choose the right executive sponsor who can resolve potential issues that may arise later in the project.

More mature organizations will have an established process and group of executives and managers designated for governance of the organization's entire project portfolio. It is their job to articulate strategy, implement policy, align projects and resources according to their priority, and make the tough decisions about risk, resource allocation, dependencies among projects, trade-offs and—if necessary—cancellation. Tools are available to support portfolio management and governance; these can be customized for the organization and can simplify the process of gathering decision data for the governance body (see Chapter 12). But governance does not require sophisticated tools. Some organizations involve their PMO—the project or program management office—in these processes. The goal is to align resource priorities and resolve risks and dependencies across projects so the organization can realize the benefits of its investment.

HOW PROJECTS GET STARTED

Project initiation begins with a business need and discussions on how to meet that need. These discussions often generate requests for additional information to make the decision to initiate a project. If management concludes that the business need cannot be met by adding this work to normal business operations, the organization decides to create a project. The value of the project may be determined by the purpose of the organization: a revenue stream, new market, profitability, or meeting a public need.

Once the need for a project has been defined and the importance or priority has been determined, project management methods and processes should be used for planning rather than the management processes used in normal operations. When management and project managers articulate that the project is different from routine operations, the project leaders can begin to familiarize the organization with the project management processes to be used.

When the project is authorized, key team members are assigned to assist in the planning effort. The roles and expectations placed on these key team members will dictate the amount of detail and the accuracy required of the plan, so they too need to understand the importance of the planning phase in creating credible estimates and believable project delivery time frames.

Managing Early Risks

Making promises as to project deliverables, budgets, and time lines in public too early—before enough is known—is one area of risk that needs to be managed from the project's earliest stages. If the project's sponsor and the customer make commitments based on unrealistic estimates when the accurate or actual numbers cannot even be known yet, there may be problems meeting expected dates, and the project may even be doomed to failure. If adequate information and data are not available to make realistic estimates, then unrealistic estimates may be made. Creating reasonable estimates that are not misleading is extremely important in planning a project. Recording the assumptions used to develop estimates early in the documentation and planning process will help to minimize later misunderstandings. As assumptions change, estimates will change as well.

Initial Estimates Are Usually Wrong

As the project progresses, estimates become more accurate. Estimates usually are proposed early in the process of project initiation to judge the project's potential magnitude and length and determine whether the project is worth doing. Since planning data become more accurate as more is known, project data are not very accurate in the project's early phases. While many organizations capture historical estimates, the accuracy of these estimates applied to entirely new ventures is even less reliable because the project team does not have a similar past experience to use as a guide (see Figures 4-2 through 4-4).

Proposed Technical Approach

The technical approach to be used in creating the deliverable, proposed by project team members, helps to gain support from the groups involved for

FIGURE 4-2   As the project progresses, the accuracy of the estimates increases.

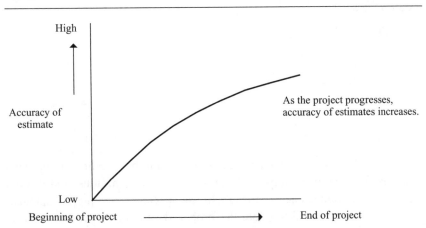

FIGURE 4-3   As the project progresses, uncertainty about project risk decreases.

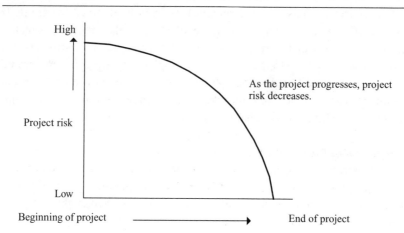

FIGURE 4-4   As the project progresses, the ability to control or influence total cost decreases. As graphs/curves in Figures 4-2, 4-3, and 4-4 demonstrate, over time the accuracy of project estimates increases, risk decreases, and the ability to control or influence total project cost also decreases, illustrating the importance of careful planning.

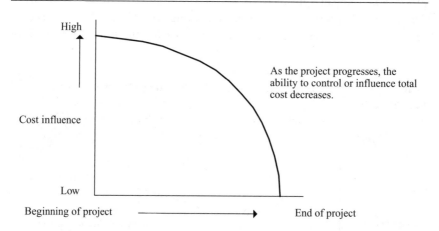

going ahead with the project work. However, the best technical approach emerges from careful analysis of the problems, opportunities, and desired results by knowledgeable experts. Technical specialists and project management professionals will validate the proposed approach or refine it based on their definition of the current state and an examination of existing processes as well as specific functions that must change to meet the stated business need. The approach proposed during initiation should be considered tentative.

Defining the Business Need

Project initiation defines business needs and sets the purpose and direction for the project. It stands to reason that you cannot manage what you cannot control, you cannot control what you have not planned, and you cannot plan what you have yet to define. The initiation phase of a project clarifies boundaries around the solution to a business need: What is to be accomplished, and what is out of bounds? What is feasible within the time frames and resource limits, and what is not? What is critical to business success, and what is discretionary?

If a clear articulation of the particular need to be addressed was not explored fully in preproject discussions, then project initiation is the place to define and document those concepts more fully. Some technical projects will need to define specific requirements. Government projects will need to examine the resource and technical implications of contract specifications. Service organizations will need to define customer needs and document expectations. Trade-offs may need to be made during planning or during project initiation, but the one trade-off that should not be made is satisfaction of the customer's real need.

The Charter

The project charter makes the project official. It is the document that puts management's limits, as well as expectations, on paper. It captures in writing all the key assumptions, critical success factors, and understandings that the project manager and team will be authorized to work with during planning. It documents any agreements discussed during project initiation, as well as the approach and approximate time frames assumed during initiation for use in high-level planning. The charter usually gives a high-level estimate of the resources that may be expended on the project. This estimate—expressed as a range—is subject to verification and review after the detailed planning process has created more reasonable estimates of what it will take to complete the project's work to the desired specifications.

A charter document will explain the business reasons for the project, record its main goals, specify the customers and their needs, name the final deliverables, and clarify what the customer wants the final deliverable to do.

It may list the names of the project stakeholders, many of whose resources may be required for completion. It outlines the business case, often providing insight into the way benefits were calculated and defined. It may propose estimated acceptable ranges for the project's budget and time frame, acknowledging that these numbers are subject to change after detailed planning provides more reliable figures (see Appendix B).

The charter establishes the organization's commitment to support the project by providing the authority and resources the project will need to achieve the intended benefits successfully for the organization. The charter confirms that the project is aligned with the organization's strategic priorities and will get support to achieve its goals. It should note explicitly, however, that the estimates made during initiation are preliminary and may change after detailed planning. Whether or not the organization requires signatures on the initiating document, routing it for approval allows all involved to voice concerns and make needed refinements.

Contracting to Perform a Project

A number of organizations that perform projects under contract to generate revenue enter their projects through a process of contracting. A *preaward document* is prepared to articulate the understandings of what the project's boundaries and assumptions are. Management consulting firms, consulting engineers, original equipment manufacturers, quasi-government organizations, and vehicle construction subcontractors may get their work by responding to a *Request for Proposal*, often referred to as an *RFP*. The response to an RFP articulates the bidding firm's understanding of what the business need really is, the deliverable, the scope of work, and the project's boundaries and critical success factors. While this document is not formally called a *charter*, it serves the same purpose. It articulates the fundamental concepts necessary for project planning. Similarly, the signatures on the contractual documents signal the approval of the sponsoring organization that those understandings are acceptable enough to proceed with development of a plan. Whether or not the organization calls it a charter, this formal initiation document is an important part of a project's initiation phase.

Feasibility Study Projects

Some organizations do not know enough about the parameters that will affect a proposed project to make clear decisions about the problem, the opportunity, or the business need to charter a project with confidence. In these special cases, a separate project actually may be created whose sole purpose is to examine and research the feasibility of proceeding with a project. (Feasibility—when discussed in relation to the product—is usually part of the earliest life cycle of the deliverable and assists with definition or analysis. See Chapter 5.) The report that is generated, once accepted and approved, provides needed clarification regarding areas of the project that were unknown or ambiguous. In some cases more than one project may be created as a result of analyzing the project's feasibility. In some cases operational changes are made as part of a larger initiative or program.

Some organizations will contract with one organization to do the feasibility study and another to do the project. The report's findings would be combined with other success criteria, assumptions, and critical success factors to prepare the formal documents authorizing the project.

THE PROJECT'S LIFE CYCLE: PROJECT PHASES

Since projects, by definition, have a beginning and an end, the project has a life cycle. The life cycle starts when it is first defined as a project (project initiation phase) and is chartered. It extends through high-level and detailed planning (project planning phase), receives management approval, and moves through execution of the plan (project execution phase) until the team deliverables are turned over to the customer. At the end of the project's life cycle, administrative and legal issues are closed out, the project is evaluated, and recommendations are made for improving projects in the future (project closeout phase). (See Appendix A for a more detailed diagram of the project process.)

While we have already touched on some of the ways projects are formed and carried to conclusion, the following provides a brief summary of a project's life-cycle phases.

Initiating the Project

The project is initiated when the sponsoring organization and stakeholders agree that the desired outcome cannot be accomplished through normal operations and decide to create a project. It extends through the processes and activities needed to define the project's purpose, business need, relationship to the organization's mission or programs, desired outcome, assumptions, constraints, and parameters. During project initiation, the project management tasks are to assess priorities for the project, consider alternatives, select an approach, outline the business case for allocating resources, document the assumptions and constraints, and obtain approval signatures that commit the organization to proceeding. Initiation concludes when management and key stakeholders agree on the high-level approach, projected timetable, estimated resources, budget, and scope of work to an extent that allows the team to proceed with more detailed planning. Briefly stated, project initiation begins with a need and ends with a charter that shares the background and specific requirements of the project. To verify that that business need can be met, a project plan must be completed first. The criteria and measurements used to determine project success in the charter should be conveyed to the project team to guide its decision making during planning.

Planning the Project

Project planning establishes the project's context, overall structure, strategy, and process. The project's planning phase begins with a charter and ends with a detailed approved plan ready to execute. Planning a project is carried out in two separate efforts that eventually are integrated into a comprehensive plan: high-level planning and detailed planning.

High-level planning is carried out to create the framework for the project's management. Discussions and documentation help to clarify the need and customer requirements, pin down critical success factors, define the boundaries and scope of work, describe the proposed approach that will be used to create the deliverable or result for the project, block out an estimated timetable for the project by project phase, propose the project's duration, and identify the types of resources that will be needed to create the business outcome and technical deliverables. High-level planning provides an opportunity for management to supply guidance to the team and for the team to refine the assumptions, boundaries, and constraints under which it must operate. It also helps to set the criteria by which the team will know it has completed its work and the project has been successful.

Detailed planning takes the scope of work, objectives, approach, and parameters already defined and uses them to articulate the work breakdown structure (WBS), tasks, activities, methods, and tools for doing the work. Detailed planning validates or discards preliminary assumptions made during project initiation and balances the expectations for quality and performance in the final deliverable with the time and resources allocated for completion. It confirms or adjusts the scope boundaries if necessary, based on changes to the schedule and effort estimates. It also creates the strategies for effective project execution, the timing and logistics of adding people and resources, links the time frames in the plan to the organization's business cycle and calendar, and sequences the relationships among dependent tasks. It creates the technical-task infrastructure that allows the team to succeed in performing its work. It lays out a cycle for oversight, and reviews and documents the methods and deliverables for project management.

Detailed planning is complete when both management of the project and the team's tasks, schedule, and methods are clearly defined, discrepancies are resolved, and all are integrated into a workable plan. The planning process addresses those stages of the product life cycle that will be included in the project's scope so customer expectations are aligned and the team can hand off responsibility for the deliverable at closeout. It also includes in the plan and project schedule the project management activities that will occur from project kickoff to turnover of the deliverable(s), including closing the project site if space has been allocated to the project or project team. Detailed planning is also when the processes for other elements of project management are carried out, such as development of the communications plan, risk plan, and quality plan. Processes for project human resource management, procurement of needed resources, and turnover methods for the product of the project are documented. The control plan specifies which methods will be applied to ensure the project progresses as planned and inserts any control and reporting cycles into the schedule that will occur either at the project or program level.

The changes that emerge from detailed planning are used to refine the timetable and cost estimates made during initiation and high-level planning. As these changes are approved by the project sponsor and—if appropriate—the project's customer or key stakeholders, the project schedule is baselined and distributed to those who will be managing or using the schedule.

Executing the Project

Executing the project marks a shift from defining what needs to happen to actually doing the work. The execution part of the project's life cycle starts with a detailed approved plan and ends with completion of the project's final deliverable. It is a cyclic process of proactive work activity, reacting to variances between the plan and actual results and controlling progress against the plan. The team's focus is on carrying out the defined tasks and working together to create the deliverables while ensuring that the business need or outcome is met. Actual effort and cost are compared against estimates, variances are identified, trends are assessed, and decisions are made to take corrective action. Planning may need to be revisited when estimates are refined and as changes are approved. But in execution the plan is being refined rather than developed. The detailed plan is "baselined" going into execution, and changes are tracked against the baselined plan to refine processes and improve estimates for future projects. Management is informed of significant variances from the approved plan's estimates. Other processes are carried out that either increase the chances for a successful outcome or manage risks. Some are designed to facilitate the work, provide support, or update information for team action. Some are continuous; others are repetitive. Some—such as communications—start as early as initiation and extend over the entire project life cycle. Others extend for only that portion of the project they address, such as technology planning or resource procurement. Still others—such as the risk plan—open and close as windows of project activity associated with those risks open and close. These processes help the project manager, leaders, and team to keep the project moving forward with all the necessary information, resources, updates, direction, and feedback needed to keep the work on course and the schedule and budget within established boundaries.

The work breakdown structure with its tasks and activities producing the deliverable or product is implemented during execution. The approach reflected in that work breakdown structure depends on the product description, the requirements, and the portion of the product's life cycle that is to be carried out in the project. For examples, see Appendix E.

Closing Out the Project

There are two main parts to the closeout phase of a project: closing out the work on the deliverable(s) and closing out the management responsibilities for the project. When the project is over and the work complete, the final deliverable or product, as well as all the resources—including the team—are sent off to other areas. The customer, sponsor, project team, and stakeholders give feedback on their satisfaction with the project and the deliverable(s). Management reports are filed and benefits are delivered to the host organization or sponsor. Management responsibility for the product shifts from the project manager and team back to operations managers. The project ends. Any lessons learned are recorded, and files are stored for future reference.

SUMMARY

This chapter provided a summary of how organizations manage projects. It described how projects get started, why initial estimates and assumptions that rely on operational precedent will not be valid for the new project, and why the iterative planning process does not lend itself to reliable estimates in the early stages of the project.

The chapter also provided a summary view of the project's life-cycle phases—initiation, planning, execution, and closeout—as well as the key elements and outputs of those phases. Both projects and products (deliverables) have life cycles, and aligning the product life-cycle stages with the scope of the project is part of defining what kind of a project it will be. Defining the kind of project—design, build, or implement—helps to define the methods and approach to be used, as well as the type of expertise that will be needed. The improved definition of expertise, methods, and resources in turn are used to refine the budget and schedule. These refinements—validated by key team members—enable a better estimate of project completion dates and product delivery windows, all of which are used to manage customer and stakeholder expectations. Although there are differences from one industry or organization to the next and differences in the processes used to develop the final deliverables, projects share common life-cycle elements wherever they are conducted.

The next three chapters address the planning process that occurs between project initiation and project execution (see Appendix A). Chapter 5 explains the concepts behind the planning process. Then Chapter 6 explains creation of the high-level plan based on the boundaries and constraints of initiation, a work breakdown structure, and preliminary estimates. The high-level plan scopes the project and is the basis for further planning. Detailed planning for execution—covered in Chapter 7—will add estimates at the team and technical levels, taking the detail of the plan and the reliability of the estimates one step further before project plan execution. Each level of planning is based on the same initial boundaries and constraints and objectives and requirements, providing even better estimates of the resources required to deliver them.

REVIEW QUESTIONS

1. Why would a project manager review the process of managing projects?
   a. to help analyze approaches
   b. to help refine approaches
   c. to adjust emphasis
   d. to implement new processes
   e. to allow the next project team to deliver more results
   f. to allow the next project team to be more efficient
   g. to allow the next project team to be more reliable
   h. all of the above

2. One of the basics of project management is to obtain agreement on the definitions of project management phases and product development stages so that everyone on the project has the same "generally accepted" understanding of terms related to project management phases and which of the product's stages will be included in the project's scope.
   a. true
   b. false

3. Issues that can affect a project's selection include all the following *except*:
   a. its financial contribution
   b. better market visibility
   c. improved infrastructure
   d. issues yet to be identified

4. Given that a good plan may be difficult to achieve, the factors that affect the ability to create and execute a good project plan include all of the following *except*:
   a. a defined process for managing projects
   b. a policy on how projects are selected
   c. acceptance criteria
   d. standards for judging a good project
   e. training
   f. a standard set of tools and software
   g. a company's fully defined product line

5. As a general rule, the best level of management oversight and sponsorship to a project is *not* the level of management that has the authority to resolve all issues that arise within the project across all levels of the organization that are integrally involved in its delivery.
   a. true
   b. false

6. A charter document will:
   a. explain the business reasons for the project
   b. record its main goals
   c. specify the customers and their needs
   d. name the final deliverables
   e. clarify what the customer wants the final deliverables to do
   f. all of the above
   g. a, b, and c only

C H A P T E R

PLANNING CONCEPTS

OVERVIEW AND GOALS

The goal of this chapter is to sketch out the planning of a single project and describe the purpose and function of the planning phase. Less attention will be given to planning that involves the product of the project and its developmental stages, except to clarify the project's work as it relates to the product, or deliverable, of the project, because such planning varies by industry or type of work.

More detail on how planning is actually carried out by the team is presented in later chapters, including how to find the information needed to plan the project and incorporate expert opinion and the use of charts, graphs, and scheduling tools to present project estimates.

PROJECT PLANNING

A project's planning phase begins with a charter and ends with an approved plan. The amount of planning that occurs between these points depends on the type and size or complexity of the project and the amount of certainty that exists in the process and definitions that planning is based on.

The process of planning takes the parameters from senior management (charter), the high-level project approach and strategy from project leadership, and the detailed tasks and resource estimates from the team and integrates them all into a comprehensive, balanced, believable plan for project execution. During the planning phase a written scope statement is prepared as a basis for project decisions. It addresses not only the boundaries of the work to be performed but also any work specified as "out of scope." (See Scope Boundaries Template, Appendix B.) The scope is defined further when the major project deliverables are subdivided into smaller, more manageable components. (See List of Deliverables, Interim Deliverables, Appendix B.) Formalizing the acceptance of the project scope (what will be delivered) with the customer and involving the customer in the review of the product or service features (quality and performance of what will be delivered) serve to verify the scope. As the scope of the project and the resources and time lines for its completion evolve during the planning process, the triple constraint evolves as well, allowing careful project delivery of the final deliverable on time and on budget.

There are variations in how different organizations divide the work of planning. The chosen approach depends on the size and complexity of the project itself and whether there is a standard process the organization chooses to follow in managing its projects. Some organizations "charter" a project as soon as the decision to explore the project is made (see Figure 5-1). In that case a project to determine the project's feasibility must be completed first. That project's deliverable, or product, is often called a *feasibility study* or a *cost-benefit analysis*, and this product fully defines the deliverables. If the product or deliverable of the project is not clearly defined (product life-cycle stage 1), then it is not possible to plan costs or schedule in detail for its design, implementation, and construction. If the full implementation is chosen as a result of the feasibility study, a separate follow-on project is chartered.

Most organizations begin the high-level planning process with a charter that spells out goals for the project. This precedes planning and development of the project approach. Budget is allocated for the planning process, and a project manager is appointed to carry it out.

Immediately following high-level planning, the charter may be refined to accurately reflect the consensus of the team and its sponsors prior to detailed planning. (See Project Charter Template, Appendix B.) The refined charter becomes the "management deliverable" for high-level planning and shapes the expectations of key stakeholders, including the project's customers and any groups that will be developing portions of the final plan.

Boundaries of the Planning Phase

The beginning of project planning occurs when management gives the project manager the authority to spend time and resources on creating a project

FIGURE 5-1   Project selection decision process. The high-level project life cycle is shown with a feasibility study at the beginning. In this process, the project is stopped prior to chartering because the findings of the feasibility study showed reasons not to go ahead with this project. A number of factors external to the project could have been involved in the decision, as discussed in other chapters.

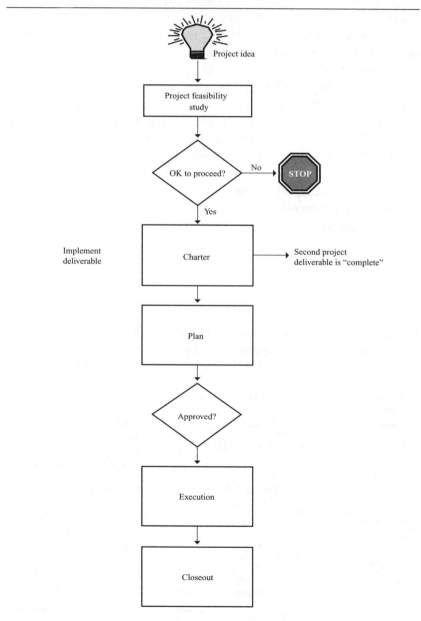

plan for the project. The decision to execute the plan (or not) marks the end of project planning. One term commonly used for this juncture is the *go/no-go decision*. Management typically considers the content of the plan together with other business environment factors before deciding to approve project execution (see Figure 5-2). Some of the issues that emerge during these discussions will need to be addressed if the project is approved. An issues list is created that will allow assignment of responsibility for each issue to some member of the team and the addition and tracking of additional issues that are identified as planning progresses. (See Project Issues List, Appendix B.)

There is a major shift in emphasis between the planning phase and the execution phase. When beginning execution, the team stops worrying about how it will approach tasks with strategies and issues and begins to actually do them. While the plan still may undergo some refinements once the project's execution phase begins, these refinements are considered modifications to an existing plan, not part of the planning process. To mark this shift in emphasis, the project plan is baselined and changes to the plan are tracked as changes. Major revisions to the plan are released when approved as new versions under configuration management.

FIGURE 5-2 Project phase inputs and outputs of project phases. Go/no-go decisions are made at various points in the project. Each project phase builds on the work of the prior phase until closeout, when the project ends.

Project Phase Input	Project Phase Name	Project Phase Output Go/No-Go Decision
Business need or idea	Initiation (sponsor)	Charter Project charter approval
Charter	Planning (project manager and team)	Project plan Project plan approval
Project plan	Execution (project manager and team)	Project final deliverables Final deliverables accepted
Project final deliverables	Closeout (project manager and team)	Closeout report

How Much Detail Is in the Plan?

A truly effective project plan is detailed enough to assign, delegate, monitor, and control work but still allows discretion in how the team chooses to carry out that work. Planning and control mean controlling against an agreed-on plan. Getting agreement on the plan usually means involvement by those who will have to pay for, implement, and sign off on it. Committing a group to deliver without its explicit agreement introduces unnecessary risk into the plan's execution.

In some plans, teams define their own detail and put it in the plan. In other plans, key players help define the high-level schedule and then major "chunks" of the project's work are handed off to others with contractual understandings. Separate technical plans may link to the high-level plan as the sequence of work requires. When separate teams contribute different parts of the plan, the project manager responsible for the project plan will need to balance and refine the amount of detail contained in the plan until it is appropriate for monitoring and control across teams.

While in some circumstances a bottom-up approach will be the first cut at a plan, the most common approach is to block out the approach and strategy from the top down using a work breakdown structure, or WBS (see Figures 7-1 and 7-2). Technical tasks and estimates then are added in detailed planning as the technical team provides specifics and the deliverables are identified. [*Note:* A bottom-up approach may be viable as a first cut when (1) only the technical experts on the project are sufficiently knowledgeable about how to go about the development of the product and (2) they do not have a consensus prior to planning on the particular approach to be taken.]

Integrating the top-down planning assumptions and the bottom-up technical estimates adds or deletes tasks and changes the overall plan. The early estimates and assumptions made during initiation and high-level planning are always subject to refinement after detailed planning is completed. Some organizations wait to collect stakeholder signatures on the document until after all planning is complete and revisions are incorporated into the original document. In this way, their support is based on the complete or current plan. Some organizations do not use a charter but have a standard documentation and approval process that performs the same purpose; they make proceeding with the project "official."

High-Level Planning

High-level planning defines the approach, the boundaries for scope, preliminary resource estimates, potential delivery date ranges, and strategies for management of expectations and quality within the team and with customers and management. The general time table and budget estimates from initiation do not contain enough detail to validate the business case until further analysis validates the project scope and objectives. But a plan cannot be considered viable for a go/no-go decision until more accurate estimates have been worked through in detail, with input from the project leaders and key technical personnel.

High-level planning consists of a number of separate processes:

- *Scope boundary planning.* What is in the project, and what is outside its scope.
- *Approach development.* The most viable project approach and structure.
- *Project duration estimating.* Elapsed-time estimates through closeout.
- *Timetable estimating.* Durations of the major project phases and product develoment stages by milestones.
- *Project budget estimating.* The overall cost of resources estimated for all phases.
- *Business case development.* Justification for the project's benefits and value.
- *Budget allocation.* Spread of the budget across project phases.

As more is revealed in defining the project and the desired outcome, greater accuracy becomes possible. If complete accuracy can be achieved, however, it will not be possible until the project is closed.

The Project Structure
The purpose of top-down or high-level planning is to use the boundaries and constraints placed on the project to create an overall structure for the project. The high-level plan serves the project's planning effort in a similar way as writing an outline serves the development of a report or a book. It is a blueprint that puts the primary elements of the larger project in their proper perspective so that as the detail of the project is developed, it holds together in a larger context.

Blocking out the project's structure allows the project manager and team first to test the concepts of the overall approach that were developed during initiation and then to align the project phases and product development stages with the time lines and resources estimated during initiation. In a large project, the linkages and relationships of subordinate contracts can be modeled at a high level into stages of development and integration, and sections of the plan can be marked for handoff to other groups for detailed development if needed. There are two parts to the high-level plan: the work breakdown structure of the project's management approach and the development strategy for the project's final deliverable. It is much easier to resolve structural issues at the earliest stages of the high-level planning process— when there are fewer dependent variables—than later in the project, when the changes will be harder to isolate and more expensive to integrate. The project's structure for creating the final deliverable needs the involvement of the people who will be developing the detailed (bottom-up) plan or technical approach. Input from the customer and key stakeholders is used to validate the definition and requirements of the final deliverable that are the basis for the high-level estimates of resources, as well as the optimistic and pessimistic schedule dates. Critical skills and knowledge can be articulated at this point and aligned with particular stages of development of the deliverable. It is at this point during planning when expert opinion can be leveraged: when are the specialists needed, and how will they be used?

Often the project's core team is brought into the planning effort to do project scope and objectives planning. (See High-Level Project Planning diagram, Appendix A.) A schedule-development session with the key team may be held to obtain input into the overall high-level plan and to validate projected phase dates. This process then leads to the development of the work breakdown structure, which, in turn, is used to develop the elements of the plan needed for project control. The project manager should by this time know what parts of the organization's standard project development process are required for this particular project and what discretion he or she has to change or tailor it to the project's unique needs. If the organization provides standard scheduling templates for project software, this is the point where those templates can be selected and tailored to contain the project structure as it is defined—after high-level planning has incorporated management's projections. While there is still a lot of detail to be worked out, the type of project has been defined and the approach is validated. The definition and requirements of the final deliverable are blocked out, as well as the general categories of resources. There is now enough information available to proceed with further planning.

Intermediate Decision Points

In top-down planning, there may be intermediate go/no-go decision points, particularly if a project contains a lot of unknowns or if there are hard dates that have to be met by certain contracts. The feasibility of meeting those dates may not be clear until a certain level of planning has taken place. Some organizations will want to know the financial return on investment of the project[1] or confirm the feasibility of the earliest delivery date before deciding to approve additional planning. If management's requirements are not met, it may decide during high-level planning to kill the project. Since planning is expensive, there is no value in continuing to plan if the overall project's profit potential or value contribution does not meet management's minimum requirements.

Resource Estimates

Once most of the high-level planning steps are complete, the question of resources is on everyone's mind. At the completion of top-down planning, only high-level estimates are available on the number and types of resources required to execute the projects. Resource categories can be added to the software template, with hiring estimates on their hourly rates, but the actual personnel are not yet identified. Their availability, cost, and sequence are still undetermined, and these elements must be decided before realistic cost estimates can be assigned to the project. The more project management maturity the organization enjoys, the more realistic and predictive are the plans and estimates simply because the organization's processes, standards, and metrics are refined. In some organizations, estimates derived from the experience of prior projects can be loaded into standard software templates to model potential cash flow needs.

Coverage of Necessary Tasks

Before moving into detailed planning, a last-minute check of the high-level documentation is in order. If there are pieces missing, categories of work still undefined, or questions without answers, it may be a good idea to obtain the data before creating the detail; otherwise you run the risk of planning rework.

The Work Breakdown Structure

The work breakdown structure, or subproject tree diagram, is a deliverable-oriented grouping of project elements that organizes and defines the total work scope of the project. Each descending level represents an increasingly detailed definition of the project work.[2] During planning, the work breakdown structure will be developed, deliverables named, and responsibility for creating the deliverables assigned to appropriate groups. The work breakdown structure (WBS) is entered into the standard software template selected for scheduling the project and managing progress against the schedule. High-level tasks and their associated deliverables are entered at key points in the WBS. Then they are linked to show dependencies. This automation process enables the first high-level estimate of duration for the project and allows discussion of a range of dates for delivery. (Those dates—optimistic or pessimistic estimates for each stage deliverable—are still subject to change, of course, because activities will be assigned to specific workers, and the amount of time needed to complete them will vary by the level and experience of the team member doing the work. That level of detail becomes available during project plan development.)

Documenting the Approach in Templates

In many project environments, software templates and formats will exist for capturing the initial ideas in early project documentation, as well as estimating tools or formulas for capturing the first estimates of the project in a standard format. Some will use a "bogey" or well-proven and accepted rate for familiar kinds of work plus ratios of proportionate resource estimates by stage based on prior experience. Ideally, there also will be standard success criteria for projects, a database of prior projects and estimates for similar efforts, and the contact points for approvals defined throughout the project life cycle. The project manager and team can use these tools and formulas to spread the work of the project over a framework created by a standard scheduling tool template. By preparing estimated distributions of resources and purchases across project phases, the team can predict scope and costs more accurately and extrapolate trends into later stages or make needed corrections. (See Staff Effort Estimate Template, Spending Estimate Template, Appendix B.) After the project is complete, capturing the actual numbers and adding them to the organization's project history database allows more accurate projections in the future.

In less mature project environments, a former project's paperwork or electronic archive can be used as an example in creating initial plans and schedules. Former project managers can provide estimating ranges for high-level planning, especially if their projects were similar in type or scope. The organization may have mandatory forms or heuristics to determine predictable levels of effort and costs per development stage for the project's end product. These estimates of effort then can be used to create a rough prediction of elapsed time and a preliminary budget. As formal as these initial documents may appear, a good amount of planning is still necessary before these documents can be considered complete (see Figure 5-3).

The project manager must have team and customer acceptance—and must believe that the plan is achievable—to lead the project team effectively and commit to the delivery of results. The project manager's challenge is to produce a plan that is not only realistic but also believable. The high-level estimate must be comfortable to both top management (who typically are optimistic) and the technical staff who will implement it on a task-by-task

FIGURE 5-3 Planning aids. This chart compares the types of planning aids available to project managers in more mature and less mature environments. Organizations that have a lot of experience with estimating generally have more accurate and more mature methods for estimating costs and delivery dates.

More Mature Project Management Environment	Less Mature Project Management Environment
Templates/guidelines	Experienced project managers or team
Estimating methodology	Required forms
Database of previous project estimates	Ad hoc planning

basis (and these folks typically are pessimistic). Even if the time frames for delivery of the project's final outcome appear acceptable, the project manager needs to get more information to have full confidence in the plan.

The end of high-level planning culminates in approval of the overall approach and a consensus on the acceptability of initial estimates; the next move is to create the detail that will either validate or refine those initial estimates.

DETAILED PLANNING

Once the project is documented adequately at a high level, a decision about whether to proceed can be made in view of the parameters given by the project champion or sponsor, key stakeholders, and customer(s). A project framework is defined, and formal approval is given to move ahead with detailed planning. Breaking work descriptions into specific activities during detailed planning makes a more accurate view of the work possible. At the end of detailed planning, more accurate effort and resource estimates can be made for completing that work. Thus, although a general agreement can be inferred from this approval to proceed to detailed planning, it is by no means a final decision to execute the plan and complete the project.

The boundaries of detailed planning can be established by its inputs and outputs. Detailed planning begins with a review of what has already been established and documented during the project's initiation phase: the project's scope and boundaries, range estimates and desired outcomes, how the project supports the organization's mission and management's current strategy, and any policy and prior project data that might be useful in doing more detailed planning. It uses the project structure and high-level tasks developed during high-level planning to generate detailed work activities by deliverable and assign resources. It ends with a detailed plan suitable for management approval (see Project Plan Development, Appendix A).

Detailed planning requires planning both the tasks to manage the project and the tasks to create the project's final deliverable in adequate detail to assign and track work. Scope statements guide the team in project plan development. In scope boundary planning, the scope of the project and the scope of the product or deliverable are defined separately. The *product* scope is a statement that describes the features and functions that will characterize the project's end product or service (often called *high-level requirements* or *scope of service*). The *project* scope is the statement of work that must be done to deliver a product with the specified features and functions in the way the customer needs it delivered. The project scope states which of the product's life cycle stages are included in the project (Design? Build prototype? Construct? Implement/test/train? Start-up/trial run? Document? Revise/refine?) and the work breakdown structure to be used for detailed project planning.

Types of Detail

Detailed planning uses the scope and objectives, together with a work breakdown structure, to create a plan that is suitable for project control and for managing the triple constraints of time, cost, and performance. The detail and accuracy in the detailed plan should be sufficient to allocate resources, delegate clearly, and measure progress. It should be accurate enough to elicit confidence and realistic enough that scheduling and reporting are meaningful activities. The refined estimates and dates developed during detailed planning are formally approved prior to project execution in the go/no-go decision.

The parts of a project that require detailed planning are:

- Effort/activities (including human resources and expertise)
- Purchases/equipment
- Subcontractors
- Task dependencies
- Decision points/approvals
- Interim deliverables
- Delivery dates

The tools to be used in project execution also need to be incorporated in the project plan, including team training on project management methods and standards. Quality standards and measures, methods and processes, forms, protocol, use of historical data, contract reviews, and appropriate use of software and other technical tools all should be determined prior to project execution. If areas of process or methods are still undecided, then tasks should be entered in the schedule or issues list to ensure that those decisions are made and that they are integrated into the overall project plan.

If the project is sufficiently large or complex, it will need to be divided into subprojects. Subteams will need to have their own detailed plans, with scope definition, budget, schedule, risk analysis, and integration into the larger plan for their part of the project and their deliverables. Tasks may be needed to prepare project policy and staff manuals. A common approach is needed across the entire project to plan for projectwide responsibilities such as dealing with client groups, government agencies, insurance representatives, financial officials, and other organizations that interface with parts of the project (e.g., utilities or external information technology support). If parts of the final deliverable from subgroups will need to be merged into a whole for the project, each subgroup will need to be provided the standards and templates to allow integration. When transmitting the work plan, the project manager is also responsible for communicating to the separate subprojects and work groups the deliverables' specifications and requirements for their part of the total work and the dependencies of other groups on both the timeliness and the quality of their work output. (See Work Breakdown Structure, Appendix B.)

Participants need to know in advance what their responsibilities are and what the overall policy is for handling unusual situations, special inquiries, or the press. The core team also may have responsibility for execution of the facilitating processes—the ongoing processes that create the project's environment for success—throughout the project (see the following pages and Chapter 9).

Project Plan Development

The structure of the project is defined by the work breakdown structure or subproject tree, which, in turn, is organized based on the final deliverable and project requirements. Examples from similar projects that have produced comparable outputs or products can provide help with the approach and tasks. Selecting the right structure for managing project work is a key decision in maximizing the effectiveness of the work process.

• The actual process that is followed will have a significant effect on the quality of the output. If best practices or specific methods have been defined for use, review points need to be identified at the early stages of the project to confirm use.

• If later stages of product development rely on certain standards being met in the early stages, then quality metrics will need to be established early and in detail and communicated to the team. What is expected, where will it come from, who sets the criteria, and under what circumstances may the output be rejected and sent back for rework?

• If customer acceptance criteria and scope management will involve certain key customers and users in decisions to accept or reject the end product, then those customers' parameters and requirements will need to be identified, understood, and then incorporated into the checkpoints (stage reviews). In addition, those individuals will need to be involved in the development of the scope and acceptance criteria up front and their presence added to quality checkpoints in the schedule.

Many of the key decisions that influence a project's ability to produce a quality outcome are made early in the project and are implemented by the choices made regarding work methods and project design. Quality approaches will need to be communicated to the team and built into the project plan. The later in the project that quality problems are identified, the more costly are the solutions.

From the very beginning, the team will need to have a vision of how the project will finish. The detail that team members enter into the plan will reflect the agreed-on version of that finish. The people who are controlling the progress against the plan also will use that vision to execute controls. To be successful, the project outcome must meet the clients' or customers' business needs, and the product must be fit for use in accomplishing those ends.

Once a project is planned and documented and the work plan is ready for execution, processes must be put in place to monitor progress against the expectations created in the plan. To be useful in monitoring and control, early in the process of initiating the project, criteria must be established for determining whether the end product of the project is suitable to meet the customers' and sponsors' needs. This means:

• The deliverables meet standards of fitness for use and conformance to specifications.

• The project is complete so that the team and the customer will know when it is done.

Criteria established during the planning phase are useful not only in determining whether the project is a success but also in developing the framework for managing and controlling quality. Risks will need to be identified, articulated, quantified, and judged appropriate to be within acceptable limits to continue the project planning process. (See Scope Risk Analysis Template, Appendix B.) In some cases, the project's processes will be familiar and risks and impacts will be low. In other cases, the risks and impacts will be significant and the project's entire approach and strategy may need to be designed to moderate and manage risk. Key points will need to be identified in the overall project or product life cycle to review and validate:

- The risk plan to minimize risk
- The quality plan to ensure quality
- Ongoing processes for creating the project's deliverable as intended

Interim points may be needed to capture lessons learned in addition to the final review at closure. Distinctions among special causes, or onetime problems, and common causes, or weaknesses in the system, can improve outcomes, particularly in longer projects. To ensure that the processes are contributors to overall quality, a final process review also should incorporate lessons learned.

Structure to Incorporate Work Packages

The sequenced tasks and milestones of the project schedule will signal when technical handoffs and quality gates for product or service development need to be placed into the schedule. There needs to be an orderly transition from one group's work products to those that depend on them.

Incorporating the Work Breakdown Structure into the Overall Plan

If the organization does not provide standard project scheduling templates or project management scheduling tools that reflect generic types of projects, the project manager and team leaders will need to incorporate the project's unique work breakdown structure into the overall plan. Some teams meet together in a massive planning session to develop the project work flow on walls, posting sticky notes on large sheets of paper that identify key tasks and necessary deliverables. The flow then is entered into a scheduling software tool. Others distribute the detailed plan for review and input electronically, sharing copies of the final plan online for collaborative development. The project manager will integrate and refine the submissions into a composite plan that has a reasonable level of detail, a viable sequence, and a logical structure to guide the work.

At this point the tasks, activities, and resources can be identified and the durations of tasks reasonably estimated so that a schedule can be produced for the work of the project.

Entering Process Review Points in the Plan

Once the project plan for managing the work of the project and producing its deliverables is complete, the plan needs to be reviewed thoroughly and checkpoints inserted for facilitating processes. The facilitating processes will be addressed in greater detail in Chapter 9, so only a quick summary will be provided here. These processes focus on the management of the project rather than the technical work of developing the product, service, or result of the project. They are also known as *knowledge areas* on the project management professional (PMP) certification test:

• *Project integration management.* This is a subset of project management that includes the processes required to ensure that the various elements of the project are coordinated properly; it is applied during every phase of the project whenever changes reshape and realign the project's progress—project plan development, project plan execution, and integrated change control. The project plan should identify key checkpoints of integration, such as when multiple streams of work converge or when decisions will be made to select one option over another.

• *Project scope management.* This is a subset of project management that includes the processes required to ensure that the project includes all the work required, and only the work required, to complete the project successfully. Scope management plays a key part during project initiation when the boundaries are set and the scope is planned, during high-level planning when the scope is defined, during project plan development when the scope is verified and the emphasis of the project is built into the plan, and again during project execution—during scope change control—to keep the work aligned with its original intent so that changes do not affect the project's scope. Scope review tasks need to be flagged at those key points in the project schedule.

• *Project time management.* This is a subset of project management that includes the processes required to ensure timely completion of the project; it is shaped by efforts such as defining the project interim deliverables and/or work activities, sequencing them into a schedule, and estimating their effort and duration—ensuring that the plan is developed properly and later executed properly during schedule control. Time management will be reflected in estimating methods and ratios, reporting policy, quality management strategy, contract management procedures, and process implementation. Time estimates and reporting cycles will need to be flagged in the plan for all these activities.

• *Project cost management.* This is a subset of project management that includes the processes required to ensure that the project is completed within the approved budget; it begins during resource planning with the identification of people, equipment, and materials in quantities needed to perform project activities. Cost estimating and cost budgeting occur when the cost of these resources is identified and allocated across individual work activities, and they are executed through cost control, budget monitoring, and quality processes. Procurement and contracting, cash management, vendor decisions and negotiating processes, human resources recruiting and retention policies, frequency of changes in assignments, use of productivity tools, and effective training all can have an effect on costs. Cost reviews can be entered in conjunction with milestones, perhaps using earned-value calculations (see Chapter 11).

• *Project quality management.* This is a subset of project management that includes the processes required to ensure that the project will satisfy the needs for which it was undertaken; it is built into the approach, standards, processes, measures, definitions, and details of the plan and implemented by the team through training and professional discipline under the direction and monitoring of those responsible for quality assurance and quality control. The quality philosophy of sponsoring organizations has a significant effect on quality, as do the quality habits and discipline of professionals brought into the project from other organizations or groups. Quality planning sets the relevant quality standards and defines how to satisfy them; quality assurance regularly evaluates against those standards, and quality control monitors compliance. Quality reviews need to be entered in the plan early in work cycles, along with control reviews at junctures where deliverables will be handed off or incorporated.

• *Project human resources management.* This is a subset of project management that includes the processes required to make the most effective use of the people involved with the project; it is based on the project deliverables, risks, and quality plan, and it helps to determine the human resources and skills needed for the project. It is implemented by the project leaders through team development and team leadership. Human resources practices can affect teamwork, team development, retention, quality, and cost, as well as legal and insurance requirements. Human resources management monitoring and oversight can be scheduled periodically, as well as when team changes occur.

- *Project communications management.* This is a subset of project management that includes the processes required to ensure timely and appropriate generation, collection, dissemination, storage, and ultimate disposition of project information; it is shaped by the leadership behavior and communications of the management team, articulated in the communications plan, implemented through information distribution of various types of media to the team and project's stakeholder audiences during the project's execution, and assessed through performance reporting, monitoring, and oversight and finally in records during administrative closure. Communications management strategy is portrayed in the project's formal communications plan. Tasks for periodic review of the appropriateness and coverage of the communications plan can be entered into the schedule.

- *Project risk management.* This is the systematic process of identifying, analyzing, and responding to project risk and is identified early during project initiation. The risk tolerance for the project is defined at management levels and recorded in the planning documents. The potential risks are identified by the team and stakeholders, quantified, analyzed, and prioritized during project planning and risk responses recorded. Risks for each phase of work finally are monitored and implemented during project execution as the work of the project is carried out. Risks are controlled as the appropriate response to risk is applied. Risk reviews can be planned in advance at key junctures of the schedule where risks will either have materialized or been replaced with new items to monitor.

- *Project procurement management.* This is a subset of project management that includes the processes required to acquire goods and services to attain project scope from outside the performing organization; it is formulated during development of the project's approach and articulated during project planning. Procurement plans finally are implemented and reviewed as resources, products, contracts, expertise, and work packages are solicited, selected, and administered during project execution and project closeout. Completion and settlement of any remaining contracts, including resolution of open items, is finalized at closeout.[3]

Cyclic reviews of each of these areas are added to the project after the plan is well developed to help the team remain on track, even as shifts in direction or changes reshape the work during execution. (See Reviews & Approvals Template, Appendix B.) The amount of time and attention paid to conducting reviews should be adjusted to the size and complexity of the project. Excessive reviews can not only interfere with the team's ability to perform work but also add unnecessary cost and effort to the budget, undercutting overall value and benefits.

Entering Deliverable Review Points into the Plan

The acceptance criteria for the project and the deliverable product serve a purpose during project reviews. They inform and remind the entire team of the objectives of the project and the desired functionality of the end product. Intermediate acceptance criteria can be set to identify the quality of contributing components during the process of development so that changes can be made early and rework prevented.

The customer who will accept the deliverable or product at the end of the execution phase needs to be involved at interim points in the development process as well as at established review points.

PLAN APPROVAL

The final process in the project's planning phase is the process that secures formal management approval and acceptance of the team's approach, cost, and time frame to deliver the project's desired outcomes.

Many of the management sponsors, resource contributors, and customer representatives will have little or no interest in the content of the project plan itself. After all, the primary purpose of the plan is to guide the team in its work. What they are interested in is that all the key factors have been considered and that anything that might prevent the project from succeeding or compromise the quality of the product outcome has been addressed adequately. For this reason a summary of the key parts of the plan and its processes is useful. This summary can include (see Appendix B for examples):

- A milestone schedule for deliverables, with interim key deliverables as well as final products described and targeted on the calendar using elapsed time (weeks, months, or years)
- A risk plan, with mitigation plan and responsibility assigned
- A deliverables schedule, which is like a flowchart showing the milestones and the interdependencies for each subproject
- Location and placement of approvals on the schedule for deliverables and how they will be managed
- A spending forecast, preferably with graphic charts to convey when financial resources will be expended
- Key roles and responsibilities and an organization chart for the project

A formal document will be prepared as a part of the project plan to formally capture management approval. Once general consensus is reached to go ahead with execution, those whose support is needed will have a line in the document on which to place their signature. The approval document can be stored online together with other supporting elements of the project plan so that it can be reviewed not only by those who signed it but also by any others who may wish to verify those approvals. A hard copy should be retained in the permanent project files.

When the go/no-go decision has been made, the team is free to proceed with the project. Planning is verified.

SUMMARY

This chapter provided a summary of the concepts that underlie project planning and the project elements that must be planned. The links from concluding the initiation phase to beginning the planning phase and the elements of dependency within those two phases were blocked out. The use of scope boundary planning documents and the work breakdown structure were explained, including methods of building a detailed plan with standard templates, and creating a work plan using a team. Adding checkpoints and quality gates was discussed with reference to the tools and software the team applies to maintain control during planning. The knowledge areas defined in the *Guide to the Project Management Body of Knowledge* (the *PMBOK Guide*) were introduced, together with their contribution to the project process used by organizations to manage projects (see Appendix A). The basic elements of how the project team will develop the product, service, or result of the project were presented, including both a high-level plan and a detailed plan, with templates of relevant information used as a reference to show how they are created (see Appendix B).

In the next chapter, the methods for planning, sources of information, and the roles of the leaders and sponsors in shaping the project will be explored.

REVIEW QUESTIONS

1. The work breakdown structure is a(n) _____ grouping of project elements that organizes and defines the total work scope of the project.
   a. activity-oriented
   b. organization-oriented
   c. risk-oriented
   d. deliverable-oriented

2. The sequenced tasks and milestones of a project schedule will signal the technical handoffs but not quality gates for product or service developments that need to be placed on the schedule.
   a. true
   b. false

3. Cyclic reviews of each of the PMBOK areas should be added to the project after the plan is well developed to help the team remain on track, even as shifts in direction or changes reshape the work during execution.
   a. true
   b. false

4. The final process in the project planning phase is the:
   a. team approach, cost, and framework to deliver the project's desired outcomes
   b. formal approval and acceptance
   c. team's agreement and acceptance
   d. team's celebration and review
   e. sponsor's review and approval

6

HIGH-LEVEL PLANNING

OVERVIEW AND GOALS

This chapter describes some of the methods the project manager and team use to capture the information necessary to simultaneously create a project plan and advance the project through its developmental phases. The project manager, assisted by key team members, seeks out the information from initial discussions and concerns until the project is sufficiently defined that it can be planned properly. Using this initial documentation, the project manager and team then complete the planning phase. A number of different roles are involved in projects, and using the viewpoints and expertise of the people in those roles provides significant value in creating a viable project plan.

In this chapter we'll look at how the professional gathers and documents the project management information needed for project planning. During this phase it is important to listen to the voices of the project stakeholders, integrating the needs and requirements of the sponsor and customer into elements of a comprehensive plan to guide the work of the team.

The emphasis in planning is on designing the entire project's life cycle of effort at a high level during the initial phase because the earlier a process is established, the simpler and more cost-effective it will be to implement. Changes and rework cost money. Once the high-level plan is sound, the process of detailed planning adds the subtask detail needed to make the resource estimates and timetable credible for execution.

If sufficient effort is put into planning the project itself, how it will be managed, and how it will create an environment of success for the team, then more emphasis can be placed on creation and management of the product or service, the ultimate source of benefits for the customer.

IT IS ALL ABOUT PLANNING

Directing and facilitating the planning process are the main functions of a project manager. The plan that is created becomes the logical platform for project management activities during the project's execution phase. Without a plan, there can be no triple constraint and no meaning to the challenge of delivering a quality product or service on time and on budget. The scope of work, the budget, and the time line are created to describe as realistically as possible what is needed to carry out the project. Each depends on the others. They are the three points of the triple constraint.

The project management professional may end up coordinating the work of other team members, vendors, contractors, consultants, and subcontract managers. He will use a variety of methods, tools, and techniques to manage and control that work. It is part of the project management professional's job to make those early planning judgments of when and how they will be used, as well as make the tool selections and design decisions so that each later stage of the project's development builds naturally on those that went before.

As we have mentioned, planning is a human analytical function that is not yet "automated" through the use of tools. Tools can be used to record, realign, track, and measure the project's activities, but tools cannot manage. The activities in this chapter are those that the project management professional, rather than the members of the technical team, is responsible for implementing. How the parameters and limits of the project are defined, where they come from, and how they are converted from interests and concerns into elements of the project's planning and control structure help to determine the project's eventual success.

HIGH-LEVEL PLANNING

High-level planning is like doing a quick sketch of the project. In a "projectized" organization, there may be a discrete set of project types that an organization performs routinely, and this project may have been placed in one of those categories as a first guess. However, there is not very much to work with at this stage of project development for creating a detailed plan except for perhaps previous estimates of time and costs from a similar project and some general descriptions about the project's purpose, end deliverable, and desired outcomes. The clarification and organization of project boundaries require time and effort.

Planning a project is not a job for the timid. There are many challenges to implementing projects that arise from doing something new for the first time. The business need or the problem being addressed does not fit neatly into the normal way of doing business. People are frustrated, and issues emerge. The project manager needs to communicate to all involved why a project approach is viable. The project approach is viable primarily because projects have specific ways to address the storm of challenges, barriers, and unknowns that keep surfacing whenever the need is discussed.

The project professional has a unique perspective that lends confidence to the planning process. By focusing on the deliverable and on the customer need, the project manager and team can handle these interferences. The project team members can take them in stride is because they know that project management is designed to handle them.

Getting People Involved in the Planning Process

A key way to generate support for a new project and build quality into the process is to involve others in the planning process. Projects do not occur in isolation, without the leadership and effort of people. People create the ideas, generate the commitment, carry out the planning, and make the decisions to implement. People carry out the assignments, create the deliverables, implement and control the processes, and negotiate the changes. People deliver the product to the customer and assess whether or not it has achieved desired results. Since projects require people, the project must provide the organization for leading those people, as well as the process they will follow to complete the deliverable and manage the project's work. The project management professional will anticipate how the phases of the project can take the ideas and concerns of people and build them into the elements of a plan that can lead them effectively.

Whether the environment is mature or evolving, and whether the processes are variable or refined, it is people who are doing the projects, implementing the processes, and making the decisions.

Communicating the Importance of Planning

In many organizations, planning is rarely used because repetitive processes are quite well defined. Operations processes have been refined gradually over time, and practically everyone in the organization is familiar with the way day-to-day business is conducted. In project management, planning is the most critical process. Because each project is unique, it is not something you can automate—people must do it. You can automate the calculations, and you can automate the data collection and storage. You can even automate the sequencing and rearranging of the project's elements and descriptions and the calendaring of events. But you cannot automate the clarification of assumptions, integration of inputs, and iterative process of analysis that we call *planning*.

Why is planning so important? Because projects are defined as creating something unique, something different, something "new." The project manager and team cannot rely solely on what has been done before. The complete processes, refined knowledge, and hands-on experience that are enjoyed in routine operations may not be available to a project. Even when they are, the previous experience must be adapted and adjusted to the new situation and requirements because each project is unique. The project manager and team will need to piece together the approaches, methods, examples, and lessons learned from prior projects of a similar nature, selecting what works and discarding what does not fit. And even when they gain agreement on the approach and the plan, there will still be new elements to deal with that were unforeseen.

Gathering Information for the Plan

During the planning process, the project manager and team will analyze and integrate the myriad complexities that arise when something new is proposed, prioritize them, and design ways to address them. Using different planning methods, they create a totally new plan that proposes to deliver the project's end result in this specific situation with the requirements, resources, team, tools, and capabilities that have been made available for this unique project. Only when the project manager and team have created a plan that is sufficiently credible and realistic to get general approval are they free to generate and manage the work that has been defined and implement the agreed-on plan.

Project managers typically are brought into a project after others have decided it is needed. Discussions may have gone on earlier, but the project manager may not have been involved in most of them. It is only when those who desire the result determine that it cannot be met through normal business operations that someone decides to "make a project of it." What you find in the early stages of project planning is a host of questions, a lot of declarations, and sometimes little definition. Everyone agrees, however, that the effort is still worth expending to create a project. Someone is asked to take it "offline" and come back with something a little more definite. This is often the project manager's cue that the organization is ready to begin the project's formal planning process.

Interviews to Confirm Project Assumptions

The project manager usually works alone in getting the planning process started. Her role is to make initial inquiries, refining and confirming the concepts behind the project's inception to be sure that the foundation for planning is valid. A few key assumptions may have been articulated but may not be confirmed fully as a foundation for planning the project approach and the deliverable. The project manager should meet with those in authority to discuss these assumptions. During initial meetings, the project manager should capture in writing management's reasons for wanting this project to occur. What was not working? What need was not being met? What is the business opportunity? What are the anticipated benefits? Why is it so important? To answer these questions, some internal research and even interviews may be needed if the answers are not apparent in documentation.

• *Business need.* Confirm why the project exists. Getting a clear picture of the project's value to management creates a solid platform for moving forward. Hearing the description from different people shows the expectations different stakeholders have for the project's success. Differences in terminology may indicate differences in expectations, while revealing nuances of benefits that can help the team clearly scope out what will truly meet the business need.

• *Alternatives attempted.* Clarify how the project got started. At some point in the early stages of project initiation, people in authority (the organization's executives or managers or the customer's executives or managers) defined a need and brought it up for discussion with others in authority. They brought the need to the attention of others because—as badly needed as this product or service may be—they recognized that they could not achieve this result alone. They may have already attempted it using routine processes with little success. They may have proposed it through normal channels of authority and met with resistance or skepticism. They even may have tried to assign it to someone and had it bounce back. There is a definite need but no clear means of achieving it. Identifying what other alternatives were attempted can flag unsuccessful routes to meet the business need, saving valuable time and effort.

• *Issues.* Seek out the real issues. For some reason, the desired result cannot be accomplished using operations. If the effort were to be attempted by those in operations, it would interfere. It might interfere with processes, with budget plans, and even with revenue production. Regulatory compliance may be an issue. The efforts to accomplish the goal without a project can provide insight into potential barriers to success. Project management methods may be enough to move it to conclusion, but issues will still exist. Creating an issues list early in project formation permits recording and tracking what has interfered in the past and may again in the future. If key people can be identified to help with resolution, the project can be ready to handle them should issues arise.

• *Organizational benefits.* Clarify how the proposed project supports the strategic plan. The strategic plan reflects management's reasons for wanting initiatives—and their associated projects—to occur. The sponsoring organization finds that the project is aligned with desired business directions.[1] The customer organization needs the product or service to accomplish strategic goals. Projects that do not support the strategic plan—either because they represent a local view of priorities or because they were created before a big change in executive leadership or strategy—are vulnerable to cancellation. Projects exist to accomplish important goals. (See Figure 6-1.)

Reviewing Early Documentation

Meeting minutes from early project discussions are a good source of high-level planning information. Minutes of meetings can provide insight regarding who has a stake in a particular project. Management is not the only group to see the need for a project. Long before a project is formed, the

FIGURE 6-1 Typical reasons for projects. The chart shows an example of why projects are formed. A customer of one of the authors, a manufacturer with plants in the United States and Asia, classifies all projects into one of three categories—revenue enhancement, expense reduction, or governmental/regulatory.

Project Category	Expected Results
Revenue enhancement	Project will increase sales.
Expense reduction	Project will decrease cost.
Governmental/regulatory	Required for compliance—may not increase revenue or profits, nor decrease expenses.

topic is discussed and people offer their opinions. People may have strong opinions and may state them. People have objections to what is not working effectively and often take the time to voice them. People have reservations and keep bringing them up.

The early stages of project initiation seem to generate many questions but few answers. If the answers are not yet obvious, it is a good idea to capture the questions on paper, distill them into their underlying issues, and record them—preferably in a living document database known as an *issues list or log* (see Figure 6-2). The questions themselves can provide structure and eventually help to create a way to address all the issues as planning gets under way. The concept documents should capture in writing not only what is intended as a result of the project but also the other approaches that were considered and why they were determined not to be viable. Discarded options communicate background information regarding why a project is needed and can help persuade those who still hold reservations about the solution.

If a template exists to propose a project, these descriptions are usually condensed and inserted into the business-case portions of that template. Scope boundaries, a description of the primary deliverable, the project's overall approach, estimated ranges for the project's duration and timetable, rough preliminary budget estimates, and the business case comprise the high-level plan's initial documents. As discussions and planning clarify more elements, they are also added. It is a good idea for the project manager to keep his own documentation, using it as a resource to complete the organization's official project charter and approval documents (see Project Charter template, Figure 6-3). Some large organizations develop the charter in two stages, Charter A for initiation and Charter B after detailed planning refines the time lines and estimates. In these organizations, there are two separate approvals—decision points—in the project process before the project team begins execution of the plan. This degree of formality can help improve quality, manage expectations of management and stakeholders, and create a better work environment for the team as they launch the project.

Developing the Risk Plan

Risk management begins early. The concerns brought up in initial discussions provide information that is useful in managing risks that might impede project progress. The goal in risk management is to maximize the likelihood and impact of positive changes and minimize the likelihood and impact of negative changes on the project. If the organization does not have a list of identified categories of known risk, the project team can create one. If it does have such a list, the project team can refine it to reflect the risks for the project.

FIGURE 6-2 Issues list. The project team can use this template to keep track of open items, issues, and questions.

PROJECT ISSUES LIST

Date Issued: _____   Project Name: _____

Issue #	Description of Issue	Person Who Needs Resolution	Person Responsible to Resolve	Date Resolution Needed	Date Resolved	How Resolved
1						
2						
3						
4						
5						
6						
7						
8						
9						
10						
11						
12						
13						
14						
15						

Used by permission. The Griffin Tate Group, Inc.

FIGURE 6-3   Project charter. The sponsor uses the charter to communicate the purpose and direction of the project to the team.

PROJECT CHARTER TEMPLATE	
Prepared By:	
Date Issued:	
Project Name:	

Project Scope	
Business Case	
Project Objectives	
Project Customers	
Customer Needs	
Final Deliverable(s)	
Customer Requirements	
Life-Cycle Stages	
Customer Acceptance Criteria	
Key Stakeholders	
Organizational Deliverables	
Organizational Acceptance Criteria	
Organizational Goals	

Project Assurance	
Scope Risk Limit	
Reviews & Approvals Required	
Status Reports Required	

Project Resources	
Team Assignments	
Deadlines	
Staff Effort Limit	
Spending Limit	
Organizational Constraints	
Project Priorities	

Used by permission. The Griffin Tate Group, Inc.

A few categories of potential risk, with subelements, can be placed in a table with number ratings in the columns entitled "Impact" and "Probability" and calculated across and tallied at the bottom.[2] Comparing comparable risks across projects can help management determine which projects are "high risk" to give them added attention and support. For a single project, it is enough to identify risks associated with each key deliverable, sort them, and develop countermeasures (see Figure 6-4).

As key deliverables are completed, the risks associated with those deliverables fade away and the team moves on. The risk analysis table provides team members a list of risks they should be alert to at each stage of the project. While old risks associated with completed deliverables are removed, and new ones added, the format of the table provides a familiar reference for the team as they work. The risk management process, repeated as a cycle shown in Figure 6-5, ensures the appropriate analysis is being carried out at each stage of the deliverable's development.

Early in the project, the project team can identify the potential risks associated with each major deliverable as those deliverables are defined. These risks can be identified as high, medium, or low impact and high, medium, or low probability. The preventive or mitigating actions for each risk are also identified. Number ratings can be substituted for high, medium, or low categories. Multiplying the numbers in the columns allows the risks to be quantified and compared. To gain the comfort of the team, some lower threshold of risk can be established as acceptable (risk limit), and only the

FIGURE 6-4 Risk analysis table. This simple chart identifies the format for creating a risk analysis for each deliverable. The rows below the headings identify the risks by name, impact, probability of occurring, and countermeasures.

Deliverable	Risks	Impact (High, Medium, Low)	Probability (High, Medium, Low)	Countermeasures
List the name of the final deliverable.	List the risks identified by the project team.	This describes the severity of the consequences if the risk occurs.	This describes the probability that the risk will occur.	This describes the preventive measures and/or contingency plans to prevent and/or mitigate the risk.

FIGURE 6-5   Risk management begins early. Managing risk is a process that extends across the entire project life cycle and repeats within phases. At a high level, the process covers risk identification, risk quantification, risk ranking, risk mitigation, and risk retirement. The process cycle is repeated as the project life cycle advances and key deliverables are created.

items with high risk ratings are entered into the risk plan. Areas of high risk may need to have a mitigation plan in place, quantifying each element and describing in brief how that risk will be managed. Eventually, during detailed planning, names of team members can be added to each category of risk to be managed. (See Scope Risk Analysis template, Appendix B.) Later in the project, these team members then can report on the status of their assigned risk area during project plan execution. When one of the risks materializes, the team member assigned to that risk area takes the specified action to mitigate that risk and reports to the team if it was successful. Risks that never materialize are simply closed in the risk plan as the project moves forward. Throughout the life of the project, the risk analysis should be revisited and the risk plan updated.

SCOPE AND OBJECTIVES PLANNING

High-level project planning begins with scope boundary planning based on management's initial estimates; then blocks out the high-level estimated duration, timetable, and budget for the project; and ends with the team's involvement in planning the project's scope and objectives in more realistic detail. By the time the person documenting the project has captured the expectations and assumptions of management in writing and can state clearly the purpose of the project, what is part of the project, and what is outside its charter and authority, the information is available to define the project's scope and boundaries in the plan itself.

The project manager will have a sheaf of information, a business case, a charter document with management's dos and don'ts, perhaps notations on scraps of paper or in notebooks, or meeting minutes and comments captured in electronic files. There may be some high-level requirements from the customer. Someone may have pulled out some legal or regulatory reference material and handed it over en masse. Budget limits will have been alluded to, but without precise numbers. Meeting notes still will contain mention of risks, concerns, technical opinions, or caveats, but these probably will be eliminated from the meeting notes when they are written up for permanent reference. There may be a milestone schedule entered by deliverable in the scheduling tool, but it lacks detail and is not yet tied to a realistic calendar. At this point the project manager may not have much information about the users.

Defining the Deliverable

During early discussions, when the problem is not fully defined, there may be talk about what the project is to produce, but there may not even be a clear understanding of what the end product or service will be called. People will have referred to it by some name that conjures up the right characteristics at various points in the discussion, and these are probably written down. But there is likely to be little agreement at this early stage as to what the product or service is, its size or capability, and how it will be deployed once it is developed. In fact, there is often no real way to know if there is common agreement until something is committed to writing. Thus part of high-level planning is simply to record these parameters and critical success factors for the project's product or service or result, as well as its desired outcome, and start using the name most people agree to call the product or service. Later, when requirements are developed fully, they can be sprinkled with the specific details into the project's plan as the interim deliverables, detailed requirements, and project activities are further defined.

Once the concepts are actually recorded in documentation and shared with others, the substantive objections will arise. People will see something in print that they either agree with or object to. Clarity can be hammered out as agreement is forged, and the project will emerge as the deliverable's scope and outcomes are defined further. Requirements and specifications emerge from discussions and should be recorded in detail. The project's scope definition emerges from this refinement.

Agreement on the deliverable and its requirements is fundamental to creating a detailed plan that can guide the team's work. There is no purpose to planning anything in detail if there is no clear agreement on the deliverable to be planned. The purpose of initial draft write-ups is to flush out that agreement, item by item, so that planning can proceed with confidence into the next stage of detail.

The actual words people used during initial discussions can provide clues about their expectations for the project. For instance, if they used the words *produce* and *deliver*, then the project is one that will be expected—at least at this stage—to generate a product or service at closure. If they used the words *further define, design, explore, formulate,* and *clarify,* then the project is envisioned as a planning or design project, not the creation and/or implementation of a full-blown end result. The outcome—product, service, or result—probably will be handed over to another project to further develop a product or service, once more is known.

Finding out who will "own it" when it is complete is a good way to identify a source of quality parameters and product descriptions. Finding out who will use it and how it will be used is a good source of product performance criteria and minimum requirements. Someone also may need to plan this transfer or turnover as part of the project; draft criteria can be captured during discussions to help define when the product or service will be considered complete by the customer and user. Sometimes the refinement of performance requirements can result in a new name to describe the project's outcome or deliverable. These changes need to be recorded in the initiation documents and communicated to all involved in the planning process.

With the scope boundaries, product or deliverable description, and initial requirements in place, the approach—planning or design or construction—can be used to create a *work breakdown structure* (WBS) that eventually will be populated with tasks and deliverables in a project scheduling tool.

The project's structure can be formalized. The preliminary schedule still will reflect the estimated overall duration and timetable proposed during high-level planning.

Identifying Team Resources

The deliverable will require certain key skills and abilities to produce. At this point the deliverable is clearly defined. While the names of people to be assigned to the project may not yet be identified and the vendors or material sources spelled out, it is possible at this stage to name the job roles, the general skill types, and the level of personnel that will be needed to staff the project. Many scheduling tools will have a place for entering these roles by type. Using the average salary for the level of staff that will be required to do the work, a budget estimate can be created that is more accurate than the general estimates offered up during project initiation. These generic categorical estimates, when saved in the archives, are useful in developing organizational resource standards and even templates by project type; these in turn are useful in more accurately blocking out future projects during planning, as well as in aligning resources across projects enterprise-wide.

At this point in planning, most of the high-level planning steps are now reflected in the scheduling template, and the resources are being identified as project staffing continues. The project is ready to move into detailed planning. However, before the core team puts in the detail, a last-minute check of the high-level documentation can identify any missing pieces or unanswered questions. It is safer, cheaper, and wiser to seek them now or document their status as "unresolved" than to charge forward and be faced later with major planning rework.

Filling the Gaps in the Project Plan

After high-level planning discussions are documented, a project plan may exist, but it is uneven and incomplete. What is known is recorded, but many details are still missing. Management and top executives have stated what they will go along with and what is totally unacceptable but not what occurs in between. The customer has described what outcome is ideal and what would not work but not how it will be implemented. The technical experts have described what exists and what might be possible but not how to resolve specific issues. The users have declared that the product or service must be available and working by a certain date, but are not able to explain how someone could get it done by that date. Even the project manager has proffered a high-level "guesstimate" as to how much time and resources are feasible to generate the desired outcome, but is not able to offer quantifiable reasons why that "guesstimate" is valid. Everyone has issues, but no one seems to have answers. Getting to the answers requires facilitation and integration of many people's ideas into a single plan that can work. A good deal of planning effort is needed to fill the gaps in the plan.

Sometimes, if the effort is a large one, a budget line item is created to fund the planning effort. A smaller project or one that is more clear-cut may require only the project manager to complete the plan, with input from the team. A larger project may include teams of leaders or skilled facilitators to move it forward. But someone has to kick off the planning process, and a project management professional is usually the one to do it.

Confirming Project Roles

Projects need many types of supporters as they are formed. There are occasionally two key roles involved when planning begins: the sponsor—that is, the person who proposes the project—will accept line authority for the project's success and will take responsibility for the results, and another high-level executive outside the line authority of the project will champion the project's formation because he is convinced of its long-range importance. While the roles have a distinct part to play, the persons who fill the roles can vary from one project to the next. Here are a couple of examples:

• Sometimes the executive who champions the project serves as a high-level "gatekeeper." Because he is not the one who oversees the group that delivers the project, he can fight for the project's survival in organizational meetings and lend it status and authority. (An example is a city mayor who supports beautification and therefore lends support to a parks project sponsor to get resources allocated for the project.)

• Sometimes the sponsor is a single manager who has the status and authority to advocate the need for the project and also pay for it and implement it under her own business unit. In that case, one person may fulfill both roles. (An example is the president of a packing products company that sponsors building a new facility in a different state.)[3]

Usually we think of the customer as the one who funds the project and receives the results on behalf of the users of the final product or service. This is most likely the case if the project is a contract or is operated by a firm that builds a product or delivers a service in return for a fee. There are variations, however:

• A public service project may have a government agency fund the project using taxpayer money, with the customer a public citizen receiving a service, a group using a building, or a truck driver traversing a bridge.
• A sports arena may have a private-sector sponsor, a local government cosponsor, with both a sports team and sports fans as customers.

For internal projects within an organization, on the other hand:

• The sponsor may be the "customer" paying for the project and enjoying its benefits when complete.
• The sponsor for an information technology (IT) project can have one group paying for the system and a completely different group or groups benefiting from it.

Whether these roles are separate or combined, both have a stake in the project's success. Including these auxiliary roles in the stakeholder management process is always a good idea.

Project sponsors usually will have been involved in the early discussions about a project and will be familiar with its background. Although the undertaking has shifted from normal operations to project roles and rules, many of the time and resource assumptions that were articulated during early discussions are still considered part of the plan by those who participated in those early discussions. Those involved do not consciously recognize that any "new" endeavor will not be as efficient or as predictable as operations that have been refined over time. Someone responsible for the project's implementation will need to remind stakeholders of the concept of iterative planning on projects, optimistic initial estimates, associated risks, and the extra time required when doing things differently and for the first time.

Confirming Management Commitment
Public commitment to continue the undertaking under new rules is a critical success factor for projects across the board. Some projects are created at higher levels in the organization using external consulting groups and then handed off for management to other units. Once the individuals who take on the role of sponsorship recognize that a project may take longer and cost more than normal operations, they still must remain publicly committed to carrying out the proposed effort. They also must create support among the other stakeholders. First, their support is needed in preventing any commitments on time or resources until a more detailed plan is available. Second, their support is needed to permit exceptions to the normal way of doing things. Because this support is so crucial at the early stages, most organi-

zations require their sign-off on the business case and proposed approach before proceeding with a detailed plan. In effect, they are committing to underwriting the expense of planning. (See Figure 6-6.)

Using Different Viewpoints

Although the project manager usually will begin the planning phase as an independent worker, at some point she will call in the identified specialists and begin a team planning process. The initial approach needs to be validated, and the descriptions of the deliverable that were developed in initiation need to be given a reality test with the technical personnel who will be charged with its development.

Planning is not a common skill, and a few team members will have been taught different formal or informal planning methods. Some team members may have no formal exposure to planning at all. Some people believe that scheduling tools such as Microsoft Project are planning tools. However, effective planning has definite methods and techniques. The project manager and team leaders are responsible for explaining the planning process, its value, and the effect that good or bad planning will have on the work of individual team members and the customer. The purpose of getting diverse input into plans needs to be explained and valued. The viewpoints of people with different technical backgrounds and job functions can identify needed fea-

FIGURE 6-6 Typical players/roles in projects. The chart shows each key player and his or her overall responsibilities in relation to the project.

Role/Player	Responsibilities
Sponsor (sometimes called *project champion*)	Accountable for overall project results Sells the project Has courage and clout

Project customer(s)
  Technical customer
  Economic customer
  User customer
	Accepts final deliverable
	Approves technical specifications
	Pays bills/funding
	Represents user's needs if not the user

Project manager or project leader	Accountable for overall project results (shared accountability)
Project team member	Accountable for his/her deliverables (shared accountability)
Functional manager	Provides resources, team members (accountable for work technical quality)

tures in the product or even spot problems in the early stages when the plan still can be refined easily. Getting those varied viewpoints later in the project may require expensive corrections that absorb valuable time and attention of team specialists. Viewpoints of executive management, the sponsor, the customer, the user, the technical designers and developers, and those who will install and integrate and maintain what is created all play a part in creating a quality outcome. Tapping a greater variety of viewpoints generally equates to better quality plans.

The team's involvement in the planning process will expose team members to the parameters of success for both the technical aspects of the product and the management of the project itself. It is important that the project's limits, constraints, and priorities be delineated, agreed to, and communicated to the team and the customer. Each will have viewpoints to consider when creating the technical approach and the plan and validating whether the work planned will be achievable and will meet the business need. A clear scope statement—one that defines what will be included in the project and what is outside the boundaries of the project, as well as how the project interfaces with functional areas, stakeholders, and other projects—clarifies the goals and benefits of the project. It helps the team plan the deliverable(s) to meet approved sponsor and customer requirements for the end product.

There are also appropriate points in the process when the project manager should actively seek diverse viewpoints. Very early in the project's initiation, the sponsor is asked to provide the statements of goals and benefits that outline the expectations management has for the project. The customer articulates the outcomes and benefits of the project's deliverable. But the team and project manager write them into the charter and build them into the plan so they are specific, clear, logical, properly sequenced, integrated, and thoroughly understood by all. When complete, the statements are approved with signatures.

Once the deliverable and scope are clear, the kind of project it is can be described, and—by description or by inference—the approach to project management can be pinned down. Based on whether it is a design or planning project, as opposed to a construction or implementation project, the project manager should be able to pick a valid scheduling tool and begin to enter a work breakdown structure based on what already has been defined in the scope statement. While there will not be much detail, the acceptable range for the project's start and end dates and the descriptions of primary project deliverables can be entered into a model to create a bar chart with phase names for the project. See Figure 5-2 for examples of deliverables by project phase. At this point in planning, viewpoints of other project managers who have undertaken similar projects can be sought to validate, refine, or change the project approach and identify tasks and risks that may have been overlooked.

Once the project type and the technical approach are incorporated into the work breakdown structure and built into the scheduling tool task list, viewpoints of technical specialists can be sought to validate the adequacy of the scope and approach. Depending on what the project is intended to develop, the stage deliverables for the product, service, or result of the project will be embedded in the task plan and sequentially linked according to the dependencies of each successive deliverable on the ones before. Projects exist to move a deliverable through the deliverable's life-cycle stages. Which of those life-cycle stages are to be included in the scope of the project, and the tasks the team will have to carry out to complete that scope, will affect the project duration and timetable. (See Deliverables' Life Cycles, Appendix E).

The verbs used to describe the scope should articulate how much authority and autonomy the project team will have. The assumptions state everyone's common agreement about what is bedrock and what is hypothesis. Writing down project success criteria helps everyone understand under what circumstances management will consider the project adequate to deliver results and under what circumstances the project will need to be reassessed or reworked.

Clarifying the Plan Through Exposure

As people become more aware that a project is needed, they are open to the possibility that it may take more time or resources simply because it will be done in a new way for the first time. Distributing the plan for review helps to get everyone on the same page regarding how much time, effort, and resources will be needed to complete it. This review for clarification is necessary for a number of reasons:

• *Obsolete assumptions.* Discussions held during initiation about the effort or activity required to produce results most likely took place before actual formation of a project was even obvious. Executives and managers may have discussed the need for some solution for their operations. The assumptions they made about how to proceed and how much time and resources would be needed often are based on standards that have their roots in operations. These standards may not apply when used on projects.

• *Obsolete perceptions.* Although the undertaking has shifted from normal operations to project roles and rules, many of the time and resource assumptions that were articulated during early discussions are still considered part of the plan by those who participated in the discussions. Projects, being new, take longer.

- *Unexpressed concerns.* To help people verbalize potential risks and correct these early assumptions, the high-level plan needs to be shared with those outside the project who will be providing support, allowing them to review how it has evolved and expressing any concerns while they can still be addressed in planning. Once the plan is developed in detail and people on the team are using it to manage their work, outside suggestions will no longer be useful.

Although the project planning phase may begin in a cloud of undefined expectations, as the project progresses, the fog begins to lift, and these things become clear. To grasp the evolution of a vague and undefined cluster of questions and needs to a realistic and achievable plan, it may help to remember that the project has phases, that planning is iterative, and that this evolution is normal.

It is the responsibility of the project manager to move the project through its phases—initiation, planning, execution, and closeout—increasing its definition and clarity for the team and communicating its progress to management and customers so that the end result delivers the project's desired outcome on time and on budget.

DOCUMENTING THE PLAN

Capturing definitions and expectations in writing is important for use in the next steps of detailed planning. With so many free-form discussions taking place during a project's early phases, it is important to write it down. People forget what they said in the past, and the project team can even forget some of the fundamental assumptions that were agreed to. A written document is like a snapshot of a building under construction. You can sometimes spot problems with the foundation and load-bearing structure by subjecting it to scrutiny from many directions. The agreement or disagreement people express with the project's early concepts—especially once they are put in writing—can help flush out potential disagreement when it can still be managed. Sometimes the project's leadership can refine the approach to make it acceptable. In other cases it is simply a good idea to move those people with disagreements into the risk planning and management process.

Structuring the plan for ease of use can simplify communications in a large project. As the project plan is begun in detail, it is important to structure it in such a way that it can respond to and manage the needs of different stakeholders in different ways. There will be at least four levels of information to be managed, and communications will need to be shaped for each of these audiences:

- *Sponsor/management.* There are managers who fund, sponsor, approve, cooperate with, and support the project, and they are interested in high-level key management viewpoints and summary reports. The high-level tasks and charts should be at a common level of specificity across the project so that when summary reports are printed, they make sense to management and use terms management will understand and relate to.
- *The project leadership.* People selected to lead the teams and produce the product will want adequate detail to assign work and an adequate structure to maintain order within the team. The stages of development and deliverable names should be labeled so that they reflect team leaders' sense of progress as the product or service advances through the stages of the development life cycle that are included in the project scope.
- *The team.* People assigned to work on the project, either in support of the project management team or in the technical development of the product, will want to know the project is planned, sequenced, and structured adequately to allow successful delivery. They will want to know what is reliable and what is subject to change. The terminology of the project management tasks, deliverables, and subprojects should be comparable across teams so each group can mark progress not only against their own technical work plan but also against the entire project's advance toward completion: the final deliverable and closure of the project.
- *The customer.* Those representatives of the customer group who are assigned to review and approve of product or service designs and deliverables at key points in the project will want assurances and schedules they can respond to. They will want to know that their customer needs are built into the plan and that they will be involved in the project early enough to affect positive change if change is needed. (For internal projects, remember that the sponsor and the customer may be the same individual or group.) Using the customer's terms for what they will be reviewing, and similarly appropriate names for the meetings they attend, will allow them to step up quickly and respond appropriately when brought into the team to help move the project forward.

Considering the interests and benefits that each of these groups will derive from the project is often called *stakeholder analysis.* If a project is large and complex, it may need to separate the plan documentation, reporting categories, and level of detail so that they can be retrieved and disbursed easily to these various stakeholders based on their interests and involvement. For large and volatile projects, secondary and even tertiary stakeholders may need to be managed—people in the community, people who have a vested interest in keeping the old methods in place, and people who will need to accommodate the results of the project in their work methods or future plans.

On large projects, a chart can be prepared that lists the stakeholders and participants, cross-indexed by their role on the project and sometimes even by deliverable. This chart is often called a *responsibility matrix*. Some of the stakeholders or participants will contribute their effort to develop the deliverables. Others simply will review them. Some will participate in implementation of the plan; others simply will be briefed on its progress. Stakeholder analysis and a responsibility matrix convert roles into reference charts that can be used throughout the project to manage the deliverables and track communications.

Developing the Communications Plan

When the roles and responsibilities of the stakeholders are clear, the information is available to develop the communications plan. Different viewpoints captured during high-level planning are of value not only in communicating outward from the project but also in communicating from outside groups into the project. A strategy that is key to quality is to interject many views into the early development stages to ensure a well-rounded product or service and to identify omissions. A serious project deserves serious discussion by all of its stakeholders. A smart project professional keeps pen in hand during these discussions and captures all the critical decisions on paper. Even if this information is captured electronically, hard-copy or permanent files need to be retained.

Communications methods can be selected for the project. The formats and content of the communications need to address the stakeholders in ways that are familiar to them. They should use familiar terminology, familiar formats, and familiar channels of communication. There also will be a need to build consensus across different types of groups. In meetings, flipcharts, which make the consensus visible to all, are better for promoting understanding and agreement than simply routing a static piece of paper or a file for people to read. When teams are scattered, teleconferencing is often the only collaborative mode for arriving at group decisions. If video teleconferencing is not available, providing a visual reference—such as a PowerPoint presentation—along with a verbal discussion responds to different learning styles of the participants and invites discussion. Again, using terms they agree to and understand speeds understanding. The consensus of those present at a meeting builds public support and quells disagreement later. Meetings also create and support positive group interaction that facilitates one-on-one collaboration later. Verbal encouragement of those whose statements strengthen the intentions of the leaders and the project's strategy and goals help to clarify and confirm group standards. One-way communication is not adequate for making decisions in a project when processes differ and the end product or service does not conform to past practice. Remember, differing viewpoints support quality! Ignoring or suppressing differing viewpoints can contribute to lapses in quality.

Where group meetings are placed in the schedule can affect team confidence and understanding and even avert stakeholder confusion. Each phase of the project can reveal important communications that contribute to a successful project outcome. The early discussions among project stakeholders during project initiation are the bricks and mortar from which the project charter is made. Customer needs and requirements define the boundaries for product development later. Risks and issues are also verbalized early in planning and represent concerns or objections that may need to be managed as the project progresses. Many of the initial issues and risk-based discussions are not likely to occur again later.

By communicating expectations during planning, the team begins the communications process. Approval by sponsors and customers of the preliminary approach and resource estimates is important because it begins to shape the organization's view of what is possible and realistic, as well as whether the project will be able to deliver business value. Reviews by team members and technical staff are important because they shape the expectations of the deliverable and the team's ability to deliver results.

There is still substantial risk in creating initial documentation that is poorly planned or highly inaccurate, however. So many unknowns exist at the early stages of project development. Accurate information on completion dates, resource needs, and outcome characteristics is missing, although this material will follow later in the planning process. Allowing unrealistic estimates to creep into initial documentation can result in these guesses being cast in concrete.

Managing customer expectations is also part of the project manager's job throughout the entire project. If the customer is using operational experience to calculate a delivery date, the project's delivery date automatically will be later owing to the new elements involved. Operational estimates can set the lowest end of the range, labeled "optimistic," and a date by which the delivery of the product is no longer valid can set the highest end until better data are available. Better data will be available after detailed planning is complete.

If there are questions about the approach and design of the project itself, it is much easier to resolve them at the earliest stages—in the high-level planning process—than later in the project, when the changes will be harder to isolate and more expensive to integrate. (See Figure 6-7.)

Project Scope and Objectives Planning

Once it is clear what is expected of the project, the team will need to know where it is starting from. Defining the status quo is one of the first responsibilities of the project leader. As difficult as it is to define reality, reality is the bedrock on which the project is built. Before official approvals are requested or accepted to proceed with the project, the project team and the project manager must determine the current state of affairs and shape the expectations for the project and the project's outcome in much greater detail. The project manager must introduce a dose of reality to the mix.

Listening carefully to diverse viewpoints is one way to get a more realistic picture of where things stand than taking any one or two people's opinions, regardless of their level in the organization. Estimates are a case in point. Changes required because of the organization's culture are another.

Discussing the next stage of the project's development—a cyclic process of creating ever more specific range estimates—is a risk-mitigating

FIGURE 6-7   Cost of change to a project. As the project progresses through initiation (I), planning (P), execution (E), and closeout (C), change affects more interrelated project activities, and therefore the cost of making those changes escalates. Changing the design is cheaper than changing all related elements of a finished deliverable. Fixing a problem identified early is cheaper than fixing all the elements that that problem may affect later on.

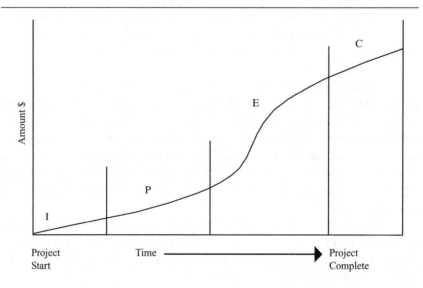

strategy. Early estimates are typically optimistic, and the team's ability to control or influence total project cost diminishes as the project advances (see Figure 4-4). The project manager's first job is to get approval to create more accurate estimates and to validate the estimated completion dates based on those estimates. Since exact estimates are not possible at this stage of the project's development, the project manager gets management's agreement to work—for the time being—within a best-case estimate and a worst-case estimate, with qualifying assumptions recorded in writing.

COMPLETING INITIAL HIGH-LEVEL DOCUMENTATION

Many organizations will require that forms be filed to get a project started— either to set up a budget line item or to set up meetings with departments or vendor groups that may be involved in early discussions. This high-level documentation contains a synopsis of the project, describes its type or structure, and presents the potential products and deliverables to be produced. Sometimes a public presentation is requested.

The business case, a budget authorization for planning, a project charter document, and criteria for postproject review give the organization enough decision information to commit to moving ahead with detailed plan development. The description of the project's scope, the product's name and performance requirements, and the initial budget estimates give vendors and departments enough information to support the project's work. Lists of resources, project roles, and a stakeholder responsibility matrix begin to shape the relationships among team members and subproject groups.

Formal documents contain condensed versions of what is agreed to and become part of the comprehensive plan and files.

• The high-level documentation (charter) provides the initial content to sections of the plan.

• The project goal statement and business case summary help to build agreement between senior management and the project team and its leaders on what constitutes success.

• Background material that is not included in the charter itself has value in risk management and communications and should be retained in the backup reference files. It may contain detail that will be useful guidance later, during detailed planning. Whether the plan is captured on paper or electronically, the records can clarify a position or trace a stakeholder's reasoning for taking a particular stand.

• The structure of the project created during high-level planning—the scope—can be used as a blueprint for doing the detailed planning. The work breakdown structure (WBS) is a decomposition of the scope definition for the project.

The scope statement, product definition, and WBS are key inputs to developing the tasks, activities, and schedule plus interim deliverables, and then assigning resources to the project. Customer and user input on product or service requirements is key to the technical approach and specific tasks. Initial creation of the risk plan, the issues log, the responsibility matrix, and the communication plan provide a framework for managing coopera-tion, expectations, and potential interference that could slow the project's progress.

REVIEW OF THE OVERALL PLAN BEFORE DETAILED PLAN DEVELOPMENT

It is safe to assume that once the project manager and team move into detailed plan development, any major changes made will be expensive and time-consuming to correct. For this reason, this is a good time to do a midplan review for verification or update.

Based on the level of the stakeholders, there are pieces of information that people will be looking for, according to their job roles and their interest in a viable project. Whenever possible, it is a good idea to use their exact terms when writing descriptions; it confirms that their input has been heard accurately, eases acceptance, and prevents needless miscommunication. Any definitions that have been agreed to will need to be recorded for later refer-ence by the team. If there are areas of ambiguity that should arise later in the planning process, these people can be contacted for their opinions. The more people can see the answers to their questions in the documents, the more likely they are to support the project.

Answering management's questions on cost-benefit analysis solidifies the project's value. It is not likely management will allocate resources to a project until people know at least at a high level what is required to carry it out. Management will not commit to fund and provide backing for a project until it knows the trade-offs. The types of questions managers will ask usu-ally will be tied to their responsibilities in the organization, their strategy, and their resources.

• Will it cost too much up front? Where is the break-even point? Are the benefits dependent on external variables that we cannot control? Is investing our money in this project going to give us other benefits that equal the value we would have achieved if we had put these resources some-where else?

  • How do we know that we made the right decision in signing off on this thing? Should we move ahead with confidence that the project will deliver the benefits everyone was hoping for when we started out? If so, how do we know? If not, why should we go forward anyway? Where is the value?

Answering the project leadership's questions on strategy and outcome builds a stronger project. Questions are asked at the project level that must be answered before good estimating can move forward.

  • Have we put enough detail into key tasks to carry out the product's development?
  • What level of sophistication is needed in tools, methods, skills, and cooperation to bring this project to successful closure?
  • What is absolutely critical to consider this project a success? What is absolutely out of bounds? What could stop it? What would ensure its success?
  • How will we know we have met the requirements of the customer, the user, and—if this is a highly visible project—the population at large?
  • Have we left anyone out? Who could block progress or undercut the team's effectiveness?
  • Are adequate resources assigned to this project to actually do the work? If someone is assigned to work on a key product element, can we be confident she will be free to carry it out without interruption?
  • Who has committed to back this effort? Can we see their signatures on the bottom line?

Answering the project team's questions on work effectiveness is one way to anticipate risks and plan the team's work environment. Once people who have an interest in the project begin to recognize that this project actu-ally will make it to execution, other questions will begin to emerge from the wings. There will be obvious questions, such as whose names are on the team list and whether their bosses approve of the assignment. There may even be a certain amount of cynicism: will we have to forgo our vacations or forget about our promotion when we work on this project? Some questions may only be implied, but they need answers nonetheless: Do we have the tools, resources, and knowledge to carry it out successfully? What are my work assignments going to look like? Am I competent to carry them out? Will I have to do this on my own, or will I get good leadership and information to help me?

Answering the unasked questions prepares the project to deliver on its promises. Less concrete issues arise that need to be addressed at some point as the project moves into detailed planning. Team members will wonder if the project has any likelihood of failure because it could affect their career progress. They wonder if their key abilities and long-range goals are going to be advanced. They worry that they will have to sacrifice family or life goals because the project is poorly planned. Managers in other groups will wonder if their resources will be diverted from their agreed priorities to this new initiative. What will happen if it does not work? Questions such as these have been called the *undiscussables* because in management one does not ask questions to which any of the answers are totally unacceptable.

For the most part, the undiscussables are not articulated at earlier stages of planning because the obvious questions get the floor. They are also questions that are difficult to discuss in public because they are not concrete or completely formed. Wise leadership will assume that these questions exist and take pains to communicate positive answers. Building team commitment and confidence starts during detailed planning, not during execution. Getting team participation in the plan, the schedule, the technical activity, and the work breakdown structure helps allay concerns and builds credibility. The details in the plan help to clear the fog and build understanding.

Project leadership also will need to consult the team about unknowns: Are there questions we cannot yet answer? How will we eventually resolve them? Are there serious challenges that we will need to resolve, and how will we tackle them? Are there risks that we will undertake, and how can we be sure they are worth taking? What happens if we end up with the worst-case scenario? Can we anticipate major problems and manage them as issues before they become problems and block progress?

These questions have been used to form the basis for the first refinement of the risk management plan. Once detailed planning is complete (see Chapter 7), detailed risk planning can be done. Until most of these questions are discussed, weighed, and resolved, detailed planning is futile.

SUMMARY

High-level planning is like a quick sketch of a project: it draws the boundaries around what needs to be planned in detail and tests the assumptions, constraints, and logic behind the planning effort. When the project is planned properly, with credible time frames, estimates, and requirements, it becomes possible to begin discussing delivery of results on time and on budget. Without proper planning, the triple constraint is meaningless.

This chapter provided a project-level view of how the project manager and team capture the information needed to document and plan the phases of a project at a high level. They use the discussions that occur during initiation, the team's and customers' questions during meetings, limitations and requirements set for the project and its product during initiation, the charter authorizing planning, the project's specified parameters, and the understandings and expectations of the stakeholders and team to create an overall plan that has the capability to deliver on the project's original promises.

If effective planning methods are used to create the project's schedule, documentation, and structure, the project plan will be realistic and supportive of overall project success.

The uneven progress in creating and formulating a successful project plan is part of the challenge to the project management professional. If the goal of a successful project is the appearance of a smooth, effortless process of structuring and managing new work in the face of change, then this chapter sets the stage for more detailed planning in Chapter 7. With a high-level overview, project approach, and associated methods and techniques, as well as the respective roles of various stakeholders in enabling a successful project, the team member—and the reader—have a more realistic framework that demonstrates how everything comes together over the project's life cycle. Completing high-level planning sets the stage for Chapter 7.

REVIEW QUESTIONS

1. The emphasis in _____ is in designing the entire life cycle of effort at a high level at the initial phase, since the earlier a process is established, the simpler and more cost-effective it will be to implement.
   a. planning
   b. executing
   c. closing out
   d. anticipating
2. Project managers typically are brought into a project after others have decided that the project is needed.
   a. true
   b. false

3. The _____ seem to generate many questions but few answers.
   a. communications involved in project planning
   b. early stages of risk planning
   c. late stages of project initiation
   d. early stages of project initiation
4. A project's initial approach needs to be validated and the descriptions of the deliverables that were developed in initiation need to be given a reality test with the technical personnel who will be charged with their development.
   a. true
   b. false
5. Answering management's questions on _____ solidifies a project's value.
   a. schedule risk analysis
   b. cost-benefit analysis
   c. milestone priority assessments
   d. resource allocation analysis

C H A P T E R

7

DETAILED PLANNING FOR EXECUTION

OVERVIEW AND GOALS

This chapter describes detailed planning—the verification of initial estimates for delivery and preparation of work plans for a project's execution. It describes how the project manager and team plan the project's work within the scope, time frames, and budget established for the project in a context of customer information, risk management, issue management, stakeholder feedback, and communications updates assembled during high-level planning. Plan development for execution of work on the project must address both the project technical work assignments and the responsibilities for the execution phase, as well as the management direction and control of the team and its work progress. The technical framework—contained in the work breakdown structure, project plan tasks, and schedule—enables creation of the product, service, or result from the team's project activities.

This chapter focuses on project plan development, the processes that define the activities, estimate their effort and cost, and sequence work tasks within the overall project framework. It also addresses how the project team prepares its technical plan to create the deliverable(s) and contributes to a realistic estimate of the resources the project will require before completion.

Assisted by project management tools, the project manager puts the detailed plan into a configuration that optimizes resources and recognizes dependencies within the paths of work leading toward delivery. It is during detailed planning that the *triple constraint* of time, cost, and project scope—the ultimate measure of project planning and performance—derives its real meaning.

Plans are put in place to address the predictable needs of the team. While the actual experience of conducting work will bring out new challenges that were not anticipated, planning to manage what will unfold is part of what detailed planning is expected to accomplish.

CREATING A WORK PLAN FOR EXECUTION

The execution phase of a project is where the plan proves its effectiveness. Some say that the beginning of a major undertaking is when the planners get their day of rest. If the plan meets its own criteria for effectiveness—predicting and controlling work, determining change, and controlling outcomes during the execution phase—the plan will contain all the tasks and resources needed to execute the work of the project and deliver its intended benefits to the customer. It also will contain all the activities needed to manage the team and its relationships with management, customers, and stakeholders.

During plan development, the limitations and constraints placed on the project during the initiation phase and the milestone targets and delivery windows applied during high-level planning are reconciled with the team's detailed estimates of effort and resources needed to carry out the work. In the management of professional projects, somehow the realities of risk and the predictabilities of tasks need to be reconciled. Formulas or heuristics frequently are used to quantify the uncertainty in task duration and effort estimates. Optimistic and pessimistic dates for completion of tasks help to determine whether any slack is built into the project to absorb that uncertainty. Arriving at a range for the estimate creates an understanding of the relative accuracy of the numbers and raises awareness of the level of risk.

The detailed planning process ends with a sequenced, balanced, and resource-loaded plan that credibly reflects what will be needed to accomplish the project. Revision and refinement, of course, still will be necessary, but these can be handled as part of change management—in the project plan for managing the project and in the product-development effort as well.

By the time the project reaches detailed planning, the work breakdown structure (WBS) has been created and team members have met to structure and sequence the work against their professional methods, calendars, and delivery dates. Key members of the team have put their tasks into the plan to deliver the intended results within the limitations of the project's scope statement.

Delegation of sections of the plan to teams or subprojects is one planning option that builds commitment and technical accuracy into the plan through hands-on involvement. The team can help define the need for accuracy and technical detail. The WBS often will reflect the work methods in terms that are meaningful to subproject teams and vendors. Charting a critical path through the project tasks can flag which tasks should not miss their delivery dates because they could delay the overall project. Decisions not related to critical-path items can be handed to team members to plan among themselves. Figures 7-1 and 7-2 illustrate two ways to convey the descending order of deliverables and subdeliverables in the WBS of two projects. Figure 7-1 is a chart with columns, and Figure 7-2 is a flow diagram. The flow diagram is quite useful for the transition from high-level to detailed planning.

The WBS provides the framework for the development and refinement of work tasks. The detail below the task level puts into play the technical methods and approaches the project's professionals will use to carry out the work. Placing these into a scheduling template using project management software allows refinements and reconfiguration of these activities to optimize not only their dependencies on each other and their integration into the larger plan but also the balancing of work among the people on the team.

Scope and Activity Definition

The scope statements and WBS contain the boundaries for planning the actual work activities. All the key tasks necessary to complete the project have by now been identified. Tasks that are out of scope will have been removed. The project management software that has been selected to manage

FIGURE 7-1   Work breakdown structure (WBS): outline format.

Project:	Management Training Program
Subproject:	Training logistics
Subproject deliverables:	Training needs assessment Training schedule Training facilities contract Certificates of completion
Final deliverable:	Trained managers

FIGURE 7-2   Work breakdown structure (WBS): tree format.

Project	Subproject	Subproject Final Deliverable	Subproject Interim Deliverables
	Subproject A	Subproject "A" Final Deliverable	Subproject "A" Deliverable Subproject "A" Deliverable Subproject "A" Deliverable Subproject "A" Deliverable
Project	Subproject B	Subproject "B" Final Deliverable Subproject "B" Final Deliverable	Subproject "B" Deliverable Subproject "B" Deliverable Subproject "B" Deliverable
	Project Mgt Subproject	Project Final Deliverable Closeout Report	Status Report Project Plan Project Charter

the schedule now contains the tasks necessary to produce the deliverables. The tasks are sequenced and linked to reflect which later tasks are dependent on completion of earlier tasks. Of utmost importance in this process is getting team input to the plan at the detailed level. Three key reasons why team input is important are:

• Team commitment and understanding are enhanced through involvement. The team represents the force enabling or hindering execution of these strategies and will be the liaison at various points in the work between the core team and the external groups supporting the project. Project elements that require the team's cooperation and commitment must be negotiated to engage the team's efforts. People are more committed to complete work they had a hand in shaping.

• Estimation of accuracy improves. The person doing the work is the best source of a realistic estimate of how much effort and time it will take. An experienced, seasoned worker who has done similar tasks in the past in the same organization may require only a few hours to complete a given work assignment; a person brought from another work context or with a different work approach may give a very different effort estimate. Each is a valid estimate for that worker for that task.

• Worker confidence and focus are sharpened. The effort estimates must be credible to the person carrying out the work to elicit her best effort and challenge her capabilities. What is adequate detail for one individual may be too general or too prescriptive for another.

After the team input is entered, the scheduler adjusts the level of detail. While individuals may contribute their activities for entry into the plan, it is the scheduler's responsibility to ensure that the detail is adequate to track work against the time reporting cycle but not so detailed that it limits flexibility for the professional carrying out the tasks.

Scope is reviewed again—just to be sure no new "out-of-scope" tasks or activities have crept into the plan. After the activities are entered, a scope-verification review is conducted to flag activities that are either out of scope or inadequate to meet the project requirements. Discussions confirm deleting some and refining or adding others. At this point the tasks sequence and dependencies are ready to be "fleshed out" in detail.

Requirements spelled out during initiation for the product or service or specified during technical planning are allocated to specific tasks, work packages, and teams. A list of milestones is created, and refinements are made to the high-level schedule. The overall schedule is reviewed against prior agreements and the organization's business calendar to see if any "deadlines" are still valid.

Resource Planning

The plan and schedule are now ready for the addition of specific resources to specific tasks. Physical resources and equipment may be required, with contracts to let and procurement requirements to flesh out. Based on the needed skills identified in high-level planning, individuals and material resources estimated for the project now can be assigned to specific tasks and activities. The added detail in the plan helps to define exactly what is needed for each work activity. Whether the project is staffed by individuals assigned from the same department, other work groups, or external contracts, the project activities are assigned to individuals by name and role. The individuals who will be conducting the work are asked to validate and refine the effort estimates and confirm that they will be able to carry out assigned tasks within budgeted ranges. Additional resources may need to be added if the time lines or delivery dates require it or if the level of expertise available to conduct the work is different from what was envisioned in high-level planning. Resources and requirements for project execution can be summarized and adjustments made to early estimates. A resource calendar can be created for the team, and project roles and responsibilities can be spelled out in charts and diagrams.

Succession in key roles may need to be planned in the event that a project extends over a lengthy period—such as a multiphase design and development project or phased program implementation over several years. The plans for changes in project leadership, vendors, or other key elements will need to be explained early in the project and executed at key points in the schedule. Including succession plans in the project planning process and announcing them early reduces political pressure within the team and prepares people to accept change in leadership as the project progresses.

Activity Sequencing

The critical path for conducting the work of the project is created by identifying and linking dependent tasks and determining their optimal relationships. Once detailed activity has been added to the plan, convergence of paths and integration points is matched to the high-level milestone schedule, and adjustments are made to the sequences. Depending on the type of work, some work may be scheduled concurrently and thereby reduce the elapsed time between the beginning of execution and the production and turnover of key deliverables. Negotiated delivery points for interim deliverables from subprojects or contracts are added to the plan and new tasks added for review.

Scheduling project tasks may require that certain skills and tools be batched together. Tasks that require different methods or processes are batched together. And tasks that require that multiple previous tasks be completed are scheduled later, so that all the necessary prerequisites are completed before the next task starts. Once activities have been sequenced, a network diagram can be created to show paths through the project.

Activity Duration Estimating

Available resources, levels of expertise, and other factors such as mandatory reviews or work commitments can affect the duration of activities. The team calendar will mark prior commitments on mandatory training, team member vacations, or resource commitments to prior projects. Refinement of the durations is carried out before the effort estimates are locked into the schedule and budget. The project manager and team may review slack and parallel activities to maximize the team and adjust the work across groups or individuals. The estimates that result are used to predict the number of work periods needed to complete schedule activities.

Schedule Development

Once the activities are considered adequate to assign and track work progress and the durations and effort estimates are reasonable to carry out the tasks, then the schedule can be created. Ideally, with experienced estimators, historical precedent, and planning models, the schedule should fall reasonably within the estimated date ranges for the project's high-level milestone schedule. If not, adjustments and discussions are in order to resolve any discrepancies.

A forward and backward pass through the schedule can identify slack between the early and late finish dates on individual tasks. The critical path is established to identify the sequence of tasks requiring active management if the project is to finish as planned. If flexibility is not available or for some reason cannot be used, then the date ranges for delivery may need to be adjusted and renegotiated with the customer and sponsor.

Cost Estimating

Once the activity effort estimates have been developed and the schedule has been determined, it is possible to make an overall estimate on the cost of the project's work. Allowances for uncertainties or risk, management contingencies, and other budget management approaches will depend on the organization hosting the project. Seller responses will need to be requested through quotations, bids, and offers. On large projects or in nonfamiliar environments, expert estimators may need to be engaged.[1] But the costs can be stated in ranges as an aggregate based on the preliminary detailed schedule.

Cost Budgeting

Spreading costs across the project is more important in some organizations than others. Organizations that manage capital and resources carefully across projects will have models based on historical data to allocate the high-level budget across the stages of development of the product or deliverables. This allocation is refined using detailed cost and resource estimates during detailed planning; planners can establish predictable "burn rates" against which progress can be measured (see Chapter 11). Once estimated costs have been budgeted over the life of the project and reconciled with detailed estimates, project funding requirements can be stated. A cost baseline and costs management plan can be prepared for use in monitoring and control during execution.

Closeout Plans

Since the plan and schedule are developed and the date ranges for use of specific resources can be discussed with more confidence, plans can be put in place for closing out contracts and releasing resources at the end of the project. Since changes that take place during actual execution can be predicted to add time and tasks rather than remove them, pessimistic estimates are prudent when making tentative commitments to customers, stakeholders, and management.[2]

Plan and Baseline Publication

When the plan is complete, the schedule developed, and the baseline established, a foundation exists for making public statements about expected project delivery dates—but still speaking in terms of delivery windows rather than a specific calendar deadline. At this point, while not all is known or can be known, there is adequate experience in the plan to predict what is likely to occur. The cost and benefit of the project are more reliable at this point in planning. The sponsor and customer (who may be the same) have adequate information now to decide whether going ahead with the project is likely to produce the intended result.

THE GO/NO-GO DECISION

The processes that began when the project was initiated culminate in a decision by the project's sponsor and customer(s) to execute the plan and proceed with the work. Approval of the plan-based estimates by the sponsor and customer means that the project is ready to enter the execution phase of its life cycle. The go/no-go decision tells the team that it can shift from planning to doing the work of the project. The plan has provided the means to validate resource estimates and becomes a work management document for the team.

The budget and time-line estimates resulting from detailed planning become a type of "contract for work" or "service agreement" between the team that will conduct the work and the sponsor and/or customer who will provide the means to accomplish it. If the organization uses formal contracts for work or service agreements, this is the point in the project where such agreements can be realistically instated. The effort and resources, the schedule, and the ability to deliver the defined tasks in the plan have created a *triple constraint* against which project progress can be measured—cost, time, and delivery of the desired scope of work at an agreed-on level of performance or quality. Once the schedule is balanced and refined, changes in any leg of the triangle will affect the other two.

The Schedule as a Communications Device

How a project is scheduled, as well as the degree of detail that is tracked for control purposes, is different from one project to the next. If we think of a schedule as having many purposes, we can make better judgments about how to create one if we focus on the various purposes a schedule fulfills.

- *Road map.* An interdependent schedule can serve as a flowchart of the project showing the relationship and sequence of project activities. It helps team members and subcontractors understand the relationship of their individual deliverables to the progress the team is making overall.
- *Discussion document.* Renditions of the schedule can serve as communications devices for a team and for project stakeholders. People can focus on issues or questions related to specific portions of the schedule, using it to reveal areas of project work that may require more clarity or cooperation or issue resolution.
- *Reference tool for project scope.* The agreed-on scope of work set out in the project charter and the WBS capture the project's scope. If it is not in the plan, it is probably "out of scope" (see Figure 7-3).

The project manager needs to consider the audience when choosing the type of schedule to display. Even when presenting the schedule to specific groups of stakeholders, the logic and clarity of the task descriptions should align with what those stakeholders would expect to see and discuss. Showing the wrong level of detail to a group can elicit challenges or invite unnecessary intervention into the decision process.

Schedule Control

Time on a project as a whole—one of the resources the project team has to work with—is controlled using the schedule, which is based on the scope definition of the project, the WBS, and the tasks. The use of a project-scheduling tool creates the mechanism for assigning tasks, getting agreement on those assignments, and then controlling effort and duration on the project by holding

FIGURE 7-3 MS Project schedule: Gantt view. Software can show schedules at different levels for different purposes. In this printout of a plan for an educational event (a symposium), the Gantt view portrays high-level progress against a time schedule, which is useful in briefing management or customers. Task-level reports communicate schedule detail more effectively to those who are working on the team.

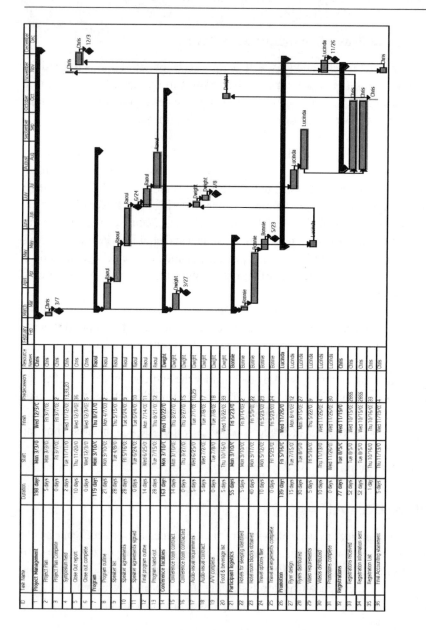

each worker accountable for completing tasks against agreed-on calendar dates and budgeted effort. Of course, since the plan is based on estimates, there will be some variance. The project manager and team leads make the necessary adjustments when variances from the plan are identified or needed changes are approved. Some tasks will take more time than estimated, and others less time, so the overall adjustments to the high level schedule may be minimal. Since, however, the plan is established at the estimates approved by management and is "baselined" for future revisions using change-management processes, when variances and changes result in significant alterations to that agreed-on management estimate, those changes are discussed at the management level. The schedule enables team coordination, trend identification, progress measurement, and collaboration with management in delivering expected project outcomes and benefits against the overall business strategy.

IMPLEMENTATION DETAIL FOR START-UP

Once the schedule is viable and the project manager and team are given authority to proceed with implementation, a number of execution-phase details still need to be worked through. Resources have to be mobilized, external vendors need to be selected and placed under contract, an infrastructure has to be set up to house the work products, and people have to have a means for accessing what they need to conduct and track their work. Placing common reference material on an accessible website allows separate groups to align their work standards and work products with those of the project as a whole. If collaborative development is used, secure access should be set up to prevent changes to elements of the plan that have been used in legal agreements. Versions of the plan should be safely archived.

Planning for Reporting

Reporting keeps the project's sponsors, customers, team, and stakeholders adequately informed to make responsible decisions in support of the project. Reporting should be planned after the detailed plan is ready for execution and should cover each area of the triple constraint: schedule, cost, and performance against deliverables. The format, timing, and submission of reports should be captured and refined in the communications plan and reflected in tasks added to the schedule. Knowing what type of reporting is useful and how it will be applied is part of the knowledge required to create a good communication structure for the project. Activities for collecting and disseminating information are also inserted into the project schedule. (See Figure 7-4.)

FIGURE 7-4 Status report plan. This chart shows a template for creating a status report in the communications plan. It names the report, identifies its cycle for release, names the person who will create the report, lists its general contents, and indicates who is to receive it on a regular basis throughout the project. If there are several status reports, each one is detailed in a similar manner in the plan. During the execution phase, the reports are generated routinely according to tasks in the detailed project schedule under the name of each person accountable.

Project name:	Project sponsor:			
Report Name	Frequency or Due Date	Person Accountable	Content	Distribution

Not every stakeholder or group will want or need the same amount of information. High-level executives will not want or need to know details of the work and its assignments but will be interested in overall performance. Team members may or may not be interested in high-level schedules or interfaces with another project—unless they are exhibited in the details of their work. Technical staff may not want cost information unless it constrains their options. The plan should be structured in such a way that different reports can be produced for different levels of project stakeholders: the project manager's report to management, the teams' reports to project leadership, and the project-level report on overall progress to the customer. Here is a synopsis of what a report's focus should be for each level, tailored, of course, to the type of project and the priorities of sponsors and customers:

• Management reports to executives summarize how work is progressing against the expectations created in the charter and its supporting charts and graphs, as well as high-level proposed estimates in the signature documents. Any significant trends are noted, and changes are submitted for approval. Issues requiring executive involvement are flagged.

• Stakeholder reports need to reflect the interests of stakeholders and external groups. Often they are limited to a high-level official overview and may provide more detail in the areas of interest for that group or stakeholder. Updates of the deliverables charts and a revised summary schedule provide an interface with external groups, customers, and line management. Their involvement in tasks and types of decisions should be flagged.

• Subcontractor reports need to reflect the priorities of contractual arrangements. If subprojects are managed by different organizations, their receipt and submission of status reports as well as their access to the actual schedule and plan at that level are negotiated as part of the contractual relationship and therefore should be tracked. Compatible technology or rollup summaries need to be established early in the planning process, especially if updates are expected from them. Management autonomy and oversight authority should be delineated clearly.

• Team reports enable and validate planned work. Plan team reports so that they provide updated information on changes to the project or the product that may affect work assignments and their interrelationships. In fast-moving projects, reports might be created daily. If cost or schedule are critical success factors, the team should get regular updates. (In smaller projects, the project manager's plan will be the same plan as the team uses; he simply will use different parts of that plan for different purposes.)

There may be requirements to submit project reports to oversight or umbrella groups within the host organization. Program manager and portfolio manager reports—grouped project reports that may include other related projects—will reflect their defined project oversight responsibilities. If data from those reports will be used to make projections or track official progress—such as earned value—the format and level of data should be specified. Data may need to be collected at similar points in the project process to be valid and comparable across multiple projects. If the project process has been used repeatedly, its process data is useful for managerial decisions. If the project process is newly established, metrics data can be captured immediately but may not be valid for decision purposes until the process has been refined, validated, and stable for some period of time.

A complete and comprehensive plan is important for credible reports. The plan needs to be reviewed to ensure that all the tasks associated with creating an environment for success are built into the overall time line for the project. Team members as well as leadership will be actively involved in these tasks even if they are not specified in the plan, so putting them in the plan is prudent. General activities such as employee meetings and training need to be in the schedule even though they may be accounted for under a separate budget category. Individuals who are involved in more than one activity need access to time reporting that recognizes their dual involvement.

For instance, there is added effort in gearing up to perform unfamiliar work or changing from one project to another. Process engineers recommend adding 15 percent to the task estimate if a person is pulled off a task for other work. Time-reporting capability and integration of reports from other contractors, development teams, or time zones may need to be added. In large or complex projects, a software tool specialist is available to help determine the most reliable method for tracking and accounting for effort against the project budget. For Internet-based plans, a specialist may be needed to be sure the tool is capable of managing the appropriate level of reporting and also capturing needed data for progress measurement. Technology and security issues should be carried in the risk plan. Any limits on team member use of social media should be explicitly spelled out, and mitigation strategies for any breaches should also be noted in the risk plan.

Planning for Procurement

Some resources will be needed immediately. Others have long lead times. Procurement needs to get under way promptly. A process will need to be in place for obtaining information, quotations, bids, offers, or proposals, as well as for negotiating a written contract with selected sellers. A single decision maker must be designated to deal with contracts, vendors, subcontractor staff, and services. This is critical. Knowledgeable decisions can make a project run smoothly, and changes must be made when they are needed. Usually the single point for decisions is the project manager, but authority can be delegated on large projects.

Subcontract management deserves special attention because the allegiance and work delivery cycles of subcontract teams and individuals are changed by their legal contracts. As the core team's integrators are put in place over multiple contractors, they most likely will manage work authorizations related to their part of the overall plan execution. The work authorizations being prepared for execution should be placed in the plan and schedule so they are proportional to the stage of the project. In this way any escalation in the consumption of resources can be extrapolated into changes in the overall project cost estimates. The team will need to track contracts to work estimates because both clients and insurance require it. Consistent guidance and policy on contract management and procurement will need to be given to all team leaders with responsibility for contract management, including delegation of authority to make changes as appropriate.

Resource usage requires a separate plan for large projects. Access to scarce resources may require bringing some experts into the project before the project is ready to use them, but the reduced risk is worth the added expense. During the human resource planning effort, the project manager can get approval from management to do things differently if the project requires it. Getting formal permissions in writing and in advance helps when dealing with operations personnel accustomed to doing things a certain way.

Budget Management

Since the budget is a type of "contract" with senior management to accomplish certain results with a given amount of resources, it is in the best interest of the team and the project's beneficiaries to accurately assess what it will take to do each part of the plan. If resources are used too soon, the results may be delayed, or resources will have to be taken from another worthy initiative to complete the project. If too much is given, waste often occurs, at the very least in that the money might have been able to leverage another time-sensitive project. Expectations for utilizing capital resources and delivering financial benefits will have been formed during management negotiations when the project was initiated. Budget management needs to align with those negotiations.[3]

Planning for Team Support

Planning for team support requires assessing the work site, technology, capacity to absorb team expansion, and compatibility of needed project information with the capabilities and limitations of the host organization's reporting systems. Project teams rely heavily on information, training, and reports. Because projects are doing something unique for the first time, reports enable them to navigate in changing conditions. Financial reports that respond to the phases of a project rather than just the operational reports for management are critical to tracking progress against the schedule and budget. Growing teams will require work space to be arranged in advance, allocating resources and budget to the appropriate stage of the work and assigning subteam organizing responsibility to an appropriate member of the team. Not having required equipment or space for new team members can not only undercut morale but also delay work tasks and status reporting. Uncertainties in obtaining the necessary accuracy in reporting should be carried in the risk plan, and management should be kept informed.

Team Policies and Standards

Normally, when we think of policies, we think of a manual or template that management sends out that covers how things should be handled in an operating environment. However, policies are simply understandings among a team as to how the management decisions should be implemented. If there are things on the project to be done a certain way, such as how to handle press inquiries, then writing it down in a "manual" makes it a continuing condition. Putting it in a central location on the team website, available to all teams—contractual or decentralized—allows team members to do things the right way from the start. Project policies can be established that are unique to the project and across all projects. The parent organization will have defined policies that affect all projects, but these often emerge and prove their effectiveness on a single project and then are adopted for all as a defined "best practice." Others are identified proactively by benchmarking against other similar organizations or industries.

Standards, whether they are project standards, work standards, materials standards, or behavioral standards, provide a "stake in the ground" for team members to compare to in doing their work. Not having standards selected, authorized, and defined confuses the team and invites the risk of nonconformance later in the project, as well as possible subjective interpretation. A good-quality plan depends on good standards. Managing strategic initiatives across projects also depends on setting and adhering to standards. Project managers can highlight areas where enterprise-wide standards may be valuable to the organization as a whole and assist management or the PMO in putting them in place.

Team Central Knowledge Bank

Team leadership should set up a location for teams to post their information and outputs. Then work output should be made available to all who need it. In an automated setting, the location may be a website. In a less automated setting, it could be a bulletin board and storage trunk indexed for quick reference.[4] The technology is less important than the accessibility of the information—available to all.

Set up a filing system for the team's central repository so that it is not created "on the fly." Ask for team help in planning not just how reference material will be captured but also what medium is simple, accessible, and transferable across geographic lines. If the team is multicultural, the title headings need to communicate contents to all groups. Team members can be asked to assume responsibility for setting up:

- A file structure for storing team reference material (provide common headings)
- Configuration of documents for permanent reference
- Status reports
- Legal, insurance, and procurement records

- Project closeout documentation
- Best practices and lessons learned

Planning to Manage Change

Whatever was in the plan, reality is usually a bit different. The key concept to remember in changing things is that change gets more complex, bureaucratic, and expensive the later it occurs in the project or the life cycle of the product or deliverable. Changes made later are extremely costly.

Planning for change is cheaper than being surprised by change. A good process for capturing, prioritizing, standardizing, and distributing changes will save time and confusion as the project moves into execution. There are two levels of change to consider: change to the project plan (baseline and revisions) being used to manage the project and change to the product's development (scope change or product configuration). Both should be placed under configuration management, and changes should be recorded against the official and most current version. The project manager and administrative team manage changes to the project; a change-resolution group will manage changes to the product. When changes to the product change the baseline plan, additional development tasks most likely will be generated as a result, with associated costs.

Adding Project Controls

Once the processes for managing the team and the work assignments are in place, the task of integrating multiple levels of control into the plan makes sense. These levels of control can be entered into the schedule in an iterative process based on passage of time, or months, not dates. They include:

- Changes to scope
- Changes to maintain quality
- Changes to the schedule and critical path
- Changes to the budget
- Changes to the risk plan as risks either materialize or become moot

If the organization uses enterprise-wide project metrics, the project needs to identify the organization's reporting requirements and be able to collect them and respond to:

- The cycle of data collection for the organization's metrics if applicable to projects

- The project's cycle of metrics tracking progress of the work against the schedule and expenditure of resources against the plan (earned value)
- Any quality metrics for product development and performance customer requirements

Control systems developed during detailed planning are put into effect during the execution phase, providing the team and assigned control professionals with the methods they need for identifying, quantifying, managing, and resolving potential variances, as well as unexpected problems, as they arise (see Chapter 11).

PLANNING FOR TEAM MANAGEMENT

The project team relies on a comprehensive project structure that defines roles, authorities, and reporting relationships; promotes teamwork; and facilitates work production. The organization chart conveys not only the team structure but also authority and reporting relationships. The relationship of individual team members and subprojects to the team's leadership needs to be spelled out and diagrammed for clarity, as well as delegation of authority to make changes in the established plan and resources. The organization's management outside the project—executive sponsors and team member supervisors—should be informed of the project's internal structure and authorities. Clarifying the project manager's role as central to project decisions can help to avert external intervention and project disruption. The number and rate of changes normal on projects are so different from what is common in operations that spontaneous outside intervention is seldom useful.

The Team's Work Environment

Physical or virtual site arrangements for the project's entire life cycle will need to be planned for quality work production for all the roles that will perform work there. Depending on the project, the team itself may or may not move to a project area. If the project is formed to produce a physical result, collocation may be necessary. If a specialist team is sent to a customer site, it will at least need a project headquarters. If the site preparation is specialized or complex, it may be subcontracted to supporting departments, vendor teams, or specific technical groups as part of their statement of work. Ultimately, however, it is the project leadership's responsibility to ensure that the work setting is ready—and supportive—when the project's execution phase begins and later at each stage before project work progresses to that point in the schedule. Integration of different teams, accommodation of differences in culture or work methods, and providing guidance for effective work are all part of the project management professional's responsibility. Management skill and communications are as much a part of good project management as the use of technical tools and controls.

Adequate hardware, software, communications technology, and backup systems should be part of the work-site planning. Space must be adequate to promote quality work and absorb staff and records expansion as the project team grows. Some projects rent temporary space with provision for expansion, provide housing arrangements in remote sites, and address safety and security as part of planning the physical site. Even on virtual projects, periodic physical meetings may be crucial to proper team collaboration and issue resolution. The simplest, least bureaucratic approach is preferred because change often adds complexity as the project progresses.

Structuring the Work

Materials and formats for the team's work products can simplify administration and work quality control. When planning for the execution phase, there are two important categories for materials and infrastructure: the initial establishment of the team's work submission procedures presented in the kickoff meeting and the team's continuous access to reference materials and collaboration infrastructure throughout the rest of the project.

Communicating work assignments and quality expectations is an important planning task. The team's introduction to the project sets the tone and pace for the rest of the work. It is important that quality materials and communications be prepared for the project execution kickoff, as well as organization charts, product charts, schedule overviews, and team assignments and structure. Some specifics can be introduced gradually, but the objectives and preliminary schedule are presented at kickoff, together with explicit leadership authority and reporting responsibilities, tools and software, reporting schedules and forms, the WBS, the deliverables and their sequences and dependencies, and expectations for quality performance, accountability, and teamwork.

Communications, training, and types and frequency of meetings will be predetermined and explained when the planning phase ends and the execution phase begins. The expectation of changes to those preliminary schedules also will need to be explained, along with the location of information on changes made to the plan.

Separate processes, channels of reporting and communicating, and responsibilities for the project leadership and the technical leadership will be established and running when the execution phase begins. Structured files, standards, databases for development, intranets for collaboration, review processes, and configuration management support also should be planned for readiness as soon as the execution phase begins.

Training to Maintain a Qualified Team

Some training will be needed immediately. Selection of the team ensures that the proper skills and experience necessary to do the work and create the deliverable are available. But training is needed to communicate the way tools and processes will be applied and to "level set" the members of the team against the specific requirements of the work. While many qualified team members have the knowledge they need to do the job, they need guidance on how that knowledge is to be converted into team deliverables. Those who have worked in large organizations may be accustomed to complex structures, while those who have worked in smaller organizations may be accustomed to greater decision authority on format and deliverables design. Depending on cultural backgrounds, one worker will not take the initiative to act without permission, while another will be competitive and assert himself to gain a more favorable position on the team. Without explicit guidelines on team cooperation and individual authority, these subtleties of work custom can cause disruption and interfere with quality team performance. A team member is assumed to be hired qualified for the job, but good team training and management practices release that capability for the benefit of the project.

Training is scheduled in advance to start the team working immediately. As the project plan is prepared, training for the team and the customer will be planned and scheduled, and leadership responsibility will be assigned within the team for both. The team will need to be trained on the project management strategy and responsibilities, as well as the formats and protocols to be followed. The technical team will need to be trained on specific methods or quality approaches for the development, documentation, and delivery of the product.

The customer and others who will collaborate on or support the project will need to be trained on what the project's processes, critical success factors, and outcomes are and the implications of those goals for the behavior of supporting or reviewing groups. In a simpler project, this training can be scheduled as a part of team meetings. On a larger project, all the materials, vendors, training package customization, sites, and schedules for training will need to be in the schedule, together with time for learning curves and resolving vendor management issues. Records and follow-up will need to be arranged to be sure the training is effective. With instructor permission, key presentations may be recorded for later use. Repeat sessions for latecomers can be scheduled in advance using the Internet, websites, or other media.

Project leadership will need training in its role in modeling quality and troubleshooting quality issues. Processes and procedures will need to be reviewed at key points for project leadership contributions to quality outputs. Decision processes will need to be set up for addressing risks, issues, and emerging problems.

After kickoff, training activities are needed in the plan to communicate any changes that may affect future work. That includes change management, the current top 10 risks being tracked in risk plans, the effects of cyclic updates, as well as any changes to reporting channels among the various teams and their members. The project team should communicate using the media and channels appropriate for each level in the management hierarchy. If the organization has available expertise in the training department, that group may be requested to assist with preparing training. Generic training applicable to most projects can be prepared in advance and refined as the project becomes more clearly defined. Web-based training accessible across time zones can be used by team members at startup or when work has slowed or groups are awaiting instruction. Specialized training can be accessed through contracts.

COMMUNICATIONS PLAN

After the project's communications strategy is developed, individuals skilled in communications can be enlisted to create the communications plan. As the project's planning phase ends and execution begins, not only the processes, tools, and activities for communications will need to be in place, but also the strategies, channels, and formats for communicating effectively with different groups of stakeholders. Some communications processes already will be in place and used before kickoff of the project itself. Others will be developed as the communications plan matures with use.

While specific communications requirements may be difficult to predict early in the project, the need for communications infrastructure is predictable as the team expands; the costs for this should be in the budget, and an update task should be entered at points in the schedule where new team members will be joining the project.

Staff changes in key roles may be needed in the event that the project extends over a lengthy period—such as a multiphase feasibility design and development project, or phased program implementation spanning several years.[5] The plans for changes in project leadership, vendors, or other key elements will need to be in the project communications plan at key points in the schedule. Including such changes in the project communications plan and announcing them on schedule prepares people to accept change in leadership as the project progresses.

PLANNING FOR STAKEHOLDER MANAGEMENT

In a context of change, the customer's role and interface with the project need to be managed carefully. Quality is impossible unless customers are involved. The project team must determine the appropriate role for the customer and must structure it for effectiveness. The earlier the involvement, the better is the response. The team needs to shape the customer's expectations. What value is the customer expected to add? What will be the customer's input? How will it be used? How will the customer be invited to participate? Preventing unrealistic assumptions keeps relationships healthy.

When planning its implementation strategy, the team can identify points in the project to involve the customer actively in the project and its execution. In doing so, it is a good idea to consider how to address and manage:

- Customer expectations of their role and potential influence
- Developing customer requirements into a format useful for team guidance
- Defining customer criteria for product acceptance
- Managing customer requirements in the actual production of the project's outcome
- Selecting tools and techniques for customer involvement during product or service development

Since the technical team, the sponsor, the project management leadership, the support groups, and the customer all will have a slightly different window on the project, part of the job of the project management professional is to ensure that the input received from one group is realigned and interpreted to be useful by the other groups and to be responsive to their different interests and needs.

Customer Involvement in Acceptance Criteria

One major way to involve the customer is to let a customer representative help prepare the project's definition of quality for the final deliverable. The customer has a key role in defining the criteria against which deliverables will be measured for acceptance. The same representative voice should have some input into the words used to describe an end state that exhibits quality (see Figure 7-5). The customer's role and responsibility include:

- Speaking for and representing the interests of the end user in defining acceptance criteria and customer requirements
- Providing timely decisions and input when the product stage requires it (some will be flagged formally on the schedule, and others will not)
- Providing input to the project plan and general approval of that plan
- Accepting and testing both the interim deliverables and the final deliverables
- Approving or rejecting key change requests presented by the team
- Providing feedback at the end of the project

Final Acceptance and the Role of Customer Surrogates

Occasionally, a project has a "customer" who cannot be identified as a single individual. An example would be a national park transportation system that will serve different park visitors at different points in time. A generic customer can be described by sampling characteristics of many different customers, perhaps through observation or by market surveys. Then a representative customer can be selected to take the part of the individual customer in the planning and review process.

For a single project, the customer roles of technical requirements reviewer, user, functional reviewer, and economic budget reviewer may be fulfilled by one, two, or even more people. Having more people involved places increased importance on coordination and communication; it often takes longer (see Figure 7-6).

FIGURE 7-5   Customer responsibilities in projects.

Customer Responsibilities
Represent end user(s)
Provide decisions and input when needed
Provide input to the project plan
Accept the final deliverable(s)
Accept or reject changes
Provide feedback

FIGURE 7-6 Typical customer roles in projects. (*Tip:* If the project manager can get one person to speak for all these roles, coordination will be easier.)

Customer Role	Authority
Economic	Authorizes and approves resources and changes to budgets in the project plan
Technical	Determines if the deliverable(s) meet specifications and technical requirements
User	Determines if the deliverable(s) meet functionality and user requirements

Other Levels of Stakeholders

Other levels of stakeholders may not be involved directly in funding the project or determining its acceptance criteria, but they have a vested interest in the project's outcome. For example, a database redesign for a government agency may affect the way data are captured and stored; researchers who have multiyear studies that use those data will want their needs addressed when the database is designed. It would be prudent to involve those researchers in the requirements process and perhaps even in the creation of the risk management plan. Customer satisfaction often extends to the larger group of customers; stakeholder dissatisfaction with tangential areas can affect the success of the project. In a large project affecting public resources—such as drilling for oil in environmentally sensitive areas, overhauling a British health care system, or restructuring of a U.S. public service such as social security—customer dissatisfaction can end up in news headlines or government hearings, damaging the sponsor's credibility.

QUALITY PLAN

A quality plan should be set up for team reference when the team begins work. A quality plan identifies which quality standards are relevant to the project and how those standards will be satisfied. In some projects quality is built into the product development process and quality gates are tracked at each stage. In some projects quality is built into the contracts so that the contractual deliverables are inspected along the way. Quality planning defines the process of identifying quality requirements and standards for the project and the product and documenting how the project will document compliance.[6]

While the methods for managing quality of the deliverables are built into the scope and requirements of the plan and controlled through scope management, a written document must be created during detailed planning to communicate to team members and any vendors or contractors the quality standards and expectations that will be maintained on the project (see Appendix B).

SUMMARY

This chapter addressed the detailed planning that the project manager, project leaders, and team members undertake to create a more credible project plan for execution. During project plan development, they add the activities, resource estimates, task sequences, schedule, and budget for the project so that more credible estimates can be conveyed to the sponsor, customer, and stakeholders who need results. The amount of detail needed in the plan now should be sufficient to control the work during the execution phase and manage the project's delivery of value against the commitment of resources. Greater detail may be needed by individual team members to control their work, but this detail usually is handled in technical team processes or subprojects; it may not need to be captured in the overall project plan.

Project plan development is also the place in the planning process where project leadership puts the infrastructure plans in place to structure the work, manage the team, and ensure that adequate resources are available when needed to begin to conduct the work. Project leaders set up processes to manage the issues, risks, and learning needs that will emerge during execution as well as during closeout. The methods and processes for quality assurance and communications are put into the plan early in the project for later use with team members, customers, subcontractors, and vendors.

The facilitating processes, covered in Chapter 9, provide the elements of project management that help to ensure that the plan—the contract the team has made with the sponsor and customer—actually is carried out.

REVIEW QUESTIONS

1. The _____ must be credible to the people carrying out the work to elicit their best effort and challenge their capabilities.
    a. scope definition
    b. effort estimates
    c. quality plan
    d. communications plan

2. When the plan is _____ , a foundation exists for making public statements about expected project delivery dates.
    a. complete and the baseline established
    b. complete and the schedule established
    c. complete and the targets established
    d. complete and the resources established

3. As the project plan is prepared, _____ for the team and the customers will be planned and scheduled.
    a. risk
    b. cost
    c. training
    d. leadership
    e. scope
    f. *a* and *c*
    g. *b* and *d*

4. A _____ is important for credible reports.
    a. detailed schedule for executing
    b. signed-off and approved charter
    c. complete and comprehensive plan
    d. team-based communications plan

5. Reporting should be planned after the detailed plan is ready for execution.
    a. true
    b. false

BUILDING AND DEVELOPING A TEAM

OVERVIEW AND GOALS

This chapter describes how the team is formed and presents some of the ways teams can be developed within a project. Previous chapters created a context for defining work, structuring the project, creating the deliverable(s), and delivering the project benefits to the customer. They explained how the team develops the project plan and the infrastructure for executing that plan. Ultimately, however, the work is carried out by a team.

In the execution phase the team puts its effort toward achieving a common goal, the project's desired results. Getting the team to face the goal of the project directly, to work together effectively, to cooperate and integrate their work, and still to finish on time and on budget is a challenge. Some techniques for team development are presented in this chapter. They involve applying the facilitating processes from project management, also known as *knowledge areas*. The facilitating processes that focus on project plan execution are:

- Communication
- Team development
- Resources management

- Information distribution to stakeholders and the team
- Contract administration
- Quality assurance

The most obvious areas that facilitate team development and a positive project culture include communication, team development, and human resources management, but to a certain extent all of them are involved in creating an effective project team. While this chapter cannot even attempt to cover all the options and nuances that professional project managers apply in developing and managing a team, it will introduce a few key concepts and provide examples of how facilitating processes contribute to the success of a project. Being able to identify these processes and use them successfully is the hallmark of a professional in project management.

CREATING AN ENVIRONMENT FOR SUCCESS

Part of planning and executing a project is proactive: the project manager and team put their efforts and energies into doing things that must get done for the project to reach completion. Because of the constraints on resources and time, some things will not get done—simply because others are more important to project success. The project manager and team are charged with delivering the end product, not with carrying out a group of activities. Ensuring that the project develops what it should and not something else and that it does not run out of time and resources before it is complete requires exercising controls in a variety of ways. The project's facilitating processes help to manage these challenging aspects of project management. The project management professional combines the use of specific project processes with knowledge and wisdom from prior experience. She must decide what must be done and what can be ignored, and ultimately she will create an environment for team success. Only the people inside the project can make those decisions. Reporting to someone outside the project does not allow free decision making for the professional. The Standard for Program Management, released by PMI in 2006, specifically states that a program manager must delegate authority to the project manager.

Planning a project requires more than focusing on the work to be done. It requires planning the processes that will result in overall project success. These processes—often referred to as *facilitating processes*—are not always in the direct critical path of the project's main activities. They enable the main activities by removing barriers, eliciting cooperation, and creating an environment of acceptance and support among team members, supporters, and stakeholders. Some facilitating processes are parallel to the phases and integrated within them. Most continue from the early initiation phase to the project's closure. Some of them—as, for example, risk management processes—are applied cyclically. The team identifies and prioritizes and retires risks as the project work progresses and those risks are no longer significant.

THE IMPORTANCE OF COMMUNICATION ON PROJECTS

Most people can take a structured task in a structured work setting and bring it to conclusion. But the people who can take a concept and convert it to action are a rare resource. It is safe to assume that not all project team members are able to take a concept from instructions or documentation and implement it. They will need help from the project leadership in converting the ambiguities into a manageable work assignment.

If team members are assigned to the project for a short period of time, much of what occurs on the project differs from their normal work. Even if the team has general agreement on work methods, standards, processes, and a deliverable to be produced, the convergence of work from other groups and individuals inserts change into the process so that even a tried-and-true approach will need to be modified. The project manager sets the pace and tone for work by communicating what is expected of the team.

TEAM DEVELOPMENT

It is easy to underestimate the importance of teams in project management. The knowledge required to manage a team is a complex mix of leadership, human resources management, common sense, people skills, political and cultural know-how, technical understanding, work orchestration, and process facilitation. While some project managers possess these capabilities, others will have to tap the capabilities of the team as a whole to successfully manage the people and direct project work.[1] As technology advances, virtual projects are becoming more common, and multicultural teams increase diverse input into the process. Keeping the team working and preserving its cohesiveness throughout the project life cycle are significant challenges, especially where a strong project management structure, such as a project management office, does not exist.

The first task in creating a team is to decide what kind of team is best suited to the work of the project. Different team combinations and structures bring with them certain types of strengths. For example, hierarchical teams work faster; teams with flat reporting structures are more creative but take longer to produce results. The team is created by deciding how many individuals or groups will be needed and their composition. Then the team will need definition of how the members will work together, including:

- Roles
- Responsibilities
- Assignment of deliverables
- Level of authority
- Organization chart indicating reporting relationships

When deciding team size, remember that more than 10 people cannot easily carry on a discussion. An ideal team or subteam is 5 to 7 people.

An additional area of team development is training. While team members are expected to bring fully developed skills and capabilities to the team, they need training not only to learn the methods and approaches the project will use but also to learn how to work together effectively. Training can include facilitated exercises, online or classroom training, and self-instruction modules. Training fills the gap between what the team members already know and what they need to learn to apply their abilities fully on the project. Training also sets the standards for how the team members will work together.

HUMAN RESOURCES MANAGEMENT

Strategies for managing the resources of the project are put into play during the execution phase. While many projects focus on material resources, in a professional project human resources often are the most costly and difficult resources to manage.

Using human resources management principles effectively, matching recruits with specified job roles, and addressing rewards and reporting relationships, the project manager will find that people's best efforts will be elicited and their ideas applied on the project. Valuable resources of money and time are spent just bringing the expertise of these diverse people to the team. Tapping their abilities early in the project maximizes the value that can be obtained by their unique knowledge, special skills, and differing perspectives. Tools and control systems can track material resources and even effort hours or the passage of time in the schedule. But tools and control systems cannot bring out the best in a team. Team leadership is the domain of the project management professional. Forging a team that can work together despite their differences and keeping team members working with focus and diligence when faced with pressures and unknowns takes not just knowledge but wisdom and managerial skill as well.

CREATING TEAMS OF SIMILAR AND DISSIMILAR PEOPLE

Teams by their very nature will have a certain amount of diversity; judicious use of diverse team member backgrounds can bring specific talents to a project. Teams with members of similar backgrounds work easily together because they understand the norms of their group; they can quickly define a process or refine a product, but they are less likely to come up with a creative solution or a new process.

Dissimilar teams can enhance creativity and generate many different ways to view a product or a process. If a specific outcome has not been decided, dissimilar teams are quite effective at assigning roles within the team based on individual talents and skills. There will be creative interplay during meetings and reviews. On the other hand, if pressure mounts and the team must generate a predetermined outcome in a specific time frame, conflict is likely to arise and interfere with progress.[2]

The project manager must be able to value, understand, and integrate these diverse points of view to explore possibly innovative solutions and at the same time stay on track, focused, and on plan. Consider the differences in thinking styles (see Figure 8-1). There are people whose dominant style is:

- Organized
- Analytical
- Intuitive
- Feelings-based

There are also different learning styles that need to be considered when conveying information to the team (see Figure 8-2):

- Visual
- Auditory
- Kinesthetic

A visual display of data may not be grasped or internalized by people who need to hear the concepts or participate in discussions to absorb the needed information. A teleconference that allows verbal interchange but does not provide accompanying visual material may not be grasped or internalized by people who are accustomed to making judgments based on what they see on a computer screen. To engage the greatest number of team members most of the time, a wise project management team will employ multimedia.

FIGURE 8-1   Diversity of thinking styles. The best solutions come from a balance of diverse thinking styles. The project manager must be able to value, understand, and integrate these diverse points of view and preferences to explore possible innovative solutions and at the same time stay on track and on plan.

Logical **Analytical** **Fact-Based** **Quantitative**	**Holistic** **Intuitive** **Integrating** **Synthesizing**
Sequential **Organized** **Detailed** **Planned**	**Interpersonal** **Feeling-Based** **Kinesthetic** **Emotional**

FIGURE 8-2   Different learning styles. Using different ways to present information to the team engages team members with varied learning styles. People can more easily take in information if presented in their preferred learning style.

Visual
Learns by seeing or reading
Likes visual information
Processes information through images

Auditory
Learns by hearing or discussing
Likes verbal information
Processes information through talking

Kinesthetic
Learns through sensing
Likes to do
Processes information through feelings or through body

Project results benefit by involving representatives of management, the customer, and the technical specialists. Their different points of view and diverse thinking styles, taken together and at different points in the project process, provide a foil against which the project team can reassess its position and stay focused and learn. There is a right time for input, of course. Broad input is sought at the beginning, using divergent viewpoints when concepts are not yet put into action and when reconfiguring an option or two is not difficult. Detailed and specific input is sought as the project moves through planning to implementation. Discussion is held to aid converging viewpoints and to seek more specific input toward closure. At key junctures during the creation and deployment of deliverables, integration needs to occur, and these junctures are also good times to solicit input from the team and from the customer. There is typically less freedom to make changes toward the end of the project. As pressure mounts to deliver what was promised, and time frames are less forgiving, adding complexity and unplanned variables increases risk. It is in the closing stages of product integration when interdependencies among deliverables and work activities would be disrupted by broader changes. On the other hand, a refinement here and there can make a difference in quality—or even perceived quality—for those receiving the final deliverables and judging fitness for use.

CREATING A PROJECT MANAGEMENT CULTURE

Because projects must be carried out differently from operations, they require a cooperative, creative, and mature culture. There is no time for hierarchy, arbitrary permissions, or distrust. Doing things a certain way because "we have always done it this way" gets little support on a project team. On a project, each best practice has a reason and a benefit. All of the team members are there because they have something valuable to offer. Everyone knows that the individuals cannot succeed without the support of the team and that the team cannot succeed unless the team members are free to perform at their best. Some organizations arrange wilderness adventures or retreats to build the kind of team culture projects create. In an individual project, the project's leadership sets the tone and environment for team trust and mutual cooperation.

Most people recognize there is a place in project execution for technical knowledge, people skills, coordination skills, and problem-solving skills, but few talk about the important role of "emotional intelligence." Daniel Goleman, author of the well-known book *Emotional Intelligence*, describes emotional intelligence in a way that demonstrates why it may well be a critical capability for someone leading a project team:

No one can yet say exactly how much of the variability from person to person in life's course it accounts for. But what data exist suggests it can be as powerful, and at times more powerful, than IQ.[3]

Goleman describes ". . . a key set of these 'other characteristics,' (of) emotional intelligence: abilities such as being able to motivate oneself and persist in the face of frustrations; to control impulse and delay gratification; to regulate one's moods and keep distress from swamping the ability to think; to empathize and to hope."[4] There is little doubt that in the midst of a fast-moving project, the project management professional relies heavily on these "other characteristics" to keep himself and his team moving forward with confidence. Individual morale and team morale are valuable resources that must be managed wisely. Pressure to perform often increases as the project nears its end. The exercise of emotional intelligence within the team is often crucial to success.

One example of the crucial role of emotional intelligence is found in records of the first transatlantic flight from England to North America in 1936. In a rare undertaking for a "team of one," the pilot left normal operations—scouting big game from the air in Africa—to make this first east-to-west flight across the Atlantic. Like any project manager, Beryl Markham needed data to gauge progress and make corrections to the plan. When the altimeter showed the Atlantic was two thousand feet below, the Sperry artificial horizon showed her flying level. She judged her drift at three degrees more than her weather chart suggested, so she corrected her headings accordingly. "I am flying blind. A beam to follow would help. So would a radio—but then, so would clear weather. The voice of the man at the Air Ministry had not promised storm." But she could feel the wind rising, and the rain fell hard. And there were other unanticipated challenges. "The smell of petrol in the cabin is so strong and the roar of the plane so loud that my senses are almost deadened." But once she got used to the conditions, it became routine.

She also has a clock. "At ten o'clock P.M., I am flying along the Great Circle Course for Harbour Grace, Newfoundland, into a forty-mile headwind at a speed of one hundred and thirty miles an hour." Because of the weather she could not be sure of how many more hours she had to fly, but she estimated between sixteen and eighteen. The tank had no gauge, but written on its side was the assurance: "This tank is good for four hours." So she had the benefit of someone's previous experience recorded for reference. "There is nothing ambiguous about such a guaranty. I believe it, but at twenty-five minutes to eleven, my motor coughs and dies, and the Gull is powerless above the sea." She wrote later, "One's own knowledge and self-management kicks in. It is the actual silence following the last splutter of the engine that stuns me." Her years of training held. "I suppose that the denial of natural impulse is what is meant by 'keeping calm,' but impulse has reason in it. If it is night and you are sitting in an aeroplane with a stalled motor, and there are two thousand feel between you and the sea, nothing can be more reasonable than the impulse to pull back your stick in the hope of adding to that two thousand, if only by a little. The thought, the knowledge, the law that tells you that your hope lies not in this, but in a contrary act—the act of directing your impotent craft toward the water—seems a terrifying abandonment, not only of reason, but of sanity. Your mind and your heart reject it. It is your hands, your stranger's hands—that follow with unfeeling precision the letter of the law." She followed her training. "I do not know how close to the waves I am when the motor explodes to life again. . . . I ought to thank God—and I do, indirectly. I thank Geoffrey De Havilland who designed the indomitable Gipsy, and who, after all, must have been designed by God in the first place."

Of course she reached America, albeit with icing in her fuel line that caused her to land in a swamp and arrive at her intended destination by land rather than by air. But reaching the North American coastline was a triumph. "I saw the cliffs of Newfoundland wound in ribbons of fog. The night and the storm had caught her [the plane] and we had flown blind for nineteen hours. . . . I was tired now, and cold. Ice began to film the glass of the cabin windows, and the fog played a magician's game with the land. But the land was there." With a protractor, map, and compass, she set her new course and proceeded south. A milestone had been reached. Her plan had worked well and just needed adjustments. The end of the project was in sight. Soon she was on the ground taking stock of her metrics: "I stumble out of the plane and sink to my knees in muck and stand there, foolishly staring, not at the lifeless land, but at my watch. Twenty-one hours and twenty-five minutes. Atlantic flight. Abingdon, England, to a nameless swamp—nonstop."[5]

Processes That Promote Teamwork

People who work well together are able to focus on their work, deliver results on time, and meet a budget. In an effective project team, the entire team's work is aligned with the project's goals. The project leaders and team members "own" their project plan, as well as the execution of that project plan. They are free to collaborate individually and as a group and address individual needs that are of concern to the team, but at the same time they focus primarily on interdependent actions. While some decisions must be made by the leader, decisions are made primarily by consensus.[6] Everyone participates, and team members feel empowered. Challenging questions are valued; conflict occurs, but people feel they are listened to and supported. The work environment honors individual diversity.

Building Trust

As a general rule, project management promotes trust within the team simply because the team is the only means to deliver the project. Promoting trust and teamwork is important to the project's success. Distrust can erode quality, slow decisions, and fragment cooperation. Trust that exists in a team is affected by the team's leadership, and the following processes—in addition to their contribution to standardization and integration of products—promote positive feelings of predictability and logic within the team. Projects need:

- Team processes
- Project management processes
- Technical processes

Open communications, clear performance standards, objective measures, and carefully administered rewards all contribute to trust.

- Open communications build trust because they assume that the information people give them is accurate, is true, and will withstand scrutiny. Limiting access to information implies that the information cannot stand up to scrutiny or that the people who are restricted from it are not trustworthy. Protecting access to information arouses suspicions.
- A commitment to quality is conveyed by the work examples shown to the team. The project team should expect all deliverables to be correct when submitted to them for their work, as well as when they are passed on after their work is complete. The occasional error is quickly corrected for the benefit of the team and without blame.
- Standards should be stated overtly, and they should be reinforced by example.

Clearly defined criteria, when written in advance, allow everyone to measure the adequacy of the work against what has been predefined as acceptable. Use of the defined measures conveys that objective measurement processes should be employed by everyone on the project.

Reinforcing Positive Culture Through Autonomy

In a mature organization that understands and values project management, the detailed schedule is a tool for the team and for no one else. Management oversight will be based on the high-level schedule, except for spot checks of accuracy or conformance with broader policy. Organizations that display the detailed schedule to all levels of management inside and outside the team may be playing politics or using fear and peer pressure to create an environment of compliance. More problems will be created by such visibility than will be resolved by it.

- Natural discrepancies in the schedule may be misinterpreted. People who are not knowledgeable about project management may expect more accuracy than is reasonable in a new endeavor and lose confidence in the team when they see normal discrepancies.
- Higher-level managers may be tempted to exert control over the detail, and their authority will allow them to do it. Micromanaging is expensive and disruptive.
- Control of the schedule is often not the problem that needs to be resolved. It may be estimating accuracy, management support, or lack of technical clarity that is causing the problem.
- Making a change may require using professional judgment about management trade-offs to choose a solution.

If the judgment of the project manager and project leadership are to have any weight, the resolution of a specific project management problem should be kept within the team. Project management is designed to be evaluated on results, not on the activity detail of getting there. If a problem is taken outside the project for resolution, it should be initiated by the project management professional in charge. His purpose in taking it outside the team is to request assistance in resolving a problem that needs outside intervention to solve it. An example would be a request from the project manager that the project's sponsor support him in preventing an operational manager's reassignment of a key team specialist assigned to a critical project task. The problem can interfere with the project's overall success, but the project manager and team may not have the influence to keep the specialist without senior management support.

In a professional environment, trust in individual performance is fundamental. In projects change is normal, and creative solutions may be needed that do not conform to traditional ways of doing things. On the other hand, if the new way is better, a new best practice may be created.

Reinforcing Positive Culture Through Rewards

Rewards convey to the entire team what behavior is desired and reinforce success when it does occur. What leadership chooses to reward conveys to the rest of the team what values are to be recognized and what behavior is considered to be above the ordinary. A good amount of the potential for quality performance still rests with the individual's own initiative. To tap individual initiative in a project management context and create a project management culture within the team, try giving rewards to reinforce these areas:

• *Prevention.* Encourage people to identify errors or omissions and to submit corrections, focusing on the process and not on the people. Do not reward heroes who jump in and fix unforeseen problems. While this may be admirable behavior, it is just part of the job, not something to reward.

• *Continuous improvement.* Negative feedback should focus on the processes. Make corrections to the process so that a responsible professional who follows the agreed-on process can deliver the work successfully.

• *Team performance.* Everyone on the team should share in the reward if the team meets its goals. Be careful that individuals do not stand out as a success if that success comes at the expense of the team's welfare.

• *Goal achievement.* Actions that contribute substantially to the final project outcome and customer requirements deserve more acknowledgment than exemplary individual tasks or early finishes that gain nothing for the project.

Encourage peer recognition so that people get satisfaction from being recognized as worthy by their coworkers and so that the rewards are not unduly exaggerated in their importance. Save the team rewards for public recognition and staff meetings. Rewarding the team in such settings also conveys progress to observers and provides assurances that the project is still on track, on time, and on budget. Teams can be objective too.

A word of caution: When very little structure exists, such as in the earliest stages of team activity, communications take on undue importance. It is prudent to select carefully what initial recognition is to be given and what that recognition conveys so that it elicits the desired response that this project team expects of every member. Then wait to deliver the recognition until the new behavioral expectations have been communicated and are understood. If quality is a critical factor, provide more oversight and reinforcement at the beginning, when team members are still developing their work habits.

To set work standards that support both the team and quality performance:

- *Establish and communicate norms for work hours, overtime, volume, and output, as well as acceptable ranges for deviation.* Protect overachievers from burnout by limiting off-hours access to the site or by turning the lights out after a certain time each night. Productive energy is just one more resource to manage! And although it is seldom discussed, excessively long work hours steal time from families, adding another hidden risk to the team's continuity.
- *Engage the team in identifying issues and provide a process for their orderly resolution.* Create and maintain an issues list.
- *Be objective, not subjective.* Keep the focus on the work standards and away from individual people.

TEAM BUILDING

When a team is formed, its members will go through stages of team development. The development stages have been defined crisply by one source as "forming, storming, norming, and performing."[7] In the earliest stages, individual team members are busy focusing on what is expected and what they are to do in their respective work roles. As dominance evolves and differences emerge, there is a predictable stage of internal conflict. Eventually the group will evolve its own norms and begin to work effectively as a group. During transition, leaders may need to reiterate expectations to reduce disruptive competition and encourage team members to reinforce positive behavior.

When a team consists of members from different organizations or different cultures, team members should spend some time learning about the various cultures and environments. Make sure a skilled facilitator moderates the discussions to keep them positive. Provide some group guidance on behaviors that are acceptable to differing groups. A mixed team of professionals in Europe arrived at a project site with different social greeting habits. Some people greeted everyone and then started to work. Others went straight to their work, reserving interpersonal greetings for the midmorning break. Team members were interpreting the others' habits as frivolous or antisocial. Such speculation eroded morale. The project manager identified the problem promptly, set a standard for all team members to work before socializing, and the problem disappeared.[8]

To shorten the evolution of an effective team, team-building activities can be organized for the team by its leadership. Expectations for behavior and performance must be established promptly and in a cohesive manner when people first come into the project. When people arrive in a new work setting, they usually are open to new approaches. They will quickly form impressions of what is expected of them—in performance, in behavior toward others, and in teamwork. Having those standards laid out and communicated early in the project is important. If new standards are not established quickly, people go back to their prior work behaviors.

One way to establish behavioral expectations is to solicit group input during the first meeting. Solicit group expectations about the project's desired environment. Open discussion allows an airing of norms acceptable and not acceptable to the group and encourages discussion. Conduct periodic reviews with the group about how they feel things are going to ensure that hidden problems are not being ignored.

Choosing to use team-based planning techniques can help form bonds to support the success of the project. Based on the type of project, certain behaviors are of greater value than others. Creativity, hard work, finishing on time, and detailed factual analysis may be characteristics that are particularly valued in a project. Each member will bring different gifts to the benefit of the whole.

ESTABLISHING PROJECT MANAGEMENT CULTURE ON VIRTUAL PROJECTS

If a project team cannot meet together, as in a virtual project, team members will need to participate in tasks using technology, contribute to common work products, and keep a trail of documentation for practically everything. On virtual projects, the team deduces norms for the project by observing who gets rewarded. Selecting the right individuals to recognize takes on exaggerated importance. Establishing best practices files, as well as 24-hour access, is just common sense.

Using an accepted project management template for reference documents, a team needs to create an online project manual for round-the-clock reference on virtual projects. Having one place to look for guidance on performance standards creates a common ground. All the team members are here to work, and common standards give them something to comply with. Measures of quality communicated up front direct the work toward agreed-on outcomes. They also enable people to be successful by defining success.

Select methods that are comfortable for team members to work with. It may be increasingly important in the future to consider the differences among groups as to how they interact with digital media and "smart" devices. People of all ages and cultures are working, communicating, navigating, reading, searching for needed information, and entertaining themselves electronically.[9]

Automation touches practically everyone. But not every culture has a project work culture, and not every age group relies on digital devices to the same degree or for the same purpose.

School systems are feeling the shift to digital media. Today's college students pride themselves on their ability to multitask and consider it a boost to their productivity. Small children stay in touch with their parents while gaming with their friends. But while some school systems now use electronic media and computers to teach traditional subjects, others balk at the "digital distraction" that personal devices introduce into the learning process. They cite evidence that basic learning skills such as analysis, problem solving, and retention appear to be on the decline.[10]

As young workers emerge from school systems that vary in their use of digital media, it is inevitable that this wave of "wired" workers will affect how projects are staffed and managed. One effect of ready electronic devices is that knowledge mastery is eclipsed by the ability of anyone to search quickly for anything he needs to know. And those who have grown up using technology cannot imagine working without it. These new workers enjoy independence and are quick to change what they are doing if they do not think it will produce desired results. They are able to work quickly in short bursts. Instead of working on one big idea, they create "snippets," paragraphs that meet an immediate need. And while many do not see the connection among quick tasks, they do not feel the need to see those connections. They can be satisfied with short-term outcomes. Others are just looking for that "next big idea."[11]

Project management would appear to fit neatly into this fast-moving stream of activity and tasks. Project management has always recognized as valuable the worker who could get things done. As long as she could deliver results, no one was particularly concerned with the "package" that worker came in. A strong results orientation is the great equalizer. Furthermore, people drawn to project management are comfortable with ambiguity and change and risk, using their knowledge and skills to quickly put order on chaos and work toward agreement and project results. In many cases they are willing to work with the technology available to them on the project and simply make it work for them.

On the other hand, a number of trends that are affecting projects could challenge project effectiveness. At the very least they will require focused attention.

Managing the Digital Team

Managing the digital team may mean the project manager will need to think through the strategy for getting workers who work electronically to "form a team." They may be accustomed to working alone with significant independence. Typically, different people with desired skills and abilities work together on a project and the mix may change as the project advances. A number of strategies are available for addressing diverse teams, including articulating the diversity and augmenting the strengths of each. But the technological mix of workers will also vary: some will be knowledgeable but not so digitally "savvy"; others will be able to make electronics do minor magic but will have little understanding of the effects of their actions on the team, the goals of the project, and the importance of the effort to the organization as a whole.

While the team may be able to use common electronic devices, their occupational training, approach to work tasks, response to direction, and even cultural communication practices can vary. Instead of assuming competence in key areas, use training to align it. And do it face-to-face. Even with all the devices to assist communications, eight out of ten people still prefer meeting in person.

Provide at least some fundamental project management training. Select a webinar that teaches what your project practices. Some people assigned to the project may not be familiar with project management and how it differs from normal operations. Just because people are familiar with carrying out tasks and reporting back does not mean they know projects. Some organizations may have provided the new team worker access to project management software and functions but do not actually practice project management according to accepted standards. Project managers and leaders will need to be explicit in communicating their team expectations.

Turnover can be a real threat to project success if key team members do not honor their commitments or complete assigned work. As mentioned earlier, workers may be quick to change their work allegiances or job responsibilities if they do not think what they are doing will produce desired results. Spend time with each worker to determine what conditions would cause him or her to leave and then manage risk accordingly. Cross-train similar team members so they can assume each other's duties if needed.

Provide more structured templates for deliverables. The quality of deliverables may require more supervision if workers are content to contribute paragraphs or short content. Multitasking using electronic devices may be creating people who are not good at analyzing or focusing on complex assignments. Pair newer workers with senior professionals to work together and share learning. Encourage people to review one another's work.

Put more attention into role assignments. The project manager or team member responsible for adding new members to the team should assess the prior experience of people assigned to the project and assign major tasks to people who have previous related experience and a good reputation for delivering results. Should a nonperformer emerge who must be cut from the team, keep good records of what and why for future reference. And put some time into capturing "lessons learned" so that both the team member and the way he or she is integrated into the work group are improved for future projects.

MANAGING TEAM RESOURCES

A project manager and team have finite resources to expend in delivering results on a project. Team members are assigned to work on the project for a specific period, and when that period is over they are most likely expected to return to their regular jobs. They need to be able to start work promptly and work efficiently. As a general rule, all the routine organization charts, job role descriptions, policies, rewards, and constraints that team members take for granted in the larger organization will need to be re-created in some form on the project. They need not be elaborate, but they are necessary. The extent to which they are created and their quality depend on the level of maturity of the team in project management experience, the complexity of the project, and the support structure of the organization. The manner in which they are conveyed and used may depend heavily on the makeup of the team and the digital devices or corporate environment they were accustomed to in their everyday work.

Maintaining the central point of authority on a project is crucial to maintaining control. Getting agreement is important when the time exists to forge that agreement, but when time is short and the pressure is on, a single source of decisions allows people to move forward together quickly. Even if the general atmosphere of the project is team involvement in everything, a single point of decision is needed, especially if there is time pressure or an emergency. Decision authority can be delegated, but centralizing control is more difficult if it is not established up front. There may be several decision makers on different areas of a project, but it is the project manager who has final decision authority, not the sponsor or customer outside the project or team members beneath the project manager. (See Figure 8-3.) Even when it is the team that decides on a new course of action, it is the project manager who will decide how it will be put into the plan.

Team Meeting Procedures

Meetings help in getting group input and facilitate decision making when these tasks can best be accomplished in a group setting. Whether the meeting is physical or virtual, make the meeting as efficient as possible by using structured processes for project management and agendas that are intended for that type of meeting. Separate status-type meetings from discussions since they have completely different agendas. Meeting procedures make meetings more productive; always have an agenda as a road map and put the most important items first. Use a flipchart or an electronic board to make work results visual and to record consensus. Take notes and promptly distribute minutes of meetings to cement agreement and items of consensus.

FIGURE 8-3 Typical players/roles in projects. The chart shows the key roles needed for most projects.

Role/Player	Responsibilities
Sponsor (sometimes called *project champion*)	Accountable for overall project results Sells the project Has courage and clout
Project customer(s) Technical customer Economic customer User customer	Accepts final deliverable Approves technical specifications Pays bills/provides funding Represents user's needs if not the user
Project manager or project leader	Accountable for overall project results (shared accountability)
Project team member	Accountable for his/her deliverables (shared accountability)
Functional manager	Provides resources, team members (accountable for work technical quality)

When leading a discussion, create a "parking lot" designation for important points that are raised but really belong in another meeting; stay on the agreed agenda. When presenting priorities on which everyone may not agree, use categories—like sticky notes on a board—to shape the hierarchy of items. The simple fact that the items can be rearranged helps to get agreement (see Appendix B). If the organization is formal and the decisions have controversial far-reaching effects, and if senior personnel will be meeting with management, run the meeting using *Robert's Rules of Order*. This method of meeting management is designed to handle controversy and create collaborative decisions, and while it may seem complex at first, many workers are familiar with it. The standard agenda addresses approval of prior minutes (and agreements within them), a review of old business, new business, and action items for the next scheduled meeting.

Post ground rules or principles that express how people agree they should work together; enforce them when discussions get out of line. Have stand-up meetings when they are never intended to last longer than a few minutes. Be brilliant, be brief, and be gone.

SUMMARY

This chapter focused on the team—creating it, developing it, and mobilizing its energies and talents toward the project's ultimate goal. When human talent is recruited to perform project work, team members often come from different work roles, different organization units, and even different cultures. It is up to the project manager to mold these individuals into a functioning and effective team. Building a team means building trust and cooperation. The project needs everyone's best efforts and can use the facilitating processes associated with communications and human resources management—plus group processes, principles, and techniques—to gain commitment and capture that extra edge of performance.

Chapter 9 covers the facilitating processes that support the execution phase and closeout. These processes correspond to the "knowledge areas" on the project management professional certification exam presented initially in Chapter 1. These knowledge areas and their corresponding processes are flexible tools that a project management professional can use to create an environment for success on a project. They are used in conjunction with the technical approach to anticipate positive and negative influences on the successful outcome of the project. The goal of facilitating processes is to maximize positive influences and minimize the impact of negative influences.

REVIEW QUESTIONS

1. The project manager sets the pace and tone for work by:
   a. doing the work by himself or herself
   b. communicating what is expected of the team
   c. providing the high-level leadership
   d. none of the above

2. The team is created by deciding how many individuals or groups will be needed, their compositions, and their:
   a. roles
   b. responsibilities
   c. assignment of deliverables
   d. authority
   e. organization chart reporting relationships
   f. all of the above

3. Detailed and specific team member input is sought as the project moves through planning into implementation.
   a. true
   b. false

4. Emotional intelligence is a key set of personal characteristics, including the ability to:
   a. motivate oneself and persist in the face of frustrations
   b. control impulses and delay gratification
   c. regulate one's moods and keep stress from swamping the ability to think
   d. empathize and hope
   e. all of the above
   f. a, b, and c only
   g. a and b only
   h. none of the above

5. Which of the following all contribute to trust?
   a. communication management, unclear performance standards, risk management, and personal reward systems
   b. one-way communications, goal-oriented standards, intuitive measures, and fair reward systems
   c. no communications, poor performance standards, objective measures, and carefully disguised rewards
   d. open communications, clear performance standards, objective measures, and carefully administered rewards

6. People who _____ are able to focus on their
   _____ , deliver _____ on time, and
   _____ a budget.
   a. work well together; deliverables; benefits; exceed
   b. work well together; work; results; meet
   c. work poorly together; work; results; meet
   d. do not work together; egos; results; meet

7. It is not the project manager's role to mold the different individuals into a functioning and effective team; this is the sponsor's responsibility.
   a. true
   b. false

8. Which one of the following can erode quality, slow decisions, and fragment
   cooperation?
   a. trust
   b. team building
   c. interpersonal conflicts
   d. distrust

C H A P T E R

9

FACILITATING PROJECT EXECUTION AND CLOSEOUT

OVERVIEW AND GOALS

This chapter describes the facilitating processes that a project leader and team use to implement a project and complete its deliverable. The project phases described in previous chapters—initiation and planning—created a context for managing the project and delivering its benefits. They are the point in the process where the parameters and requirements for the project are identified, developed in the project plan in adequate detail to manage a team, and built into an infrastructure for executing that plan.

In this chapter—addressing project execution and closeout—the project manager and team use the work plans and infrastructure created during planning to carry out the work of the project. However, there is still a good deal to be done to ensure a smooth execution. They must determine how the project management knowledge areas of the professional and their associated facilitating processes can best be applied to ensure the success of the project. Some of the knowledge areas that facilitate project execution—scope management, time management, cost management, risk management, communications management, human resources management, quality management, and procurement management—also enable and advance development of the product or deliverable during execution. Since knowledge is applied in many ways, and facilitating processes are not sequential but rather are used throughout the entire project, each facilitating process area must be defined, developed, executed, and closed out. Some cover the life cycle of the project. Others apply mostly to execution of the work. Each process must be integrated with the requirements of the project and specific tasks or activities added to those parts of the project most affected by them. Some must be linked to the organization's defined procedures that affect the project.

Part of planning and executing a project is proactive—the project manager and team put their efforts and energies into doing things that must be done for the project to reach completion. Other parts are reactive—ensuring that the team works on what it should work on and not something else and that it does not lose focus or run out of time and resources before the project is complete. Facilitating processes help the team manage these challenges. The project manager combines the use of specific project processes with knowledge and wisdom from prior experience to create an environment for success. When the deliverable is complete, it is turned over to the customer, and the sponsoring organization and the customer organization can realize the benefits of the project. (Processes that are focused primarily on monitoring and control will be addressed in Chapter 10.)

CREATING A SUCCESS ENVIRONMENT WITH PROCESSES

Planning a project requires more than focusing on the work to be done. It requires planning the processes that will result in overall project success. These processes—often referred to as *facilitating processes*—are not always in the direct critical path of the project's main activities. They enable the main activities by removing barriers, eliciting cooperation, and creating an environment of acceptance and support among team members, supporters, and stakeholders. Some facilitating processes are parallel to the project phases, integrated within them. Most continue from the early initiation phase to the project's closure. Others are confined to a specific phase such as project execution.

Project integration management focuses on the interrelationships of the parts of the project, ensuring that one area does not negatively affect another and getting the parts to perform effectively together. The key documents that mark successive phases of the project's initiation, planning, and execution provide evidence that project integration is taking place. The processes and assumptions that result in a charter, scope statement, project management plan, and changes to the project scope or the product's requirements must be integrated and revisited throughout the project to ensure their alignment.[1] The processes that are used to develop the project's deliverables also need to be identified, planned, and integrated into the plan and schedule so that they advance the project's goals and intended outcome.

COMMUNICATIONS

The communications plan created during detailed planning is put into action when the execution phase begins. Start-up information is distributed to members of the team, and announcements of the project's implementation are sent to sponsors, customers, and stakeholders. Reference materials are made available online for team members, and work methods and processes are explained. Immediate training is scheduled to inform the team of the project management process and how methods and tools will be applied. On a small project, much of the work related to communications is performed by the project manager. On a large project, specific members of the team will be assigned to carry out these responsibilities including individuals trained in communications.

Reliable, sound information is essential to a project's success. From the beginning, the team must have a vision of how the project will finish and what criteria must be met to declare the effort a success. The team also will need a variety of information regarding the project, its success factors, the business case, the deliverable's requirements, and the technical methods and procedures that will result in a successful delivery. The entire project team also needs to be given a clear idea of what the client's or customer's needs are so that those needs are not compromised when the team faces minor trade-offs during execution tasks.

Processes and templates from prior projects may be used on the current project, and the organization's standard project management process helps to establish what the sponsoring organization requires. In some cases the sponsor, technical lead, or customer will prescribe a process to ensure that the result of the project—its product, service, or plan—conforms to the acceptance criteria. Deciding how much structure is necessary requires a lot of knowledge, creativity, judgment, and wisdom.

As a general rule, standardization will help to reduce the stress of ambiguity and the challenge of newness. Training the team in its work processes, both project management and technical work, helps to get the team working together more quickly. The project manager should specify which processes and templates everyone must follow and which are optional. Standardizing forms conveys knowledge through their design. Since not all team members will be effective writers or skilled communicators, work production can be speeded up through use of templates. Partially developed forms for agendas, e-mails, reference file categories for the team, and reports can contain generic information from the start so that only specifics such as subtitles and dates or agenda items need to be added when they are used (see Appendix B).

Identifying members of the team who are knowledgeable about communications methods and strategies can be useful when designing standard formats. If central files for standard communications templates are set up in advance, valuable team effort is not wasted on overhead activities when the project is in full production mode on the deliverable.

Always presenting communications in the same format also helps the receiver quickly identify what is being presented and go right to the essence of the message. The format conveys what is there, how it is to be used, and in what context. If good form design practices are used, errors are reduced: the data can be entered quickly and even added to later. Configuration control methods should show the proper version.

Communicating clearly is a way to manage risk through common understanding. Since creating, editing, and managing communications takes both time and effort, here are a few tips:

• *Keep communications simple.* In written documents, such as e-mail, put the message in the heading and first paragraph and clearly specify any action the recipient is expected to take after receiving it. When responding, add the new message to the response heading. In automated voice messages, specify urgency and how someone is to apply the information before giving the message verbally. Repeat action items, due dates, and contact numbers at the end if the message is lengthy. Convey temporary information verbally and reference material in writing.

• *Prioritize everything you communicate (watch out for overload).* Decide in advance what must be communicated and what is discretionary. When sending information, the sender should put the most important information first in case the receiver is interrupted or is in a hurry.

• *Pay attention to the meaning of words.* Define unfamiliar terms. Use them consistently. Do not overpromise; stay factual.

• *Standards of communication.* It is better to make a "good" communication now than a perfect one later. Tell people whom to contact if things remain unclear.

The project's central team can manage the routine aspects of communications. Repetitive tasks—such as keeping meeting minutes—can be assigned to specific individuals on subteams or rotated within the group.

Minutes should be retained for meetings where managerial decisions are made that affect project outcomes.

Communicating Through Reports and Data

The project communications plan should include a chart of what reports will be conveyed to the project's stakeholders and team and who will be receiving the team's reports. Some reports will be cyclic, and others will be event-driven. (See Figure 9-1.) Since many people interacting with the project will be receiving information in formats different from what they are accustomed to, the project needs to set up definitions and possibly symbols to convey the importance and finality of that information. Symbols can be useful when project team members come from different language backgrounds. When people are asked to submit reports and data for the project, they also must know how accurate the data are or should be.

Distributing the Schedule

The deliverables schedule, as well as other versions of the schedule with target dates and tasks, can serve different purposes for different audiences. A particular view of a schedule can be used as a sales tool, a nagging device, or an excuse, depending on how it is perceived and presented. The project

FIGURE 9-1 Communications plan example. The communications plan lists key project management documents, the recipients of those documents, and the frequency of their release.

Document	Recipients	Frequency

Project plan
  Schedule
  Budgets
  Scope
	Project sponsor
	Management team
	Project team
		As needed

Project status report	Project team	After each team meets, usually weekly
Project change Log/status update	Project team Project sponsor	Weekly
Sponsor project status review	Project sponsor Project customer	Before each sponsor review, usually monthly

management team will be using the schedule to promote desired behavior by selecting how it will be used with different audiences of stakeholders.

The high-level schedule, once refined, is a better tool for communicating to the public than a detailed schedule. Usually only the team members will report or use detail or need to know it. As a general rule, stakeholders should be provided with only the level of schedule detail that is appropriate to the amount of control they are authorized to execute if they do not like what they see.

Distributing Information to Stakeholders and the Team

An effective communications process takes an assertive stance to managing changes between what people expect and what is really relevant to complete the project. The plan identifies who will need what type of communications when, as well as the channels or medium to be used. If people are accustomed to receiving important information using certain channels or modes of communication, information received differently may not be taken seriously, and the communication may not achieve its intended goal.

The plan itself can be lean and simple. It lists the team members by type (technical or project management, subproject or contract), program manager, stakeholders, and support team (information technology, training). It records the communications methods, media, and schedule for distributing specific types of information to various project stakeholders. Whether it is a blanket announcement by e-mail or a personal address by executive management in a group meeting, the medium conveys information to the team as well as the content of the message.

The project manager needs to convey some principles of communication to the team in the plan to keep the process effective. The parts of a communications plan all serve a purpose; key people need to be involved in key areas of the project for the project to be effective. The plan should specify who is to be involved through communications, how they will be informed, and what purpose their involvement serves in the project's success.

Communication is everyone's job, and significant changes and issues during project execution need to be communicated upward from project team members to team leadership, and direction, changes, logistics, status, and resolutions need to be communicated downward to the team to guide their work. Even with an effective process and a plan, a certain amount of miscommunication occurs on projects. The goal is to minimize the negative effects through systematic communications management.

MANAGING QUALITY

Ensuring quality on a project is a much larger topic than can be addressed in this chapter. Quality—meeting the agreed-on customer requirements—is a result of the convergence of many levels of effort on a project and is covered under scope management (see Chapters 6 and 11). A quality plan, established as part of the overall project plan, is the location for recording the project's defined quality strategy. If standards, tolerances, and methods are defined for the organization as a whole or are particularly applicable because of the technical area used to shape the product or final deliverable, they also should be referred to in the quality plan (see Chapter 12). Any special applications or conditions required for the project to create a product or service that is unique or different need to be spelled out.

The quality plan needs to define what is considered to represent quality on the project, how it will be managed, and how it will be tracked and controlled. The definition of quality generally accepted in project management means meeting the agreed-on customer requirements. How effectively the team members communicate and capture what they hear can affect the quality of the deliverable and the project's final delivery of desired benefits. Clearly defined customer requirements and managed customer expectations also are shaped by the organization sponsoring the project and the maturity of the organization's process environment. (See Chapter 10 for more on quality and Chapter 12 for more on organizational project management maturity.) However, quality is also a result of quality processes, particularly in project management. While the processes used to create the deliverable may be new, the processes to manage the project have evolved over time and should be performed well and consistently.

The definition of the desired state of the outcome or final deliverable on the project must be documented and agreed to so that when the project is complete, the deliverables can be judged adequate. The team needs this acceptance criteria as soon as possible to know what to create on the project. If changes are made to the acceptance criteria while the project is in progress, those changes must be communicated promptly to the team, and the implications of those changes on the work process or outcomes need to be explained.

While the entire project team is responsible for quality, the project manager, working with the team's leadership, takes explicit responsibility for the quality plan. And the definition of what represents quality in the sponsoring organization is the explicit responsibility of top management.

MANAGING COST

In many organizations, how money is managed can affect the profitability and financial health of the company. If the project can predict when resources will be needed, the organization can keep money in revenue-producing activities or investments until it is needed on the project. Cost-allocation formulas applied to the resource management plan during project planning can help predict when needed resources must be available to the project to pay vendors, contractors, and fees, but adjustments and refinements need to be made throughout the execution phase to keep those predictions on target during changes. In government, the availability of funding in the budget cycle must be anticipated and managed, and the fiscal year often differs between private sector organizations and public sector organizations. Contracting and procurement may need to be carefully managed to keep resource use and resource availability aligned.

Allocating the appropriate costs of project staff, financial resources, and material to each element of the plan, including subplans, makes it possible to predict when capital and material will be needed and to extrapolate overruns to dependent tasks if necessary. Since corporations usually move money to make payments, knowing when the payments are due is useful for cash management. In profit-making organizations, staying in touch with financial managers throughout the project can help the project manager and team keep one finger on the pulse of the organization and address any special financial conditions, including fluctuations in currency, that need to be accommodated during the project period.

Accountability

Estimating and forecasting prove their value during the execution phase. Whether or not members discuss it explicitly, the project team is accountable for responsible use of resources to every stakeholder, including other teams. If the project is to be successful and deliver its desired benefits to customers, it must be completed. Running short on resources inevitably will cause delays and can even cause project cancellation. While this is usually more of a concern to the organization as a whole than to the project team, it is important that team members recognize the negative effects of poor accountability. Executive sponsors may have specific legal accountability (Sarbanes-Oxley Act) that can affect how projects track and report financial information.

Administration is also part of project management accountability, particularly when it comes to contracts, subprojects, vendors, and legal advisers.

Tracking work produced to expenditures, purchase orders to contracts, and budget allocations to actual work performed allows the project team to hold each vendor, contractor, and developer accountable for the revenue received (see Chapter 11).

Logistics

In a construction project, logistics can mean getting the right materials to the right place for the tasks at hand. In modern professional projects, however, it also can mean not only getting the right people to the project at the right time but also getting the project sent to the right people. The dawn of computer-managed development or services has brought with it the potential for sending parts of projects to offices in other countries and having their workers perform tasks while the sending office team is asleep. In time-sensitive operations, producing the project result sooner by leveraging time zones can provide profitable benefits. Planning and managing these transfers is a complex new task in project logistics.

Logistics planning needs to address not only the product development tasks but the project management tasks as well. Both need to be integrated for effective execution. More than one large project with several subprojects under it has found itself in trouble because the project plan included product development activities in its logistics planning but not the project management activities. In one military facility, the impact of simultaneous subproject tasks on multiple teams (stakeholders) was overlooked as was the capacity of the facility to train them. Some schedules had analysts from many projects being trained in a single facility without adequate training space for all the teams. Some had several implementation dates from different software projects overlapping in the same organization. This meant that the various projects' deliverables were being implemented separately, without considering the cumulative impact of change on analysts who had to use those multiple new tools in a short period of time. Ideally, program management and portfolio management would be used to integrate projects (see Chapter 12). But if the organization does not have either, the project manager will need to assume responsibility for logistics integration.

Contracts and Procurement

The use of contracts (or outsourcing) allows the project team to off-load some of the planning, supervision, and risk inherent in a group of related tasks to another group or organizational entity. The many configurations of reward and penalty in contracting options can shape the cost and benefit of the contract to the project's needs. It is important to remember, however, that the burden of communication can be increased, particularly if the work is not repetitive, standardized, and stable. Different interpretations and cultural expectations can wreak havoc on cooperative efforts, as well as create volatility when dependent deliverables eventually must be combined. The bottom line is that moving work to outside organizations contributes to risk and actually can raise the risk of delays, errors, or increased costs if not managed carefully and well.[2]

Specialists knowledgeable in contracting options and legal ramifications are a valuable resource to the team, but only after the project management professional has analyzed the "make or buy" decision thoroughly. The contractual arrangements always should be designed specifically to motivate and reinforce desired supplier behavior and compliance with requirements. Many organizations follow specific processes and procedures to be sure contracts are sound.

MANAGING TIME

Many projects lose some or even all of their value if delivered late. This is particularly true of products in a competitive market, where market share goes to the first entry. Others count cost by effort expended, access to desired resources when needed, or time wasted in delays. Project management considers time to be reflected in the project schedule and to be tracked by hours against task completion on that schedule. How team members and other personnel use and waste time affects the project. A concept important to project management is the time value of schedule delivery against agreed-on date ranges and the importance of managing time on a macro level against value produced. Time is a resource. When an organization has decided that a need must be met through a project, the value of meeting that need may be amplified or diminished by time. Considering time efficiency when setting up work rules and methods can streamline results delivery.

The Project Management Schedule

The duration of a project's sequenced tasks is used to define the time window during which the project will create and deliver its product or service and its benefits. Sometimes the duration of the project will be influenced by external elapsed time in the critical path of delivery: government reviews, external market influences, or delayed access to critical resources or approvals. The team is expected to anticipate these delays—to the extent possible—and include them when estimating tasks in the schedule. By the time the go/no-go decision is reached, the schedule is expected to be reasonably accurate.

Once the execution phase begins, the project management detail and general technical methods are already built into the plan through the work breakdown structure (WBS) and task list. Often it is a simple task to use software to refine calendar dates, add names and costs to the tasks, extrapolate from these when the creation of deliverables is likely to occur, and make refinements to the tasks, effort, duration, and sequence to optimize the resources available to the task at hand. Some scheduling can be done using automated tools; others—such as work leveling for professional assignments—must be done by analysis. Uneven workloads can put undue pressure on valuable employees, affecting their relationships, health, and even their desire to remain with their employer. Many modern organizations prohibit project teams from making up for poor project planning and estimating by asking team members to work overtime "off the clock."

Communicating the Schedule

There are various ways to communicate the allocation of time in projects, including Gantt charts, flowcharts, sequenced processes, deliverable schedules, and resource time reporting. Even the time value of money and earned value tracking against a plan imply the expenditure of time. (For more on earned value, see Chapter 11.) As the project progresses, schedule risk diminishes because many tasks have been completed and ensuing tasks have become more predictable. (Figures 4-2, 4-3, and 4-4 show the trends in a project toward increased accuracy, decreased schedule/time risk, and reduced ability to influence total cost as the project progresses.)

MANAGING RISK

Given the "newness" of project initiatives, a certain amount of risk is inherent in them. The risk of unknowns is the lack of ability to predict and control those unknowns. Using systematic methods of identifying risk, quantifying risk, prioritizing and tracking risk, and controlling the loss associated with risk-based problems helps deliver projects successfully. Depending on the risk tolerance of the organization sponsoring the project, the subject of risk management may or may not be a challenge. As in most other areas of project management, the ability to predict and prepare for exigencies is a critical success factor.

Risks can be categorized and compared with the project's critical success factors: scope risk, schedule risk, financial risk, and so on. Since not all risk can be managed owing to the constraints of time and effort, creating a risk management plan and strategy helps to keep real risks in the forefront and manages emerging risks using a process.

During planning, the initial list of risks is assembled. During execution, the project team members allocate these risks to specific areas of the project and create countermeasures and a method for tracking and reviewing them periodically. Discussing risk with the project's sponsor and customer prepare them for what may arise later. For the team, predicting and controlling risk releases valuable time, resources, and energy to more critical functions of execution.

Not only the team but also other groups that interface with a project need to understand the importance of risks to project success and ways to manage risk. Management in particular needs to be aware of the role of risks in projects, and a thorough understanding of risks is needed before attempting to use risk measures to extend or cancel projects. The primary purpose of risk management is to prevent problems by predicting and avoiding them. Some team members will resist risk management because avoiding risks that actually never happen does not merit much attention. On the other hand, fixing risks once they become problems allows someone to be a hero.

Taking a proactive approach to risk means anticipating potential disruption on a project and identifying ways to prevent such disruptions from occurring by taking specific actions. People often find it easier to focus their attention on abstract areas when they are quantified and ranked according to how serious they are and how likely they are to occur. This is why projects create and use risk analyses (see Appendix B).

Methods for Managing Risk

Managing risk throughout the project requires that team members get involved in the risk management process. One method of defining risk is to develop a list of potential threats to a project and to involve skeptics from the project initiation stage in the definition of those risks. To get technical team members active in the risk management process, use definitions and terms already familiar to them from their technical work so that they quickly see the value. Executives will be more comfortable seeing risks presented in charts or numerical rankings similar to the briefings they receive daily.

High, medium, and low risk ratings are enough to elevate some risks to the current radar screen and place others behind the scenes, freeing team members to focus on other areas of the project that may need immediate attention.

The organization can predict certain risks in projects based on prior experience. Categories of risk—such as organizational risk, technical risk, environmental risk, or legal risk—can be standard in every risk plan, and the particular instance to be managed can be placed in a subcategory under one of these headings (see Chapter 12). The chart grows when project-specific risks are added, augmented by input from people who identified issues earlier during initiation, from team members, and from the customer or specialists. As the project progresses and some anticipated risks fail to materialize, they can be eliminated from the risk plan, and replaced by new ones identified with later stages of project execution.

Putting numbers to risk is an exercise in quantifying subjective judgments thereby making it easier to arrange them in their appropriate priority. Once risks have been categorized, two numbers can be assigned—likelihood (probability) and seriousness (impact)—and multiplied for all the risks in a given category to determine which risks deserve the greatest attention.

Some risks are highly threatening but unlikely to occur. Others are not so serious individually but collectively can add up to a serious concern. Some projects develop a symbol of emerging concern (such as the green, yellow, red stoplight motif) to alert the team to the level of concern of particular risks for particular tasks or stages of the work. If such a method is used, written agreed-on definitions are necessary so that the symbols can be used effectively over time.

A reasonable cycle can be established to revisit risk management as a team to confirm or retire risks on the risk plan. On projects that last more than a year with a changing environment, monthly recalculation is probably a good idea.

Allocating and Tracking Risks

Individual subprojects or teams within a large project may be assigned to track risks most likely to emerge in their area of the project. They are also accountable for the countermeasures, mitigation, and contingency resources associated with those risks. Individual managers may be willing to accept responsibility for specific areas of risk that relate to their area of work. Some risks can be spread across the entire team, with individual team members responsible for tracking their status. In covering a risk associated with a specific area, for instance, specific team members can be assigned to communicate regularly with individuals who are involved in that area and keep on top of any issues that emerge.

Too many risks on the tracking list divert attention from the project's work. Ten risks are a good number to track, winnowed down from a larger list of 20 identified risks.

Responding to Risk

There are a number of ways to respond to risk. Sometimes the risk passes without incurring any problem; the avoidance plan or mitigation plan was successful in preventing the risk or reducing its impact. Taking out an insurance policy to transfer the risk (referred to as *risk transference*) or seeking legal advice may be called for on some projects, and even regular communication with specialists may be required in particularly volatile environments. Not only do these measures need to be in the risk plan and schedule, but also their cost needs to be in the budget. If specific documentation or compliance is required, the team needs to be informed. If the risk predicted does occur, then the project must cover it out of contingency reserve funds or time.

A good fallback is to visit risk often and keep it up to date. Identify the types of risks, quantify the risk impact, and determine countermeasures. The countermeasures can be prevention, avoidance, transference, and mitigation. Select the most appropriate countermeasures to implement. Once the countermeasures have been decided on, put them in the schedule and the plan, with appropriate tasks and resources.

POLICY AND STANDARDS

The management policy and standards guiding the team need to be articulated and communicated so that they convey a common view to the diverse groups interacting with the project's members. The core team most likely will be dealing with many different audiences. For internal projects, they will be interacting with managers, internal customers, technical teams, support personnel, and operations teams. For external or public projects, the core team is also likely to interact with:

- Client or citizen groups
- Government agencies
- Insurance representatives
- Financial officials
- Others (utilities, equipment vendors, etc.)

Each group has different priorities guiding its work and its view of the project. If these groups are to support the goal and mission, they need to have a common understanding of how their support will be needed. The policy and standards that apply to the project may differ from those that apply in operations, or they may be applied differently because the project is creating something unique. Conveying that difference to stakeholders eases concerns and creates better understanding and support for the project.

PROJECT INTEGRATION MANAGEMENT

Project management is an integrative undertaking. The complexities of iterative planning and definition require periodic integration of core processes with facilitating processes and of stable standard processes with processes that have been changed and adapted to fit the project. Integration is an analytical process performed by the professionals in charge. For the project, there are a few natural points for a concerted effort in integration: the transitions between high-level planning and detailed project plan development, during project execution when changes are made to the baseline plan, and when changes are made to the project scope statement and quality plan (deliverable requirements and acceptance criteria). For the product or deliverable, there are natural points in the project where integrated change control makes sense: at the end of each product development stage, at the end of lengthy consecutive tasks that are interdependent, when subcontracts deliver results, and when different paths of the project converge. Changes, intended or not, occur as work progresses. Those changes may affect subsequent work and are best controlled if identified in advance.

Integrated change control is a review process to ensure that changes made to the deliverable product or processes are analyzed for potential negative effects on the requirements and desired outcome of the project. Some product development processes used in operations do not lend themselves to application on projects. New or changed processes from the project need to be documented and refined for turnover to operations. Project management integration requires each project and product process to be aligned and connected appropriately with the other processes to facilitate their coordination within the project and with operations processes for ongoing use of the improvements after the project is closed. These process interactions often require trade-offs among project objectives and alternatives.[3] During integrated change control, the effects of changes on other portions of the plan are reviewed, and adjustments are made if needed. Requiring management and customer approvals before making those trade-offs is one way to confirm that project goals and product value are not compromised if scope statements or acceptance criteria must be adjusted.

A final key point for integration occurs at the close of project execution. At this point the product or service that resulted from the project is turned over to its customers and users—or to operations or another project—and must be reconciled with the requirements and limitations agreed to during the initiation phase.[4] Approved change requests made during the project may modify the project plan, including scope, cost, or scheduled delivery dates. The new product or service created by the project team may also modify accepted operational procedures, policy, or ways to implement management goals in the future.

Integration is a skill that finds similarities, dependencies, and convergences by looking at a situation from several distinct views and aligning them into a comprehensive whole. When planning, the human brain shows activity in four separate quadrants.[5] The amygdala, or switching station of the brain, is the dominant thought center for integration, a capability individuals can develop with use. Integration of convergent areas of the project is a necessary function. Without integration, the complexities caused by separate definitions and different work processes could render a project too complex to provide value. With integration, adjustments can be made to make one part of the project complement another and the work of one team converge with the work of another. Team members can work with confidence if they know the impact of their work has already been reviewed and integrated.

With integration, estimates and "actuals," promised dates and delivery dates, and resource budgets and resource expenditures all become more credible as the project progresses. The term used to describe this phenomenon is *progressive elaboration*:

> Progressive elaboration of product characteristics must be coordinated carefully with proper project scope definition, particularly if the project is performed under contract. When properly defined, the scope of the project—the work to be done—should remain constant even as the product characteristics are progressively elaborated.[6]

Future direction that results from project integration management shapes the work still to come and steps over unnecessary complexity and confusion, focusing efforts—as always—on the end result.

ALL PROJECTS HAVE A BEGINNING AND AN END

Project closeout is a time when the value of planning and execution is demonstrated. When the project's deliverable—product, service, process, or plan—is turned over for use at the end of the execution phase, the expectations and promise that emerged during initiation are evaluated against actual results and the benefits of the project are realized. If the project is part of a larger program tied to the strategic plan, the program management office may report on the delivery of benefits and integrate them with the benefits of other concurrent projects or recent operational changes.

It is prudent to plan the project's closing process in advance. Expert opinion and precedent are useful in planning the closeout phase. Other projects will have lessons to share, and improvements made in the planning phase can simplify the process. The complexity and structure of closeout vary depending on the size and type of project.

TURNOVER OF RESPONSIBILITY FOR DELIVERABLES

Turning over the project deliverables to the project customer occurs at the end of the execution phase, and during the closeout phase the responsibility for the deliverable shifts to another group. At this phase of the project, technology transfer, training and operations functions, and maintenance responsibility all shift to the operational owner of the final deliverable. If acceptance criteria were clearly defined in planning, the customer and the team will know when they have met the requirements, and any minor issues that remain can be resolved.

Delivering the Product for Use and Closing Technical Work

The task of closing product work on the deliverable sometimes is "owned" by the lead technical team. Sometimes, however, it is handed off to a maintenance or support group. Specific responsibility needs to be established in advance as to who will complete the package of information, instructions, product start-up, support, and services and make sure the deliverable is operational. Sometimes these decisions are made when defining which stages of the product life cycle fall within the scope of the project. In other cases, these decisions cannot be made until the deliverable is fully defined, requirements are fully agreed to, and technical decisions made during development have been allowed to take their full effect. If the information for making some of these decisions is not yet clear, the sponsor may arrange shifting some of these functions to the operational group assuming responsibility for the new product or service after project closure.

Delivering the Business Value

The value of the project was established when it was first initiated. At closeout, any variances are identified and explained, and "lessons learned" from the project are documented. Just as many levels of the organization have expectations about the project and its product, several levels are involved in closing out a project. The most obvious one is the closure of the work on the product, but there are actually two levels of value to be assessed when a project closes: the value of the project to its sponsoring organization (strategic, portfolio, and program value) and the value of the project to its customer and user. While it is possible that they are one and the same, usually they are different. The sponsoring organization most likely had strategic objectives that were to be met through the project's achievements. There may have been a strategic goal that would be advanced, a customer relationship established, a new market gained, or a service objective met. The organization's investment of time, resources, and attention to the project's completion are returned when the business value of the project is realized. The achievement of these goals is presented in the final closeout report. Typically, the close of a successful project is welcomed by the project's sponsors and beneficiaries because they had already decided that the risks were worth the benefits. Seeing the project deliver the benefits is the payoff for taking those risks. If change must occur, at least it can be done well, in a professional manner, with minimal disruption to existing areas.

Releasing Technical Resources

Resources that were important to execute the project are no longer necessary once the project team has completed its work. While the people who fostered the work, funded it, and supported it through various changes are glad to see the project reach its conclusion because the benefits are likely to be realized at that point, team members, who have bonded and become involved in the daily affairs of the project, often are not so eager to see the project end. People who were assigned to the team most likely will be expected to transfer promptly back to their old job roles, and people who were contracted from outside will move on to another assignment. Ideally, the date estimates given for their release were accurate, and their new assignment is waiting for them. Sometimes, however, there are discrepancies, and preparations are needed for their reentry into the new/old role.

Announcing Project Completion

Announcements to stakeholders and customers that the project is complete prepares line management to retrieve technical workers assigned to the project and the customer to apply the deliverable in its work site. Public meetings on the deliverable(s) help to link key personnel across functions, transition team members back to their line functions, and recognize group achievement.

Administrative Closure

Members of the project management team often remain to close out the management tasks after the technical team is released. Legal and administrative closeout duties include disposal of unused resources and materials, addressing of contractual agreements, administrative release and reassignment of technical team members to their other jobs, and update of personnel records. Evaluations are filed, data are submitted to higher-level data files, and required documents on the project are sent to archives in case they are needed in following up loose ends or challenges. Recommended changes to processes are forwarded to operations. All these processes, forms, and data files need to be tasked to someone in the project plan before the project comes to its end so that they are completed before closure. These tasks, being anticipated in advance, are already in the project budget.

Team celebration also is an important task. It serves several purposes:

- It helps team members say good-bye to their fellow workers.
- It signals to other groups that the project is over.
- It conveys a sense of success despite any ambiguities or unfinished issues.

Also, a formal announcement of closure needs to be made to all who interacted with the team and process. Communicating a closing team event is one way to make such an announcement without the expectation that anyone needs follow-up.

LESSONS LEARNED AND PROCESS IMPROVEMENTS

It is natural that the focus of the project will be on satisfying the business and functional requirements of the product itself more than on the lessons learned because this is what the team is rewarded for doing. Creating or refining the deliverable(s) has been the primary focus for some time. However, now that the product or service is complete, there is still a technical responsibility for capturing the important lessons that will improve future project efforts.

The project plan should specify responsibility for the final review and capturing lessons learned on the project. There also needs to be a process to capture improvements and best practices as part of closing the work associated with the deliverable. Closure is also the last opportunity to capture lessons learned for improving project management organizational processes to repeat the success in future projects. Some of the lessons learned can include refinements to the standard project process, estimating methods, historical data, and resource planning methods and tools, as well as metrics data collection points and streamlining of overhead tasks.

Technical and administrative support should be planned for the last phase of the project. Most of the documents filed, contracts closed, and balances collected are handled routinely. But some require special handling or follow-up.

While the project budget is prepared during planning with an emphasis on delivery of the project results and deliverables to the customer (product closeout), it is important also to include in the budget a task for managing and disseminating project data within the sponsoring organization (administrative closeout) when the project is formally closed.

SUMMARY

This chapter covered the facilitating processes that support the core processes, particularly management processes used in the project's execution phase. These processes correspond to the "knowledge areas" on the project management professional certification exam presented initially in Chapter 1. These knowledge areas and their corresponding processes are flexible tools that a project management professional can use to create an environment for success on a project, and they are used to anticipate positive and negative influences on the successful outcome of the project. The goal of facilitating processes is to maximize positive influences and minimize the impact of negative influences.

The primary emphasis in professional projects is on completing the project and delivering its intended outcome, value, and benefits. Communicating the information and technical context for work, using risk management to prevent negative influences on the project, and adjusting the use of time and effort help the team complete the scope of the project and the deliverable(s) in the estimated time frames. Standards, policy, processes, methods, and documented expectations shape the work of professionals, and communicating in ways that make sense to different groups helps to enlist their support and commitment to complete the project.

As project work is completed at the closeout phase, the requirements and success criteria are used to evaluate the project's effectiveness and communicate the value of the effort to the customer and sponsor. The technical team disperses, the responsibility for upkeep and maintenance of the deliverable(s) shifts to external groups, and the project work and lessons learned are closed. Improvements are shared with future projects through best practices files and project archives. Stakeholders are notified that the project is over, and people return to their regular assignments.

In Chapter 10 the focus shifts from executing the work of the project to controlling the progress. Many of the elements from facilitating processes become controlling processes as well when applied with control priorities at the forefront. If proactive prevention—which is less costly—is effective, there is less need for control. Control can be focused on the areas where positive management of the critical path and critical success factors shape the final deliverable and ensure that it meets project requirements.

REVIEW QUESTIONS

1. Why does the team need acceptance criteria for the project's final deliverable?
   a. to complete project records
   b. to satisfy the customer
   c. to know what to create
   d. to abide by the project manager's rules

2. All risks can and should be prevented or avoided.
   a. true
   b. false

3. Changes to the project plan should be reviewed at natural points in the project such as the end of each product development stage.
   a. true
   b. false

4. Team celebration at the end of the project:
   a. helps the team say good-bye
   b. signals that the project is over
   c. conveys a sense of success
   d. all of the above

5. The entire project team also needs to be given a clear idea of what the client's or _____ needs are so that those needs are not compromised when the team is faced with minor trade-offs during execution tasks.
   a. customer's
   b. sponsor's
   c. team's
   d. project manager's

6. The quality plan needs to define what is considered to represent quality on the project and how it will be:
   a. controlled
   b. tracked
   c. managed
   d. managed, tracked, and controlled

7. Communication is everyone's job, and changes and issues need to be communicated upward from the project worker to the team leadership, and direction, changes, logistics, status, and resolutions need to be communicated downward to the teams.
   a. true
   b. false

8. The complexities of iterative planning and definition require periodic integration of core project management processes with _____ and of the stable standard processes with any processes that have been changed and adapted to fit the project.
   a. process stabilization
   b. facilitating subprocesses
   c. core processes
   d. project management

9. Project closeout is a time when the value of _____ is demonstrated.
   a. initiation and planning
   b. execution and closeout
   c. planning and execution
   d. deliverables and execution

C H A P T E R

10

THE CONTEXT FOR PROJECT MANAGEMENT

OVERVIEW AND GOALS

This chapter describes the environment of quality and learning established for the project team. This context for project management enables the project management professional and team to capture and maintain the elements required for quality execution of a successful project. A carefully drawn scope statement establishes the boundaries within which the project team will conduct its work. The autonomy established for the project allows the team to operate freely within those boundaries. They may draw on any relevant processes, resources, and procedures from business operations to create the deliverables and outcome, but they also enjoy a freedom of internal decisions that encourages creative solutions to unexpected challenges. This autonomy is balanced by methods and processes of project management that ensure that the project team—while acting autonomously—engages the external realities of the business environment, as well as the priorities of the sponsor and customer.

The team creates an environment within the project that serves as a check and balance system for the sometimes almost chaotic atmosphere of doing something unique—creating the project's deliverable for the first time. The organization should create an environment that supports the smooth creation and transition of the unique deliverable(s) to the sponsor and customer.

A knowledgeable and effective team working within a supportive environment from the sponsoring organization will increase the likelihood that the project will deliver results successfully and smoothly.

The project management knowledge possessed by the organization and the project manager is an underpinning for creating this environment. Knowledge provides a foundation for independent actions within the team and a common platform for developing strategy and group consensus on decisions and plans of action and desired outcomes. However, the project also must operate within the context of the sponsoring organization. The sponsoring organization helps to shape the project's expectations. The project team must stay in line with management's strategy, conform to organizational policies, and realign its work with shifting priorities as they change over time. It also must know, acknowledge, and respect the different expectations of quality the customer may have of the project deliverable(s).

The knowledge, skill, and ability of the project manager and project team are not the only determinants of context for project management. The proximity of the team members to each other and the physical location in which the project's work takes place can affect the team's productivity. In addition, the organization sponsoring the project creates the project within the benefits or constraints of a larger business or organizational work environment. The project team can bootstrap itself to a certain extent. If the larger organizational environment is not supportive of quality project management, the project team will have limited ability to succeed. (The organization's support for the project and the challenges in its physical environment will be addressed in greater detail in Chapter 12.)

Ultimately, it is the responsibility of the project professionals—the project manager and team—to create an appropriate context for the project with the limited resources available. Creating this context can make all the difference in seeking and achieving quality.

While this chapter addresses methods and processes for establishing the context for quality on a project, it also touches on how to shape quality by directing the manner in which individual members of the team go about their work.

QUALITY ASSUMPTIONS

Over the past decade, most organizations have adopted the concept that designing quality into products and services is a significant way to reduce costs and expedite results. People talk about how quality is "designed in, not inspected in." The project's approach can be established to address quality and prevent problems from being discovered too late to deliver a quality product or service. Rather than fixing things after they go wrong, the project team should focus on ways they can prevent problems from happening in the first place. Anticipating and preventing problems, weighing the costs and benefits of prevention, and choosing the appropriate actions is fundamental to project management. It is beneficial to challenge, ask questions, and bring issues to light. There likely will be enough unforeseen problems to fill available time once the project moves into execution.

This concept of preemptive prevention definitely holds true in projects, where the timeliness of a solution can be key to project success. According to Professor Mihaly Csikszentmihalyi, a University of Chicago researcher, one minute spent planning saves three to four minutes in implementation.[1] Some U.S. companies use this formula in dollar terms—one dollar spent in planning saves six dollars in execution. Research projects have tested the cost-effectiveness of planning and have come up with similar conclusions.

However, the question remains: how does the team determine what "right" is when there is so little precedent and so much is new? One way is to get insight from external sources—best practices and technical standards—and to put proper processes in place. A second is to solicit input from carefully selected people outside the project. External views are useful in shaping project priorities, particularly at the beginning. When plans are just forming, ideas are welcome, suggestions are useful, and improvements are likely to bear fruit at a later stage in the project. Another approach is to investigate all aspects of the deliverable and how it is expected to perform, including the success criteria by which its users would judge it. Explore how the product or service interfaces with other, similar products or services and how it will be maintained over time. Get insight into the definitions of value others would use, as well as the business benefits expected from the project.

Processes that bring quality workmanship to the project can help the team do what is "right" when performing work. People who have worked on similar projects are a good source of perspective. Planning processes should address as many facets of quality as possible to prevent the team from being blindsided downstream. Technical expertise can shed light on hidden issues. The team should reference these "lessons learned" from prior projects during planning. It can record the issues in the risk plan until more is known about the conditions and requirements under which the project will be operating.

There is always a process, even if it is a default process. Organizations in which processes are defined and used, and where the use of those processes is emphasized and enforced by management, get better results. There are both technical processes and project processes on a project. Both need to be managed consciously. Technical processes are brought into the project by the technical experts doing the work. Some project processes are defined by the organization. Others, however, will need to be created by the project manager and team.

A clear description of the intended business outcomes of the project as a whole, as well as a general description of the product when it reaches its end state, helps to align team consensus on what is important and what is not. While these descriptions are captured and recorded during project initiation, they need to be reaffirmed and repeated during planning and execution to keep the focus on the outcomes.

Constantly challenging assumptions, raising questions, and looking for potential problems before they happen "clears the air." Actively looking for challenges helps to make the invisible visible so that it can be managed.[2]

The Project's Risk Profile

There is a significantly different level of effort in managing risk between projects that are very risky and those that are more routine. In relatively routine projects, the risks that are present can be identified, analyzed, and ranked to focus on the most troublesome or the most threatening. In high-risk projects, risk management becomes part of every team process, and the entire team must be risk-focused in its work. In most organizations there is a "process owner" for the technical processes. For those technical processes that contain more risk, that person will need to be engaged somehow in defining the proper approach to mitigate and manage those risks. If internal process specialists are not available, external sources can be found to provide advice on the risks and how they might be managed. They will need to be integrated into the project's technical decision process, and their ideas will need to be weighed within the risk context of the overall effort. The decision-making process will need to be monitored and managed carefully to ensure that people do not revert by habit to "doing things the way we have always done them." Rote behavior in a high-risk environment can be dangerous.

The frequency of reviewing risks also will increase in a high-risk project. Rather than establishing a weekly or monthly cycle for risk review, daily risk briefings may be needed. New insights and new sources of information can bring new risks to the fore, changing the game plan while it is in progress.

Deliberate Managing of Change

Another key area for maintaining a positive context for project success is the acknowledgment and acceptance of change as a normal part of projects. Outside projects, a benefit of repetitive operations is that ineffective practices are eliminated from the process, streamlining the effort toward results. While project management processes are being defined more clearly for specific industries and specific types of projects, there is still a lot that bears refining. On projects—particularly high-risk projects—whenever a process is identified as ineffective or counterproductive, it must be changed promptly to prevent wasted effort. The team needs to be alert to this priority of change and responsive to team leadership direction.

Frequent change management briefings help to keep everyone working together and their priorities on track toward completion. Some people welcome change, but most do not accept it so readily. This resistance to change is part of the human condition—not knowing what the future will bring, still wishing to control it. To stay on top of this natural reluctance, teams need to make change more acceptable and break down resistance by making change management part of the project process.

Most people, when faced with change, feel awkward, ill at ease, and self-conscious. Some will focus on what they will have to give up if change occurs. People are at different levels of readiness for change. Some will be concerned that they do not have enough resources. If you take the pressure off, some people will revert to prior behavior. On the bright side, if everyone else is going through the change, some people will feel lonely, increasing the likelihood that they will stop resisting and join the others.

Some principles for encouraging increasing acceptance of change include:

- Identify people who are comfortable with change and have them serve as "early adopters."
- Explain not only what is going to happen but also how people will be affected.
- Be explicit in describing the advantages of the proposed change.
- Anticipate people's questions and answer them publicly for everyone.
- Do not try to implement many changes at once; people can handle only so much.

There are a number of tactics for implementing new initiatives. In preparing to implement something new and different, such as a new product or service, ask a number of questions to assess readiness:

1. Is there a perceived advantage to the user?
2. Are the consequences minimal if it fails?
3. Is it easy for the user to understand?
4. Can we implement the change in small steps/incrementally?
5. Is it compatible with the current method? Does it have a familiar look and feel?
6. Is the messenger/designer credible in the eyes of the user?
7. Does it work without breaking down? Is it reliable?
8. Does it function as promised?
9. Is it easy for people to try it out?
10. Is it easy for the user to revert back to the old way and get out if he does not like it?

Effective change requires a number of ingredients:

• *Resources.* If any change is to be effective, it needs not only people to put it in place but also the resources to train people, adapt current systems, and reinforce adoption.

• *Vision.* If people are to accept the change, they need to be able to conceptualize the desired state that will be in place when the change is over. Describe or diagram that desired end state or allow a group discussion to define it.

• *Training.* People need to hear about the benefits and processes, but they also need to know how and when their own behavior is expected to change.

• *Management support.* Without official reassurance that a new way is part of management's plan, people will be hesitant to make the change. Get management involved!

THE PROJECT CULTURE: CONTINUOUS LEARNING AND IMPROVEMENT

If a project team is successful at making management of change part of the project, the members of the team begin to look for improvements. At the end of every project, of course, good practice says the team should get together and capture the lessons learned on the project. Immature management environments look for people to blame. Mature management environments look for ways to make everyone a success on the next project. (Organizational project management maturity will be covered in Chapter 12.)

People who take personal pride in their work use continuous learning and lessons learned to improve their own performance. Their ego and personal pride are tied up in their work. They understand that project team members doing something unique for the first time are unlikely to "do things right" all the time, and they accept the possibility that errors and problems will occur. Then the challenge is no longer finding someone to blame but rather finding ways to prevent these problems from happening in the future. Some problems and errors are not crucial and will simply be ignored. In some work environments, seeing no problems at all is seen as an indicator that people are working too conservatively and are not addressing risks head-on.

Once people accept problem identification as a valued contribution to the project, the behavior and skills that are valued are pointing out problems and articulating their potential influence and possible resolution. This is one of the core skills in project management—finding problems before they happen, focusing on process and not people, keeping the project work on track, and achieving the expected project results.

PROJECT DECISIONS AS AN ELEMENT OF QUALITY

Some decisions are straightforward and can be made without collaboration. Others require careful thought and the input of several people. How decisions are made on the project is one area where quality can be built into the process. In a project management context, there are effective and ineffective ways to make decisions. Using a good decision process is critical in the project environment, where so many decisions must be made. Academic researchers have examined decision styles to determine the impact they have on the effectiveness of decision outcomes. Here are some of the findings:

• Many executives approach decision making in a way that neither puts enough options on the table nor permits sufficient evaluation to ensure that they can make the best choice. The reason for this is that most businesspeople treat decision making as an event—a discrete choice that takes place at a single point in time, whether they are sitting at a desk, moderating a meeting, or staring at a spreadsheet.

• The classic view of decision making has a pronouncement pop-ping out of a leader's head based on experience, gut, research, or all three. An event leader would mull in solitude, ask for advice, read reports, mull some more, then say yea or nay and send the organization off to make it happen.

Leaders who make good decisions recognize that all decisions are pro-cesses, and they explicitly design and manage them as such. Studies have shown that there are two distinct approaches—inquiry and advocacy—and that inquiry will produce better outcomes. David Garvin and Michael Roberto outlined these processes in a *Harvard Business Review* article in 2001.

Inquiry is "an open process designed to generate multiple alternatives, foster the exchange of ideas, and produce a well-tested solution."[3]

• An inquiry-focused group carefully considers a variety of options and works together to discover the best solution.
• While people naturally continue to have their own interests, the goal is not to persuade the group to adopt a given point of view but instead to come to agreement on the best course of action. People share informa-tion widely, preferably in raw form, to allow participants to draw their own conclusions.
• Rather than suppressing dissension, an inquiry process encourages critical thinking. All participants feel comfortable raising alternative solu-tions and asking hard questions about the possibilities already on the table.

Advocacy is a process that treats decision making as a contest where the participants advocate for their position without considering other points of view.

• Participants are "passionate about their preferred solutions and there-fore stand firm in the face of disagreement. This level of passion makes it nearly impossible to remain objective, limiting people's ability to pay atten-tion to opposing arguments."
• "Advocates often present information selectively, buttressing their arguments while withholding relevant conflicting data. Their goal, after all, is to make a compelling case, not to convey an evenhanded or balanced view."[4]

Considering a variety of options and working together to find the best solution creates a proper context for anticipating, avoiding, and managing risk while staying focused on results.

Although one might envision a team making decisions in a conference room, quality decision making can occur wherever the project takes place. A great example is the Wright brothers' approach to decisions when creating a way to control powered flight. It was a hundred years ago. They were a team of just two, but they did not let their limited numbers get in the way of quality decisions.

THE WRIGHT BROTHERS' PROJECT TO CREATE CONTROLLED FLIGHT

In 1903, Orville and Wilbur Wright became caught up in the flight fever of their day. For the previous two years they had been actively watching other people in the air using balloons; some had even done some pretty spectacular things with gliders. The brothers became convinced that humans not only could fly but also could control powered flight.

Some people say that it was the model helicopter they got from their uncle as kids that gave them the inspiration,[5] but as they matured, so did their vision.

They used their experience in a booming technical field of their day, bicycles, to experiment with the dynamics of flight. They were in the bicycle business with their father. The mechanics, balance, aerodynamics, and personal control of bicycles were familiar to them already. They simply lacked the ability to get the contraptions off the ground.

Orville and Wilbur Wright were both tenacious inventors. They were much more than the popular image portrayed of them—bicycle vendors dabbling in flying machines. They were cutting-edge engineers. For the state of manufacturing technology of their day, they demonstrated considerable creativity and technical expertise. But they also were more than creative geniuses; they were aeronautical engineers without an occupation to work in.

Throughout 1899 and 1900, they had experimented with creating a glider capable of carrying the weight of a man. Wilbur—his creativity sparked by observing birds and idly twisting a box—saw that control and stability were related and hit on the idea of "wing warping" to stabilize flight. He and his brother built a prototype airplane glider and ran a number of tests of its capability. They experimented with options for power and the ratios of power and lift. At some point in moving from testing the concept to high-level planning, they decided that they actually could do it. They decided to embark on a project to prove the viability of powered flight. Together they created a general plan of how it could be done.

During the detailed planning phase of the project, they corresponded with other experimenters and the U.S. Weather Bureau. They realized that they needed a wide-open space with steady, brisk winds to conduct their experiment. They found several potential sites that had suitable space and winds of predictable constant velocity to support testing and flight. Eventually they settled on Kitty Hawk, North Carolina, "largely because it was the closest to their Dayton home."[6]

In planning project execution, the brothers had a project development site and a project execution site that were in completely different locales. This was not done by accident. It actually was the result of careful planning. "In Dayton, Ohio, they had a place where they could find everything they needed as they built their aircraft," says Tom Crouch, a curator with the Smithsonian's National Air and Space Museum in Washington, D.C., and a noted Wright scholar. At that point in history, Dayton was at the center of all sorts of precision manufacturing. A person could walk down the street and find a foundry that could cast an aluminum block for an engine (when casting aluminum was a fairly rare thing) and find experts in the use of various materials to ask for advice.

Bicycle manufacturing was "high technology" in the early twentieth century, a perfect springboard for two brothers interested in flight. The emphasis in bicycle manufacturing was quite relevant to starting a project to prove the feasibility of controlled flight.

• It focused on minimizing weight so that the human energy of powering a bike went into distance, not moving equipment—a focus that transferred well to airplanes.
• It was profitable, giving them the financial means to conduct extensive research, make models, and then spend time elsewhere testing their equipment.
• It was machinery-intensive, requiring them to buy equipment that they would use to build their first airplane.[7]

The brothers had technology to their advantage and even access to supportive resources. The newness of the project concept, however, left them with little precedent to use in planning their project. Their project had all the standard challenges of doing something unique for the first time. There were a lot of unknowns. The decisions they made would affect the quality of their experiment, but they had no way to test the concepts on others because they were so new. Furthermore, it was dangerous. The wrong decisions could lead to disaster.

The brothers created a series of quality processes to guide their project. One was for decision making.

For them, decisions that were free from bias were a challenge. Since there were only two of them on the team at the time, they developed a unique method of creative decision making. One took one side of the argument, and the other took the other side. Each would argue a point until they slept on it, switched sides, and concluded that it was the "right thing to do." Then they did it.[8]

Once the brothers had historical data from a prior glider project and proved its reliability, they could use those data for future estimates. They created a technical process for the project, refined it using experts and historical information from nonpowered glider flights, and tested it in parts and in process before embarking on the final design, construction, and test of their airplane. The flights of the 1902 glider demonstrated both the efficiency of their system and the accuracy of the laboratory work on which the glider design was based. Only then did they feel prepared to predict the performance of machines, demonstrating a degree of accuracy that had never been possible with the data and tables of their predecessors.

The brothers went back and forth between Dayton and Kitty Hawk, conducting tests and perfecting their designs. They used different instruments and different vehicles to prototype and test them. They knew that as time passed winter drew near. They had a window of opportunity to carry out the flight. If too much time passed, they would be facing winter winds and weather. With the risks, everything had to be ready. And if everything was ready too late, they would have to wait until the next year.

The project execution phase—controlled flight—meant moving to a new location. In the summer of 1903, they built a more sophisticated aerodynamic airplane with the help of Charles Taylor, a machinist hired on from the Dayton Electric Company. Its engine was a water-cooled four-cylinder in-line engine with a four-horsepower propeller. The propeller was better than any marine propeller in existence. The plane's 40-foot wingspan was too large for their Dayton shop. They could have used a runway, but there were none in the entire country.[9] They found a hill—a bluff with sands below—that would allow the wind to capture the plane and carry it without obstruction for some distance. They shipped the 675-pound machine they had created to Kitty Hawk and added trim, and at 775 pounds it was ready to fly.

Throughout the fall of 1903, camped at Kill Devil Hills (dunes to the south of Kitty Hawk), the brothers conducted additional tests, trained themselves using a glider, and made repairs to their new aircraft while waiting for favorable winds. When they had to send back to Dayton for a tube shaft for the propeller that had cracked, it took five days' travel each way. They installed the new propeller on December 11. They ran a test, took Sunday off, and found the wind on Monday too light for horizontal takeoff. They had set up a 60-foot "rail" as the runway. They and the team took the flyer up the dunes, headed it into the wind, tossed a coin to see who would pilot the craft, and then started a 45-foot roll. The flyer lifted off. The pilot pulled back too much and stalled the plane. It settled into the sand 130 feet away.

The Wright brothers had already set their quality standards for project completion before beginning execution. The plane had to respond to wind using controls, the pilot had to be on board handling the plane, and the aircraft had to land higher than the takeoff point to prove that they were not just leveraging gravity and winds, something gliders had already accomplished. The first attempt lifted off the ground, but it landed downhill. The landing point being lower than the takeoff point, they determined it had not "proved" powered flight. Considered unsuccessful, that flight by Wilbur was written off and not counted. By default, it was Orville's turn in the pilot's seat when the good run occurred.

In a single day they made four successful flights from level ground. They carefully observed and recorded their metrics: The average speed was 31 miles per hour, and the ground speed was 10 miles per hour. Each flight was an improvement as each pilot gained more experience in control of the aircraft. Finally, the wind picked it up and turned the craft upside down, damaging it too severely to fly it again. Eventually, years later, it was reconstructed and used in tours to promote aviation. The actual plane was housed for a while in London and now sits in the National Air and Space Museum in Washington, D.C.

The brothers maintained detailed data and evaluations but no narrative until after the significance of the event was recognized and people wanted to hear about it. Eventually, Orville wrote his own account of the events associated with his project, giving us much of the detailed project information available today (see Appendix D).[10]

The Wrights' design solution—lift, propulsion, and control—continues to be used today in every aircraft from a Cessna 150 to a giant Boeing 777. Their invention changed the world to a three-dimensional space "where conventional boundaries disappeared."[11] Their spirit of discovery was invoked in the first privately funded space flight, *SpaceShipOne*, by designer Burt Rutan and pilot Mike Melvill in 2004, and continued with flight testing of *White Knight Two* in 2009. The enduring influence of the Wright brothers on the future of flight shows no sign of flagging.

Orville's comments in his own record of the flight 10 years afterward contain the essence of their "lessons learned." He wrote:

> With all the knowledge and skill acquired in thousands of flights in the last ten years I would hardly think today of making my first flight on a strange machine in a twenty-seven mile wind, even if I knew that the machine had already been flown and was safe. After these years of experience I look with amazement upon our audacity in attempting flights with a new and untried machine under such circumstances. Yet faith in our calculations and the design of the first machine, based upon our tables of air pressures, secured by months of careful laboratory work, and confidence in our system of control developed by three years of actual experiences in balancing gliders in the air had convinced us that the machine was capable of lifting and maintaining itself in the air, and that, with a little practice, it would be safely flown.[12]

The first powered flight of human beings truly was a project. It used conceptual development, initiation, research, specialists, planning, quality standards, use of prior project experience with nonpowered flight, site selection, team selection, quality-based decision methods, and metrics to establish quality gates for project completion. Once in the execution phase, it used controls, measurements, problem resolution, communications, risk management, and team management. The life cycle of the "product"—the aircraft—did not end with the project. It made many more flights to promote aviation, and finally, retired, it provides history and inspiration to us today. The Wright Brothers National Memorial at Kill Devil Hills, North Carolina; the replica of their aircraft displayed at the Experimental Aircraft Association AirVenture Museum in Oshkosh, Wisconsin; the "History of Flight" exhibits at the Chicago Museum of Science and Industry; and the display of the original refurbished craft at the National Air and Space Museum in Washington, D.C., continue to tell the story of this monumental achievement.

Darrell Collins, a seasonal ranger at the National Park Service and Wright Brothers National Memorial at Kill Devil Hills, North Carolina, says that "Achieving the brothers' dream of the first successful powered flight has had tremendous consequences for the United States and the world." Collins acknowledges that a university (Wright State) and an air force base (Wright-Patterson) have been named for these heroes but still believes the Wrights have yet to receive full recognition for their accomplishments. "No major aeronautical research facility is named for the Wrights, and history books don't always give them their due." But exhibits all over the world are now honoring these aviators, project managers, and aeronautical engineers. Today they are considered breakthrough innovators. "True pioneers, the brothers possessed a combination of intellect, curiosity, and just plain gumption that exemplifies the best of the American Spirit."[13]

And, we might add, the best of project management. Remember, in 1904, the project management books we have today had not yet been written. The Wright brothers ran a project with rigor and discipline, planned and executed systematically. While they may not have had the process documentation or terminology, they ran a real project. Their team was, like all teams, soon forgotten, and their sister—who was the business brains behind the effort—is rarely mentioned. The public remembers the product, not the project.

PROJECT MANAGERS DO NOT ALWAYS GET HIGH VISIBILITY

Project managers do not always get visibility and often do not seek it. Results are what they are looking for. They apply all the knowledge, skill, planning, process, measures, controls, and team management needed to get results. When the project is over, they move on.

From stories like the one about the Wright brothers' project to prove that powered flight was possible we can learn much about creating an environment for quality in project management. We have many best practices in project management today that emerged from early experiments such as this. Some of the methods used on this project are still best practices from which we can learn:

- Do not be afraid to tackle something big. Someone has to do things for the first time.
- Dig into the concept, test it, and challenge it. Then develop the project approach.
- Seek different opinions, use expertise, and keep asking questions.
- Have a clear vision and define what the end state will be when you are done.
- Plan resources that suit the project, and set it up so that it can succeed.
- Pay exquisite attention to detail. Double-check your numbers.
- Plan, revise, plan, revise—and then commit to execution.
- Keep risk management foremost in your mind; identify and mitigate risks and fix problems when they occur.
- Be fair and equal on the team. No team member is more important than another. You need the whole team to succeed.
- Take as long as it takes to succeed. Use windows of opportunity to make progress.

- Measure yourself against your own preset criteria to declare a success.
  - Learn from errors. Take the lessons into the future.
  - Make sure that somebody takes a picture if you want publicity.

Any person or group who has not been on a project team before may not recognize or acknowledge what it takes to do a good job of project management. They are more likely to focus on the end product, the service, or the final achievement. It is important to remember, though, that they more often will remember that something did not work than if it was late or over budget.

The project management professional must integrate the goals of executive management with the goals of the project. Often executive management gets the credit if the project is successful. It is probably a good thing that the adventure of project management has its own rewards.

STAYING ALIGNED WITH THE EXTERNAL ENVIRONMENT

While it is tempting to focus just on the work of the project and to perform the tasks laid out in the project plan, the environment can change, affecting the overall success of the project. With the first powered flight, weather is an obvious example. Whole schedule shifts were necessary due to changes in the wind or the weather. However, projects also encounter changes in the political or legal climate, shifts in resource priorities, and organizational upheavals. A wise project manager will specify how these changes will be addressed, especially if working under contract. If a project team is committed to the long-term benefits of the project's outcome, it is a good idea to check for changes in the external environment throughout the project. Knowledge about competing initiatives, impending changes, or threats may not change the actual tasks for completion, but they may have a significant effect on the communications plan.

SUMMARY

This chapter presented the importance of creating an environment of quality and learning on a project. Creating a context for success on a project means defining what quality means for each project situation and using a variety of ways to engage the team in performing quality work. Leadership sets the standards and environment for quality on a project, and the focus should stay on producing results of value to the customer and the sponsor. Working with management, outside experts, and customer representatives requires awareness of their different performance viewpoints. Taking a proactive approach to quality frees the professional team to get consensus on what a good job looks like so they can work together to define the best strategy and deliver a quality deliverable with all its associated benefits.

Once the team and management recognize that results provide the real value, the motives to hide problems, blame others, or dodge emerging issues drop to the wayside. Challenging assumptions, seeking different viewpoints, and capturing best practices through "lessons learned" all pay off in benefits for the entire team. The team's leadership must decide how best to leverage the ideas, talents, and expertise available on a project, working with management, outside experts, and customer representatives.

Once the project context has been created for quality performance, timely results, and team efficiency, the problems that emerge are no longer defined as individual personal problems; they are team challenges. Everyone works together to produce a quality end result.

Once a common vision has been agreed to and a common approach has been designed to deliver quality, controls can be established to ensure that the project reaches closure, still balancing schedule requirements with performance requirements and costs. The project context has been created that will allow success. Chapter 11 deals with ways to control deviations, interruptions, and risks so that success can be realized. (For more detail on the Wright brothers' records of actual flight, see Appendix D.)

REVIEW QUESTIONS

1. Some principles for increasing the acceptance for change include:
   a. identify people who are comfortable with change and have them serve as early adopters
   b. explain not only what is going to happen but also how people will be affected
   c. be explicit in describing the advantages of the proposed change
   d. anticipate people's questions but answer them only privately
   e. a, b, and c
   f. all of the above

2. People who take pride in their work use continuous learning and lessons learned to improve their own performance.
   a. true
   b. false

3. The team creates an environment within the project that serves as a check and balance system for the sometimes almost chaotic atmosphere of doing something unique.
   a. true
   b. false

4. The determinant(s) of creating a context (the environment for quality and learning established for the project team) include(s):
   a. the knowledge, skill, and ability of the project manager
   b. the physical location where the project takes place and the location of the team
   c. the sponsoring organization
   d. the project team
   e. all of the above
   f. *b* and *c* only

5. Some of the practices that determine what is right in terms of quality include:
   a. planning processes that address as many facets of quality as possible to prevent being blindsided downstream
   b. relying just on people actions
   c. setting up a "lessons learned" process
   d. not standardizing what works
   e. *a* and *c*
   f. all of the above
   g. none of the above

6. The concept of preemptive prevention definitely holds true in projects where the lack of timeliness of a solution is a key to project success.
   a. true
   b. false

7. A clear description of the project's intended _____ , as well as a general description of the product's end state, helps to align the team with what is important.
   a. business outcomes
   b. business needs
   c. strategic needs
   d. business priorities

8. **Inquiry is:**
   a. not part of project management
   b. an open process designed to generate multiple alternatives
   c. an open process designed to reduce the exchange of ideas
   d. another process designed to produce poorly tested alternatives

11

CONTROLLING PROJECT WORK

OVERVIEW AND GOALS

This chapter describes a variety of strategies project professionals have at their disposal to control how project work is carried out. Control consists of identifying, understanding, and correcting variances. The project manager should develop a control strategy for the project and put the elements in place to make it a reality.

    •   Some elements of a control strategy consist of facilitating processes focused on control—performance reporting, verifying scope, change control, cost control, schedule control, and monitoring and controlling risk.[1]

    •   Some elements of the strategy are proactive approaches to controlling work and results—such as identifying the potential effects an action may have on changing the scope of the project or on interdependent elements.

Control strategies are necessary to keep the work of the project moving forward and to alert the project manager and team when the work is not advancing as intended against the plan.

If the project manager wants to finish the project on time and on budget, there will need to be ways to identify and resolve variances from the project plan. The project plan is the "picture" of success. It is the best definition of the road map that leads to successful completion. But the list of tasks and activities can prove incomplete. Every time a missing task must be added, there may be costs associated with that new task. Because of this, the costs of a project are seldom predicted accurately, and budgets at the beginning of a project tend to be optimistic.

In white-collar or professional projects, most of the estimates turn out to have been optimistic. Quantifying and predicting how a professional will resolve a technical challenge does not have a lot of historical precedent, and work habits vary from one professional to the next. It is probably a good idea to remember when working with professionals that "not everything that can be counted counts, and not everything that counts can be counted."[2]

In an environment of independent professional workers using varied professional methods for performing their work, scope creep and budget creep are difficult to identify before they happen. The project manager and team members may find it difficult to maintain some semblance of control because a professional at work who is working outside of scope looks just like one who is staying within it.

The implication of technical challenges or even the need to add or replace staff is not what people are focusing on during planning. Unless there are systemic ways to calculate and control the cost of project scope creep, projects tend to get bigger as they progress, and schedules always get longer.

To control a project during execution, the project manager must:

1. Make sure the plan is sound
2. Compare actual activities and numbers to what is in the plan
3. Identify and understand the variance
4. Determine how to react

Many of the proactive strategies for establishing and maintaining project control include:

- Communicating to the team the interdependent relationships among two or more tasks in the schedule and the effect their work may have on completing those tasks
- Updating and implementing the risk assessment and risk response plans
- Refining the staff effort estimate and budget
- Adjusting the spending estimate and/or budget

There are reactive strategies as well that can help to maintain control:

- Reducing activities
- Reducing functionality
- Reducing cost or resources
- Simply tracking items one-to-one against the estimates and adjusting tasks and costs by priority

The project manager should choose how much information to track during execution by evaluating the costs and benefits of capturing and analyzing the information. Risk assessments are also a means for identifying areas of the project that may need to be adjusted.

While this chapter will touch on these types of control strategies, whole books have been written on each one of them. For this reason, the point of view of this chapter is to cover the concepts, place them in perspective, and get you involved in making judgments about the appropriate controls to establish on different projects. Once an appropriate control strategy is selected, you can go more deeply into each specific approach.

PROJECT CONTROL AND THE TRIPLE CONSTRAINT

Project control means controlling against a plan. Executing a project successfully requires tracking how the work progresses against the project plan, assessing how accurate the plan is at predicting and guiding work, and making necessary adjustments to the plan to keep it useful. Project control also means paying attention to how resource expenditures compare with the budget for each part of the plan. Controlling performance on the project consists of looking for a reasonable match between the intended functionality and characteristics of the deliverable—described in the scope statement and produced via the plan's activities—and the likelihood of the deliverable producing the desired business outcome in a timely manner.

If a particular approach to doing the work is part of the quality strategy, then tracking how work is performed is also part of the control strategy.

It is helpful to recall the triple constraint we discussed in previous chapters (see Figure 11-1). Projects are scoped in such a way that the time required to deliver project results, the resources and costs that will be consumed, and the production of desired performance benefits should balance out. Project control will need to be exercised on each leg of the triangle. How this is to be accomplished is the subject of this chapter.

FIGURE 11-1   The triple constraint. The performance leg of the triangle is contained in the scope—the tasks and activities of the project plan—as well as the requirements for the final deliverable(s). The cost leg is based on the cost associated with performing each task and/or purchases in the project plan. The time leg is contained in the schedule, derived from analyzing the most efficient sequencing and arrangement of the plan's interdependent tasks.

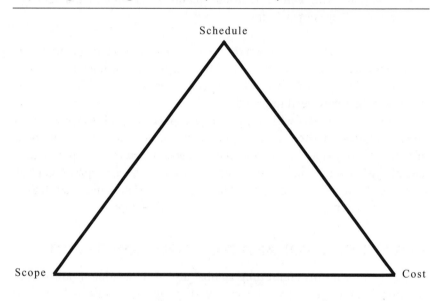

Project Status Reporting

A cycle of reporting, planned during project development and implemented during execution, establishes how the status of project performance will be communicated to the various stakeholder groups. The most common way to do this is through the issuance of regular project status reports.

Both the performance of the project as a whole and performance of developing the project's product or service deliverables should be tracked and reported. The careful effort that went into proper development of the approach and work breakdown structure, the staff selection, the effort estimates, and the carefully sequenced and condensed project schedule provide confidence in the plan's accuracy. Management expects completion according to the plan, and managers want to feel confident about the reliability of the status information. They also will want to know if the project is proceeding as planned, if the estimates are reasonably accurate, and if the delivery dates and estimated final costs are likely to change. Most project sponsors and team members are familiar with the risks and unknowns likely to surface when doing something for the first time. Teams whose tasks depend on the conclusion of other tasks will want to know if they can still expect the same deliverables on the same schedule or if changes are anticipated. The customer will want to know if the final deliverable(s) and dates are on track and, if not, what action is identified to meet those expectations. Estimates within tolerable levels of variance can produce this level of comfort. A thorough, well-thought-out plan and careful cost and resource estimates provide the foundation for successful status reporting and for confidence in the success of project delivery during execution. (See the "Project Status Report Template" in Appendix B. When project specifics are added to it, the template tells the recipient of the report what has changed, the effect it has on meeting the criteria and schedule initially agreed to, and areas that deserve attention.)

Controlling Scope

Part of creating a project is defining adequate scope boundaries around what is to be accomplished and what is not part of the plan. The work of the project needs to be described so that any unauthorized add-on tasks can be avoided. The initial scope of the project is defined in the charter or, if the project is a contractual subproject, a scope-of-work statement. The work tasks and deliverables needed to produce the desired outcome and results are detailed in a work breakdown structure (WBS) and elements that are out of scope have been removed. Once the WBS is converted to tasks and activities (usually by entering the plan into a scheduling tool) and resources such as money, materials, and people are tied to performing those tasks and activities, then completion of the project's final deliverables can be scheduled or earlier estimated delivery dates can be verified.

Scope Verification

At key points throughout the project, or when major changes are necessary, the project team will need to verify that the scope of the project—what it was supposed to be doing and what it was not intended to do—is still valid. Inspection is one method to identify scope changes; variance analysis is another. If changes in scope emerge that appear to add to the initial scope, signatures of the sponsor and the customer are needed to verify that the cost and time implications are still valid.

Scope Change Control

As potential changes are needed, a list of changes should be maintained and reviewed periodically by a change management review group. When decisions on such changes are made, the team will have to determine in detail whether they are additions or deletions affecting scope. Changes must be analyzed before the team can proceed to implement them. Changes that will affect time, cost, or performance will need to be communicated to all involved, with concrete explanations of their potential impact on the project's remaining work tasks. (See both the "Project Change Request Template" and "Project Change Request Log Template" in Appendix B.) When a reviewer sees the proposed changes entered into a change request template, the information is available to decide whether the change is beneficial or will have a negative impact on another aspect of the project. The log provides a history of each change's disposition.

Status Reporting Priorities

The team regularly tracks completion of deliverables against the target dates, the expenditure of resources against the budget, and completion of the whole project against the intended business benefits and results. There are also various types of management review addressing both the project and the product or service being produced. While these are not called status reports per se, they in fact report status of other key areas of interest to management.

In larger organizations or complex projects, management review occurs predictably at specific phase gates for the program that may be providing oversight to ensure that the project aligns with other, related projects and that the benefits of multiple related projects are being realized. There is a "phase gate" review with management at completion of each of the project's life-cycle phases (completion of the charter, approval of the integrated plan, completion of plan execution and delivery, and project closeout). These reviews get managerial approval to expend allocated resources and to confirm that the project has completed the managerial requirements for that phase and may move to the next. There are technical reviews when the approach for creating the product or service is selected, when the development methodology is confirmed, or at stage gates for the development of the product or service as interim deliverables emerge in the course of work. There is also a random calendar-based review, perhaps more appropriately termed *governance* or *oversight*, that the organization schedules that are not tied to the project's individual phase completion or schedule. These oversight reviews confirm resource priorities and alignment of projects with the strategic plan or resolve broader issues or problems across active projects. For this type of review, the stakeholders or governance members with an interest in the project are invited to participate. In large projects, the cycle of high-level executive oversight of projects may be quarterly, semiannually, or as events show the need. Since they are regular and cyclic, the team can add these predictable management review points as tasks into the detailed plan.

In smaller organizations, these reviews can still occur, but they will probably be agenda items in a comprehensive review at project life-cycle stages or at governance meetings, with managers from key areas present at the review meeting.

There are seldom status meetings just to control project scope; it is usually an agenda item in a project status meeting. Controlling scope is the process of monitoring the status of the project scope and product scope and managing changes to the scope baseline.[3] This is a project team task rather than an external management responsibility—unless project changes affect the overall product or service or will influence the project's end result. The project scope is somewhat controlled by entering the WBS, tasks, and activities into project scheduling software and limiting work to those tasks. If during the course of the project it becomes obvious that more detailed breakdown is needed to specify and control work, then subordinate tasks are added and the budget and resource allocation for the higher-level task is divided among them. If changes or new findings—such as added requirements to the final product or service or a legal review—require that new tasks be added, then additional budget and resources will be needed. The project manager must approve them if there is an allowance in the project budget for project-level changes. If the changes are large enough, they may have to be approved by the sponsor. If changes to the product or service emerge from project changes, then a change control board—or a similar review process with the customer—places those scope changes under a controlled review and prioritized approval process. The process varies by industry and technical field, but the concept is similar across most fields.

A key feature of this process is assessment of the change on the system. Placing review tasks at cyclic points in the project management process allows the team to carry out integrated change control. Whenever substantial changes are made (either to specific deliverables or to sequences of tasks that depend on prior tasks), a review probably should be conducted. *Integration* is the term used to describe the process by which teams look at the effect of changes on a project's big picture and the impact those changes will have on other areas of the project.

Controlling the Project Schedule

Controlling the schedule is the process of monitoring the status of the project to update project progress and manage changes to the schedule baseline.[4] Project schedules provide a certain amount of status-tracking information when updated periodically, and that status information can be used for control decisions by the project leadership. Since you cannot control what you have not planned, a rigorously planned schedule lends itself to better control of time. A number of tools are available for crafting such a schedule: precedence diagramming, schedule network analysis, critical path method, schedule compression, critical chain method, and resource leveling are just a few. Some projects are dependent on a well-crafted schedule.

An Olympic planning team once used a computer to list sequentially all the tasks required to run a three-day Olympic event. The length of time required to complete the tasks in sequence was about three years. When identifying the critical path, the team linked only tasks that depended on each other and created parallel paths. Each path was linked with other, dependent paths to create a "network." The total length of the "network" of tasks got shorter and shorter—and admittedly more complex. Eventually, the team crammed all the necessary Olympic execution tasks into the three-day space required for a formal Olympic event.[5] Sequenced schedules allow the multitude of tasks in a project plan to be aligned with a calendar and tracked against the passage of time. In the Olympic example, the project team's control over the schedule is crucial. The critical path through the project is defined carefully, and changes to any element of the triple constraint will affect the other two. The amount of control a different project team will place on the schedule will be based on whether the tasks are discrete and predictable or are softer estimates bordering on the professional discretion of the person responsible for completing the task.

Project control of progress against a plan may be more complex than simply reminding people of tasks and deliverable targets to which they have committed. Part of the analysis needs to address whether the initial plan was reasonably accurate and whether the estimates were aligned appropriately with the capability or the availability of actual resources. Such alignment is not a responsibility of the individual team member but of the project manager and team leads who created and validated the plan and the managers who approved it.

The complexity of a schedule can be meaningful information to team members involved in the work, but schedules communicate best when they are presented in their simplest formats to those outside the project.

Controlling Project Costs

Controlling project costs is the process of monitoring the status of the project to update the project budget and managing changes to the cost baseline.[6] On some projects, particularly those performed by one organization for another in exchange for financial compensation, the expenditure of time is linked to cost, effort, and the use of financial and material resources. Financial and material resources are identified and controlled more easily than effort owing to the procurement procedures that control the purchase of equipment and services. Such resources usually are estimated and captured in a line item in the management budget associated with the project. Cost management parameters are seldom within the control of the project team on a professional project. Such parameters rely heavily on the organization's formulas for project estimating and budgeting. For instance, many organizations that perform all of their projects using professional staff will "load" the hourly billing rate of the professional with her share of the organization's overhead expenses: salary, benefits, space, legal costs, and other organizational expenses. The budgeted hourly billing rate will thus appear much higher on the project plan than one would expect for the person's level in the organization.

Some external sources of cost to the project team—such as moving a key expert from one project to another, delaying progress, and accumulating overhead expense—may not be under the control of the project manager, but he can do a variance analysis and alert senior management of the cost implications of such actions. When work is interrupted, industrial engineers would typically add 15 percent to the effort estimates to allow for closing the active work and another 15 percent for restarting the tasks that were interrupted. Multiplying the additional effort hours by the standard hourly rate puts a cost value on that work. Quantifying the impact of the interruption simplifies discussion.

Sometimes timely communication of cost information can avert unwanted costs. Forecasting project costs that may accumulate due to external causes can focus attention on threats to project benefits and engage senior management's help in controlling them.

Earned value (explained in the following section) is an excellent method for control but relies on having a lot of accurate detail available to use the formulas effectively.

How Much Detail Do You Want to Control?

An experienced manager can often tell quickly if the schedule is detailed enough or too detailed based on the work and the time trade-offs of tracking and reporting. If the time expended tracking details is more time-consuming than the value of the information, then the reporting is too detailed. Depending on the complexity of the project and the experience level of the team, a subproject level of detail may be needed to fully outline the work and to maintain schedule control. Some organizations have a policy in place to exempt small projects from complying with the organization's formal project management process, simply because the value of the reporting data is less than the value of simply completing the small project and capturing its benefits.

There is another element to consider. Schedule may not be the controlling factor in delivering a project at the professional level. There is not a lot of difference between the control value of a high-level schedule and the control value of an activity-level schedule if the people carrying out the work do not respond to schedule control. Some areas of work such as pure research contain so many variables and unknowns that projects are difficult to schedule with any degree of confidence and people may not believe the estimates. In those cases, a high-level project plan with range estimates may be adequate for tracking progress against milestones. In other cases, training is the answer if lack of skill is the problem. Likewise, a more detailed schedule is the answer when the problem is lack of understanding. If the problem is management's project priorities, then no amount of detailed control will be likely to correct the problem.

Estimating Accuracy on Professional Tasks

Producing accurate project time estimates requires both technical expertise and understanding of the time required for performing the work, for coordination, and for documentation. Experienced individuals can estimate how long it will take them to produce a deliverable with reasonable accuracy.

Inexperienced people who have not had the benefit of carrying out similar tasks in projects or have not already performed the work at hand may miss the estimate completely. The project team should check the accuracy of estimates against delivery of results early in the project to assess their ability to meet their estimates and deliver on time. When shaping work behaviors, vigilant status reviews with individual workers and control reviews of human resource efforts in the early days of a project provide repeat benefits later. Accountability of line managers for the project performance of their employees prevents them from "dumping" less productive employees onto projects without addressing the real reasons for their low productivity. Guidance, on-the-job training, or more detailed activity breakdowns may be needed to tighten control. Ultimately, a functional manager should be accountable for loaned team members and the results of their work to ensure that commitments in their area are met.

Cost Control Strategies

Costs on projects in the professional sector are primarily labor costs. Integrating top-down effort estimates with bottom-up estimates by subject-matter experts helps to build more accurate cost estimates for labor. Other methods used to predict and track costs more accurately—and thereby control them more effectively—are analogous estimating, parametric estimating, and reserve analysis.

Costs in traditional project management often are associated with the purchase and expenditure of tangible resources so as to deliver the project's final product or service. Tracking inventory, providing just-in-time access to needed resources, and reducing scrap and waste traditionally were ways to reduce cost on projects. On sophisticated and complex projects with substantial inventory and material resources, cost engineers are able to predict quite accurately what financial resources will be needed and when and where they should be available. Cost engineers, whose work focuses on cost management, get their information from either subject matter experts or from the project team.

Clearly, organizational or departmental priorities affect resources and resource use. Enterprise-wide project cost-effectiveness rests with efforts to manage programs and project portfolios at a higher level of management than the individual project. (For information on how managing project portfolios and programs differs, see Chapter 12.) To realize the value of their investment in project management, senior management must examine the investments to ensure expenditures are tied to those areas of project management that deliver on strategic objectives and advance strategic goals. In some cases the organization must invest in infrastructure and governance to advance capability to deliver projects and sustain quality. Just cutting costs will not position an organization for future success: delivery capability must be advanced as well.

If cost-cutting is a strategic goal, scheduling software is a useful device for managing project costs when a trained and committed team with adequate resources and tools is held accountable. The schedule will be resisted if it is unrealistic, unintelligible, or out of sequence with the work that people feel is necessary to complete the project. It will be honored where people have been engaged in the planning, where pride in the result already exists, where everyone understands the deliverable, where management supports the priorities, and where work norms have been accepted and agreed to.

Without these elements, a scheduling tool for time and resource controls will not do the job alone and may be used as an excuse for nonperformance.

Replanning the Project

If the project plan—schedule, budget, and estimated deliverable milestones—is not working, and the cost of team effort is significantly exceeding estimates, there may be a need to replan the project to make it realistic.[7] One of the sure indicators of a need for replanning is that the work the team is doing is not the work that is showing up in the task and activity lists for the work period—or that task completion is driving people into overtime to stay on schedule. The first place to tackle replanning is with the project leadership team.

- *Identify the problem.* What are the symptoms? Are estimates and actuals too far apart? Does the plan no longer align with the work to be performed? Are tasks not converging, with some team members waiting for work until others finish?
- *Present the problem.* Identify areas where more attention is needed to keep the project on track. If too long a period was allowed to perform a given task and the project manager or leaders feel that it is not under control, they have the option to insert control points in the schedule and manage accuracy using features of the software packages as well as supervisory authority within the team.
- *Prioritize the risk list.* If risks have materialized and are preventing progress, reprioritize the risk list, hone it down to about 10 current risks, assign responsibility for tracking and mitigating those risks, and resolve existing problems so that progress can resume.
- *Adjust tasks and resources.* If the staff assigned to do the work does not have either the skills or the experience to perform the task as intended, arrange a teaming approach for on-the-job training or replace the less experienced person with a more experienced one. Adjust the tasks and resources on the schedule if staffing is not right.
- *Develop alternative methods.* In some projects there may be alternative methods to get the same job done. If meeting the schedule is critical, some projects will have a custom alternative under development and a less desirable but workable alternative identified for purchase in emergencies. The financial loss caused by a late product delivery is much greater than the cost of creating two project tracks for the same milestone.

High-Risk Projects

A common approach to managing potential problems is to place them under the risk management plan. There they can be recorded, assigned for tracking, and eliminated if the time for their occurrence passes without incident. Once risks actually do materialize and become a problem on the project, they are transferred to an issues management process. An issues list and a method for resolving issues—such as decision review by an advisory group or a change management integration process—can be another means of resolving conflicting demands caused by emerging problems. Some issues can be traced to existing practices, such as contracting and procurement procedures; resolution of the issue on one project and changing organizational practices can benefit other projects as well. If the issues stem from internal political pressures, contracting the work to an outside organization can defuse the problem.

There are situations where the critical path is risk-based rather than calendar-based, such as the critical paths found in information systems/software development projects. In such cases the risk management tasks from the risk management plan—mitigation and countermeasures—should be entered into the project's plan as tasks and later tasks should be linked to them as dependent tasks.

A key project management method for managing the impact of risk on the project's cost and schedule is reserve analysis. Building adequate reserve into the budget and schedule to address the effects of risk allows the team the option to finish on time and on budget. As organizations identify recurring risk and analyze the impact of risk on the organization, they become more able to predict the appropriate reserve for a project's overall risk rating.

Quality Control

On projects, quality control is the process of monitoring and recording results of executing the quality activities to assess performance and recommend necessary changes.[8] As mentioned previously, quality is achieved through a complex interaction of team member experience, organizational policy, work standards, defined processes, training, tools, human resource behaviors, and the host organization's culture and project management maturity. Management sets the environment for quality. The applicable standards and definitions of quality will vary by industry and by functional discipline. Project management professionals will define the appropriate quality elements for the project and share them with the team.

Generally, the project management plan will contain a quality plan, and related tools will be made available to the team—first to help them identify areas of quality vulnerability and then to define actions to ensure quality results.

- Project management analytical techniques useful in managing quality include cost-benefit analysis, benchmarking, design of experiments, and quality audits.
- Job aids such as metrics, checklists, performance measurements, acceptable ranges of deviation, approved changes, and interim deliverables will be applied by the team as they are trained and directed to do.

Quality is designed in, not controlled in. The quality plan should focus on early detection to reduce the cost of quality. Empowering the team is key to quality. Controls can help to identify variances indicating the need for correction or for management action.

One of the quality elements to monitor in managing a project is the temptation to reduce quality and functional performance in a trade-off between requirements, meeting the business need, and staying within time and resource constraints. Inadequate planning or unrealistic estimates or time lines add risk in this area. Unless organizations encourage accurate estimating, rigorous planning, and tracking status against an approved plan, little is being done to improve the practice of making last minute trade-offs—a sign of low project management maturity. Monitoring progress against all three elements of the triple constraint can prevent surreptitious cuts to scope or quality performance to meet a visible deadline or budget line.

Some teams may be lulled into a sense of complacency by highly consistent quality.[9] Keeping team members performing well and remaining vigilant to quality threats may require focused discussions of the importance of high quality to the organization's overall market position as well as the implications of each team member's performance on the quality of the project's end result.

If repetitive tasks occur and measurable numbers are monitored, random oversight reviews should be scheduled to keep people alert to their influence on the quality of the final deliverable and the customer's ultimate satisfaction. The people involved in quality control need to believe quality control is meaningful for them to perform it effectively. If management takes time periodically to confirm quality control is being performed, it is more likely to be performed in a meaningful way.

In high-quality environments, members of senior management will pop their head into the doorway at a review meeting and say, "I don't have time to stop to talk, but I just want you to know that what you are doing is important."[10] It is amazing what a word from management will do for quality.

EARNED VALUE AS A MEANS OF CONTROL

Earned value is a term used to describe the evolving relationship between the expenditure of resources on a project and the value being produced by work in relation to that expenditure. Earned-value formulas provide visibility in that relationship by arraying recent project data in a standard format for analysis. The earned-value formulas that look back at trends in current data, used together with risk management Monte Carlo projections that use statistics to predict the likelihood of future events, provide a basis for forward-looking corrective decisions.[11]

Delivery of value is not a sliding scale. The value of a deliverable is accrued when that deliverable is completed (e.g., 100% complete). Formulas for tracking earned value use cost and schedule information in relation to the project plan to identify the value actually being produced by the team against the plan's resource estimates.

Why Earned Value Is Used

In projects where costs are large and/or under tight scrutiny, earned value is a way to identify variances in the established plan during its execution. A number of assumptions are inherent in the use of earned-value methods. One assumption is that the project plan is an accurate description of how the project team will be able to achieve success. Based on the nature of the work, there may be variation in the accuracy of the project plan.

Knowing that its plan is only an approximation, the project team relies on what is actually occurring during project execution to insert reality into the predictions of the plan and to measure the validity of the plan. The goal of earned value is preventive action, updating the scope plan and baseline, managing time with quantitatively based durations and contingency reserves, specifying attributes of activities, using computerized tools, relying on publications for estimates of cost, calculating and applying "cost of quality," and using reports and presentations to confirm compliance with requirements at closure.[12]

Earned value uses data to spot variations early. If the results of actual data collected during project execution (e.g., reality) show results that are different from what was predicted in the plan, the project manager must know why they are different before she can take corrective action. The actual data may differ from what was expected for several possible reasons:

- The plan is wrong, or the estimates in the plan are not reliable.
- The performance is different from what was expected, or the work is being performed more or less efficiently.
- Undocumented changes, either additions or deletions, have been made to scope, schedule, or budget.

With an accurate plan and a trained team, effective use of earned value improves project performance. The project team relies on the project plan to provide guidance during execution. If the team is expected to produce timely and cost-effective results, and the project plan is found to be inaccurate, then corrective action is needed.

When faced with identified variances, the project team must make a number of choices to return the plan to reliability and predictability once again. The team can replan based on current information or adjust the plan and continue in execution using the adjustments as the new basis for guidance and decisions.

How Earned Value Works

When project teams apply earned-value methods, they want earned value to do specific things for the team. Thus earned value:

- Identifies schedule or cost variances when comparing estimated completion dates and estimated costs with actual completion dates and costs
- Calculates cost and schedule performance indices when calculating the ratio of earned value to actual costs

Project managers monitor earned value, both incrementally to determine the current status and cumulatively to determine the long-term performance trends.

The *PMBOK Guide* provides the following definitions for earned value and related terms:

- *Earned value (EV).* The value of work performed expressed in terms of the approved budget assigned to that work (for an activity or work breakdown structure component). It is the authorized work completed, plus the authorized budget for this work. Previously called the *budgeted cost of work performed* (BCWP).
- *Planned value (PV).* The authorized budget assigned to the work to be accomplished (for an activity or work breakdown structure component). It includes the detailed authorized work, plus the authorized budget to accomplish the scheduled work, allocated by phase over the life of the project. Previously called the *budgeted cost of work scheduled* (BCWS), the PV is sometimes referred to as the performance measurement baseline (PMB).
- *Actual cost (AC).* Total costs actually incurred and recorded in accomplishing work performed (for an activity or work breakdown structure component). The AC must relate to whatever cost was budgeted within the planned value and earned value (e.g., direct hours only, direct costs only, or all costs including indirect costs). Previously called the *actual cost of work*

performed (ACWP), the AC will have no upper limit; whatever is spent to achieve the EV will be measured.

Earned-value methods identify cost variances (CVs) or schedule variances (SVs) when comparing estimated completion dates and costs against actual completion. They give the cost performance indices (CPIs) and schedule performance indices (SPIs) when calculating the ratio or earned value to actual costs. Earned value can be used to predict in advance the estimated cost at completion (EAC) by calculating the ratio of budget at completion (BAC) to the cost performance index (CPI). The most widely used formulas are:

$$SV = EV - PV$$
$$CV = EV - AC$$
$$EAC = BAC/CPI$$
$$CPI = EV/AC$$
$$SPI = EV/PV$$

Calculating and publishing earned value at key points in a project defines and quantifies variation. The project manager and team then can use the information to make decisions on how best to proceed. In general, that which is measured improves. When the team knows that its performance will be tracked, members are more likely to meet the schedule and budgets.

A number of industries are mature enough to use these formulas and to gain value from them. Others simply are not ready. Most can benefit by considering deliverables to be complete only when they are delivered and then marking them at 100 percent complete. Partial credit for completion does not benefit the project and can create unrealistic expectations and deceptive work practices. Frequently, the last 10 percent of the completion effort takes as long as the first 90 percent.

If an organization has not established standard processes, formulas, and predictive estimating ratios, learning the formulas will be an exercise in educating the team for future projects or for passing their certification exam to become project management professionals.

PROJECT MANAGEMENT TOOLS

Tools that support the project manager are labor-saving devices to insert systematic thinking and processes into the complexity of managing a project. A very broad array of tools is available to the professional, including tools for scheduling, modeling, estimating, and analyzing; tools for knowledge, team, process, and configuration management; and tools for communication, collaboration, and administration. The challenge in managing a project is to select tools that simplify the process and do not add unnecessary complexity or overhead burden. Tools for large or more complex projects are available on the market, but they may not adapt well to smaller projects because of the overhead in administration they require. Even the number of scheduling tools allows selection of those that present a view of the entire project network versus those that present more specific detail and individualized reporting. The most common project scheduling and tracking tool probably is Microsoft Project (MS Project). While MS Project, like other tools, was created for tracking single projects, it has been adapted to track multiple projects in an organization (such as a program) and in large subcontracted projects across multiple organizations. New project management tools are being created on a regular basis that are adapted to use of the Internet, to virtual teams, or to specific types of projects. Many of them can be explored through books, online, through research centers, or by visiting professional conference vendor exhibits.

A key concept in project control is to acknowledge the purpose and value of tools so that the right tool is selected for its desired function. Viewing a schedule-tracking tool as the primary tool in establishing project control is putting undue emphasis on the problems that scheduling and tracking tools control.

LEVERAGING TECHNOLOGY

Technology—the science of applying knowledge for practical purposes, including electronic or other mechanical equipment—is becoming increasingly important to projects and has a direct effect on how projects are being managed and controlled. What project management professionals did manually in the 1970s and 1980s is now built into project management scheduling and tracking software. Knowledge used to be gleaned from books or hands-on experience over a project management professional's career. That knowledge now can be accessed online by computer at any time of day. Professional jobs that used to collaborate through meetings are now working in concert using the Internet and collaborative software. Some project teams today never meet face to face. The increasing use of *virtual projects* to replace bringing teams together has implications for management style and the amount of planning and structure needed before executing a project plan (see Figure 11-2).

Managing projects also requires more technical knowledge about the types of technology best suited to the project. Technology can educate teams,

FIGURE 11-2   Tips for virtual teams. When a team is not located in a single site, technology allows virtual meetings. These can be conducted by telephone, through conferencing and simultaneous computer slide shows, by using shared spreadsheets, or with other electronic and digital methods.

Tips for Virtual Teams

- Be on time.
- Open the meeting with a review of the ground rules and a roll call.
- Announce presence—both entrance and exit.
- Identify yourself when speaking.
- No personal business—stay on agenda.
- Use a "parking lot" for any nonproject business issues; cover these last.
- Don't place the call on hold; use mute (the team doesn't want to hear hold music).
- Mute phone when not speaking.
- Distribute handouts well in advance of the meeting—use version control.
- Choose variable times for meetings so that everyone is not inconvenienced every time.
- Be explicit about what you are "pointing" to in the handouts—page number, paragraph number, etc. (Paragraph numbers are helpful.)
- No whiteboard when speaking unless all participants in the conference call can "see" it.
- Allow 10 to 15 minutes before the meeting starts for social/networking.
- Be specific about time zones.
- Test clarity of your speech. Speak loudly and clearly into the phone.

---

integrate activities, and reduce risk by allowing access to the huge amount of information now available digitally. Integration of technology into project plans is more important than it used to be. It is important to understand the implications for the project approach of various changes in technology or the limits of using certain technology if all team members are not on one site. Project managers can leverage time zones for team development as well as work efficiency. Scheduling access to training by teams in different time zones allows more flexible self-development. Handing off work that was accomplished by one team member to another team member around the world allows the project as a whole to maximize the schedule. Preparation, execution, and review of tasks can be compressed. But empowering a team to work independently without mentoring or direct access to other team members for issue resolution requires the project's leadership to know more about how people absorb and retain information. There are limits to human information processing through only visual senses—the computer screen. People need to apply new concepts quickly, or they promptly forget them. Project managers also need to know how people are likely to make decisions in the absence of definitive information. Without clear direction, people rely on what they already know and believe, whether or not it applies on the project assignment.

Depending on the type of project, technology can be the great equalizer, placing information from team members with different cultural and functional backgrounds into a common format. One effect of technology is to limit interaction of the team outside their involvement in tasks directly related to the project. Limited interaction can have both advantages and disadvantages. Sticking to task-related activities can save time. Many interpersonal and cultural issues that might surface if there were face-to-face encounters never advance to that level. However, cultural attitudes toward time and accountability and authority and quality must be understood and managed. Some projects rely on human interaction for creative ideas and customer or stakeholder understanding.

Complex problems may need to be resolved through interactive discussion, and the application of different viewpoints, functional backgrounds, and professional experience. Defending the cost of face-to-face meetings in a cost-sensitive environment may require defining and quantifying risks and arguing the case for preserving the project's original business benefits. Projections of the role of project management in the future emphasize the importance of both right-brain and left-brain thinking, wisdom as well as knowledge.

We are at a point where both project management technology and product development technology must be planned explicitly into the project and selected for use based on the knowledge and ability of the team to use it effectively.

SUMMARY

In this chapter we covered new ways of looking at project control. In 20th-century projects, when managers first codified and expanded project management as a way of controlling complex new endeavors, the techniques of identifying a project's critical path, quantifying and tracking resources, and creating incentives for timely delivery were very concrete.

In today's professional world, the "soft side" of project management takes on increasing importance. Some projects are more subject to risk interference, increasing the focus on defining and managing risks rather than scheduling logistics. The ability of the project manager and leadership team to establish and maintain control depends on the knowledge and common cultural backgrounds of the team members. Mixed teams with different functional or cultural backgrounds insert a great deal of complexity into a project. Teams that work virtually using communications technology add new challenges to team management. And digital devices, while ubiquitous, are not utilized uniformly. All these elements amplify the importance of the facilitating processes in the success of projects and focus attention on the leadership skills of the project manager.

While many of the old tools and principles still apply, how they are managed is becoming an increasingly complex field of professional work for project management. Wisdom is as important as knowledge when managing the project team.

REVIEW QUESTIONS

1. In white-collar or professional projects, most of the estimates turn out to have been:
   a. pessimistic
   b. right on
   c. optimistic
   d. wrong
2. The project control strategy will need to be exercised on each of the three legs of the triple constraint (scope, cost, and schedule).
   a. neither true nor false
   b. true
   c. false
   d. neither completely true nor completely false
3. A _____ is the picture of success, and it is the best definition of a road map that leads to successful completion.
   a. project schedule
   b. project plan
   c. deliverables list
   d. subproject tree

4. A key feature of a project status reporting process is assessment of the effect of the _____ on the system.
   a. cost
   b. risk
   c. change
   d. all of the above

5. Tools that support the project manager are labor-saving devices to insert systematic thinking and processes into the complexity of managing a project.
   a. true
   b. false

6. *Earned value* is the term used to describe the evolving relationship between the expenditure of resources on a project and the value being produced.
   a. true
   b. false

7. There are situations where the critical path is _____ rather than calendar-based.
   a. risk-based
   b. scope-based
   c. resource-based

8. Calculating and publishing earned value:
   a. defines and quantifies risk
   b. establishes and controls scope and sets strategy and development
   c. defines and quantifies variation

9. Project control reactive strategies include:
   a. reducing activities
   b. reducing cost or resources
   c. reducing functionality
   d. simply tracking items one-to-one against the estimates and adjusting tasks and costs by priority
   e. all of the above
   f. *a, b,* and *c*
   g. *a* and *b*

12

ORGANIZATIONAL PROJECT MANAGEMENT MATURITY

OVERVIEW AND GOALS

This chapter looks at how an organization's environment can positively or negatively affect how a project is managed.

One element of project success is the role management plays in strengthening the project's environment for delivery. The operational structure and culture of the sponsoring organization, the priorities and expectations of the customer, the environment, and the physical realities of the project site all shape the project. The composition and competence of the project team also have a great deal of influence on how the project unfolds. However, the amount of effort the project manager and team must expend to create an environment for project success is affected by the project management maturity of the organizational environment. Anything the host organization does not provide to make the project environment supportive must be provided by the project manager and team. A more mature project management environment allows the team to focus on project results and reduces wasted effort and inefficiency across projects.

A more mature project management environment ties the project to the organization's capability to deliver results. Projects that deliver performance and quality results on time and on budget help leverage strategic objectives.

Implementing management strategy is the foundation on which a new project builds its success. As stated earlier, organizations that are good at implementing strategy are also good at implementing projects.

Improving organizational project management maturity, implementing the tools and options for its advancement, and removing some of the barriers to project success takes time. Governance, program management, portfolio management, and a project management office are some of the managerial methods being used to create an infrastructure capable of aligning projects with strategy, allocating resources effectively across projects, managing stakeholder expectations, and ensuring that management's intended benefits from the project actually materialize.

There are many different ways to improve the enterprise-wide management of projects. What is considered effective project management in one industry will differ from what is considered effective project management in another. Some industries are highly innovative and utilize team-based projects to design and launch products or services that generate significant revenue. Others must be efficient, since they are profitable only if teams excel at controlling all areas of the project. This chapter will address some of the challenges organizations face in aligning projects with strategy and business need, as well as ways contemporary organizations enhance their organizational project management maturity and strengthen the organizational framework for project success.

Of course, good project management cannot be delivered by infrastructure alone. If that were the case, organizations would not need projects—operations would be able to meet the need. Highly qualified professional project managers are critical to project success, and not every operations professional has the capability to become a project manager. Organizations that effectively recruit, develop, and promote competent project managers will be better equipped to address the internal challenges a project can bring. Projects are filled with risks and unknowns. The toughest projects require a truly seasoned professional.

The individual project management professional can help build and sustain a better project environment. Project managers and teams contribute the understanding of the complexities they have faced on projects, and they need to share that understanding with the managers around them. Promoting and supporting project management best practices and conduct preserves the profession. Contributing their advances to the profession through presentations and papers builds the professionals around them to form a more mature project management community.

Worldwide, the demand for project management talent and leadership is growing faster than the supply. Rapid change in the business environment spawns more projects. The pressures of a competitive business climate leave little leeway for individuals to "finesse" project success if the organization is not behind them. The project manager is charged with not only delivering project results for the sponsor and customer, but also doing a quality job of project management among peers. By taking personal responsibility for professional self-development and contributing to the practice and understanding of project management, the individual project manager helps prepare the workplace to manage projects more effectively in the future.

MANAGEMENT STRUCTURE AND CULTURE

The operational structure and the management culture of the sponsoring organization shape the project team's ability to deliver quality results. The more the organization's projects are tied directly to the organization's revenue stream and business success, the more likely the organization is to have put a more mature project infrastructure in place.

While technology continues to advance, the organization's ability to utilize those advances does not always keep pace. The team's access to technology and tracking software, flexible communications capabilities, and adequate physical resources is enhanced or limited by the organization's management environment. If a project is to remain focused on the deliverables and not on the organizational barriers to success, it needs processes, people, facilities, resources, tools, technology, and team support directed toward successful projects. And to manage the trade-offs needed to deliver something new for the first time, the project manager and team also need management support.

A number of project elements in the organizational environment will need to be considered in creating an environment for success for each project, such as:

- Management commitment
- Project management method
- Project alignment with strategic plans and steering councils
- Project sponsorship
- Optimized processes for deliverables
- Cross-functional alignment of goals
- Accountability for success

In addition, the management of the organization as a whole will need to improve the environment for success across projects, such as the:

- Business or work context for conducting projects
- Implementation environment
- Sponsoring organization's project management maturity
- Subcontractor organizations' project management maturity
- Project management support systems
- Team's physical work environment
- Priority of other competing team member responsibilities (other projects, operational responsibilities)
- Organizational or management culture

Ultimately, the project team must create anything that management does not provide for project success. Over the last few decades project management has trained a spotlight on consecutive evolving views of project success. As each area got the spotlight, leading organizations adopted the view and proceeded with projects in that light. Gradually, other organizations followed suit. Gradually the project management community has progressed. The recognition that project management was important to business success was an unspoken driver to continuous improvement enterprise-wide.

Early in the previous century, project managers were not even recognized as a distinct role. People look back on the Great Influenza Pandemic of 1918 for insight into how to manage society's response to an epidemic. When relating the story of how the medical profession shifted from country doctors to a scientific field of medicine, one man was credited with spearheading the movement. But he himself was not a doctor, and no one was sure what role he actually played in the medical profession. All they knew was that he got results, and they were glad he did it. We can look back today and see that he was in fact a project manager.

Project management has been called "the accidental profession." People in various occupations have been identified as particularly good at delivering results and "promoted" to the role of project manager.

In 1969, five of those professionals, convinced that project management was a profession much like medicine, law, and accounting, created the Project Management Institute as a member association for the professional. Chapters were formed in the United States and Canada as well as on different continents. Professionals in the field of project management collaborated to capture and share the knowledge they needed to do the job well.

In the 1970s the project manager was expected to be the "hero." He delivered project results through teams of colleagues and coworkers, relying on his own management knowledge and capability. At the same time, several universities began to add project management to the curriculum to support those fields of work that depended on project management for their business success—construction, engineering, and aerospace. These organizations had already adopted project management disciplines as an outgrowth of their roles as contractors on large federal projects.

Although in those years computers were still the territory of major research projects, project management tools began to proliferate. Analytical methods were formalized for detailed project planning, scheduling, estimating, and status reporting as well as for decision making and problem resoluton.[1] These methods were considered routine practices among project managers. Contests at PMI chapter meetings awarded prizes to the fastest project managers to properly place in sequence the separate steps of the project management process (see Appendix A). Almost everyone at the meeting knew it by rote.

In the 1980s many of those large organizations—the U.S. federal government and its contractors—began to see their performance aided by project management. They began to strengthen the links between the organization's performance management systems and project management practices. Measures were developed to gauge progress and predict deviations from well-developed project plans. Automated tools for project scheduling were developed by original equipment manufacturers, and software designers began to create project management software for the average professional's desktop computer. The results of team planning and scheduling and estimating could be entered into computers to assist with tracking against the plan. Many variations of those tools are in use today.

In the 1990s the certification of the project management professional— PMP certification and other professional certifications in countries around the globe—grew rapidly. Developed in the 1980s by early leaders in PMI, the PMP credential began to spread across industries. The PMP designation began to be used in selection and promotion of project managers as well as other project specialists, such as schedulers and cost engineers. Some organizations, such as original equipment manufacturers, conferred greater decision authority on senior project professionals who had obtained the PMP than was given to other project specialists who had not earned the credential.

By the year 2000, capability maturity models came into broader use. The early ones—such as the software engineering institute's capability maturity model (SEI CMM) at Carnegie Mellon University in Pittsburgh— were developed over 20 years with federal funding. They helped align the infrastructure and capability of the project's sponsoring organization with its vendors and contractors, resolving many of the contractual problems that emerge when aligning work produced at differing levels of technical process maturity. Assessments were developed to validate their adoption. Since PMI found few of them addressed project management, a capability maturity model for project management, OPM3, was created in the late 1990s by PMI. Tested and applied in large organizations, this model considers the elements of project management necessary to a given organization and industry. It is used to identify related areas of process maturity and create a maturity baseline for continuous improvement of project management processes and practices.

In 2010, project management operated in a global environment and became more strongly linked to executive strategy execution. When projects were expected to deliver results across time zones and cultures, project management was recognized as a leadership linchpin to project success. Efforts to manage natural and manmade disasters using traditional operations processes highlighted the inadequacy of ad hoc efforts to resolve a catastrophe. The time sensitivity and risk implications of slow resolution to hurricanes, tsunamis, and oil spills begged for a single point of resolution: a seasoned manager with the knowledge, gumption, and accountability to plan and integrate a multifaceted solution. Leading experts around the world began to discuss ways to make the unique capabilities of project management more visible to world leaders.

Innovative applications of the project management process spanned industries and revealed new benefits to managing organizational initiatives systematically. In 2020 and beyond, research currently under way will shape how project management is deployed and leveraged in the evolving global business environment.[2]

The project environment will continue to change with advances in technology, shifting economic conditions, stable and unstable political environments, legal incompatibilities, and competitive contexts. The integrative skills of the professional will be in high demand as information from multiple sources feeds high-level conceptual decisions.

Advances in automation will enable not only detailed control of progress measures by the team, but also trend analysis across multiple projects. Integration of projects across the enterprise and geographic borders will be not just possible but expected.

The project management community is poised for a period of extraordinary productivity, efficiency, and integration due to technological advances. But not every organization will be prepared to take advantage of the capabilities technology offers. Early adopters will forge ahead, while laggards will struggle to incorporate changes into their tried-and-true methods. Some will lapse and fall behind their peers. Still others will fail before they can even identify the challenges they face. It is not uncommon for spectacular project failures to capture news headlines, turning all heads toward the executives who are called on to explain the failure to their sponsors, their shareholders, and the public.

All organizations will be asked in some way to adapt to the changes that are sure to come. As a key function of their role, executives are responsible for the organization's viability and continuity. Like other functions critical to the future success of the organization, project management and project success are the responsibility of top management.

Management will have to determine what strategies will need to be developed and implemented to facilitate survival and growth.

Many people see project management growing in importance as the global marketplace continues to bring changes to current methods of doing business. If there is any consensus at this point, it is likely on the view that the traditional methods of enterprise-wide project management—project planning and control, use of governing bodies, leveraging of decision options, and evolution of managerial controls—are currently evolving slowly in the business world. They very likely will not evolve fast enough to adapt to the changing wave of innovation in projects.

Those organizations that actively manage change may reap the benefits of technological advancements in project management. Project managers themselves may be a driving force in navigating those changes. Because each project will select those methods most important to individual project success, and projects capture and share "lessons learned," the knowledge, capability, and competencies of project managers will evolve, as will the understanding and delivery capability of team members.

But the broader context in which projects are managed very likely will not keep up with the changing risks, increasing technological complexities, evolving expectations of stakeholders, and complex human interactions across cultures and legal barriers. While the future calls out for leaders, many managers will cling to prior management paradigms, reacting to crisis rather than preventing it.

The project manager in a future global project may find herself back in the 1970s again—project manager as "hero." The ability to search out relevant decision information, distinguish relevant information from "chaff," and distill leadership guidance for the team's benefit once again may depend heavily on the professional's own capability, knowledge, wisdom, and business savvy.

IMPROVING THE PROJECT ENVIRONMENT

The effectiveness of an individual and team is enhanced or limited by the maturity of the management environment in which they operate. While project management has been used for centuries, many modern organizations have not recognized that projects are the way they implement strategic initiatives today. In his book *Quantifying the Value of Project Management*, William Ibbs heads a chapter with the words "companies with more mature project management practices have better project performance."[3] Editor James Pennypacker declares after compiling results from many research sources that "what is good for the team . . . is good for the bottom line."[4]

What is organizational project management maturity? There has been a lot of focus in recent years on improving organizations' *management maturity*—much of it stemming from government initiatives similar to the one that documented the project management process in the 1950s (see Chapter 1) and extending it to specific functional areas like general management and information systems in the 1980s and 1990s. However, it is not always clear what is meant by that term. At the risk of oversimplifying, *maturity* in an organization's management environment means the managing of the strategic goals of an organization—or part of it—with as much holistic planning, organizing, control, and goal achievement as a team does on a well-managed project.

The Project Management Institute, in the *PMBOK Guide*, fourth edition, 2008, does not address organizational project management maturity explicitly, stating that the standard is limited to single projects, instead referring the reader to its other published standards on program management, portfolio management, and the Organizational Project Management Maturity Model (OPM3) for information on the broader context in which projects are accomplished.[5]

DEFINITION OF ORGANIZATIONAL PROJECT MANAGEMENT MATURITY

The Organizational Project Management Maturity Model (OPM3) Knowledge Foundation defines organizational project management as "the systematic management of projects, programs, and portfolios in alignment with the achievement of strategic goals."[6] The organizational project management maturity concept assumes a correlation between an organization's capabilities in project management, program management, and portfolio management and its effectiveness in implementing strategy. The degree to which an organization practices this type of project management is referred to as its *organizational project management maturity.*

To improve an organization's project management maturity, people need a model that demonstrates how project management can and should apply, as well as what elements need to be in place for it to work effectively. Working through the Project Management Institute (PMI), volunteer professionals in project management in countries around the world collaborated to create models and standards for the organization's leaders, as well as practitioners who carry out projects. Some of the standards are for managing projects, programs, and portfolios of projects—and for identifying an organization's project management maturity. They also created references, tools, and publications for the individual practitioner and for the broader project management community (www.pmi.org/resources). Among them are:

- A professional refereed publication for best practices, the *Project Management Journal*
- A standard guide to the project management body of knowledge needed by project management professionals, documented in the *PMBOK Guide*
- A knowledge foundation for determining an organization's project management maturity and an interactive best practices database for planning and tracking progress called the Organizational Project Management Maturity Model, or OPM3
- Standards for program management and portfolio management
- A model for competency in the profession
- Other special focus references such as books, research guides, work breakdown structures, forms, and analytic tools to apply on projects

One sign of a mature management environment is the documentation and maintenance of processes. Just as organizations have established processes for managing operations, they need processes for handling nonoperational work, or projects. The project management process documented in the early versions of the *PMBOK Guide* represents a simplified conceptual version of the project management process used at the project level in hundreds of organizations worldwide. (A process model based on the *PMBOK Guide* is presented in Appendix A.) Later versions of the *PMBOK Guide* have added substantial detail on associated processes with inputs and outputs, creating almost a methodology. While individual organizations will add detail for large projects or reduce process steps for simpler projects, they ultimately will tailor their unique version of a process to suit their needs. The standard core process presented in Appendix A provides a common base that extends across organizations, industries, and cultures worldwide. Its focus is on management of projects, not the procedures used to conduct them.

To help organizations assess how they address project management at the organizational level, PMI released its standard for assessing and improving maturity, the Organizational Project Management Maturity Model (OPM3) in late 2003. Over the course of several years, teams of volunteers from all over the world cooperated in developing the model to address projects within the organizational setting. OPM3 was created as a knowledge foundation for gauging an organization's understanding of and infrastructure for the effective management of projects. It uses hundreds of proven best practices from leading organizations globally; identifies a wide range of related, dependent elements of effective project management; and allows objective identification of those that already exist and those that are missing.

Through self-directed surveys, OPM3 provides a means by which organizations can select the best practices most suited to their type of organization, examine the maturity of their enterprise processes for managing projects, verify existing best practices using key performance indicators, compare their practices with best practices in other organizations, and select appropriate ways to improve the project environment over time.

While less mature organizations manage projects separately on an ad hoc basis, a structure for managing multiple projects helps to smooth the process. It also enhances management's overall control over strategic goal achievement. Increased visibility of projects across organizational lines improves managerial decision making.

OPM3 addresses the management of projects in three enterprise domains: the projects themselves, programs that manage together projects that share a common goal, and portfolios that provide a means for managing a variety of projects in a similar way (see Figure 12-1).

According to PMI's definition, "Organizational project management is the application of knowledge, skills, tools, and techniques to organizational and project activities to achieve the aims of an organization through projects."[7] It is the systematic management of projects, programs, and portfolios in alignment with the achievement of strategic goals.

To explain organizational project management maturity, PMI's standard states:

Depending on the organization's size, complexity, and sophistication, it may initiate or manage multiple and interacting projects simultaneously. Groups of projects sometimes constitute a *program*, which is a group of related projects managed in a coordinated way to obtain benefits and control not available from managing

FIGURE 12-1   Organizational project management processes depend on project management, program management, and portfolio management.

them individually. Programs may include elements of related work (e.g., ongoing operations) outside the scope of the discrete projects in the program.[8]

The work of the program manager focuses on benefits management, stakeholder management, and program governance—three themes that permeate all activities of a program. The program management and technical infrastructure records, tracks, and evaluated benefits from projects and subordinate programs to ensure the organization's investment is realized. Stakeholders for multiple projects are tracked at the program level, and governance is applied to ensure the delivery of coordinated benefits and resolution of issues caused by changes within the program and its projects.

Similarly, a *portfolio* is a collection of components (i.e., projects, programs, portfolios, and other work such as maintenance and ongoing operations) that are grouped together to facilitate effective management of that work in order to meet strategic business objectives. The projects or programs of the portfolio may not necessarily be interdependent or directly related. Organizational leaders, who are focused on the overall effectiveness of the entire organization, understand that projects, programs, and portfolios are well suited to helping them achieve their strategic goals.[9]

Using the accepted path of process improvement—standardize, measure, control, and continuously improve—the typical assessment for maturity of project management processes will sample existing artifacts created by active processes to validate their use, conduct individual interviews to confirm knowledge of best practices by project team members, and document elements of the company culture to capture snapshots of the organization's current state, thereafter noting areas where project management practices have made significant improvement.

The PMI standard, OPM3, also states that "as important as it is to accomplish individual projects successfully, additional strategic value is generally realized by treating *most endeavors* as projects—managing them individually and collectively in alignment with strategic objectives."[10] It goes on to say, "Likewise, an organization should allocate resources—financial and human—in alignment with strategic objectives."[11]

HOW PROCESS IMPROVEMENT APPLIES TO PROJECT MANAGEMENT

Projects always have collected "lessons learned," but when those lessons are applied to a common process, improvements that are made can be measured. Variations are predictable and can be managed. Many organizations apply continuous process improvement to operations but do not apply it to projects. As projects become more frequent owing to the increasing rate of change in the business environment, they are using an increasingly larger share of organizational resources.[12] As executives push to maintain better control of those resources, they are recognizing project management as a key and core business process. The resources and improvements applied previously only to operations processes are now being turned to the project management process as well. But those improvements must be of a different kind. Much of what has been established for operations does not transfer directly to projects and in fact can work in opposition to project success. To ensure that organizational project management maturity is managed properly, a better understanding of the nature of projects and their proper alignment with process improvement is needed.

When applying process improvement concepts to project management, several areas of process maturity should be addressed:

• Management's involvement in the leadership of project management as a core business function, shown by its support of the PMO, enforcement of project management standards and policy, training, and reliance on project management to produce strategic results for the enterprise

• The project process itself: initiation, planning, execution, control, and closeout processes that apply to managing the project, regardless of the product or service being created, and management's involvement in approving the formal charter and plan that authorize the project's use of organizational resources and commit human resources and management support to the team's achievement of approved goals
• The processes that the organization uses to support the unique functions of projects, most of which are somewhat different from those of operations (project cost management, project time management, etc.)
• The process the organization uses to capture and apply lessons learned for continuous process improvement in how different types of projects are planned, managed, and controlled

In a mature project environment, the host organization is supportive of projects. If changes and exceptions must be made to ensure the success of the project, a means is provided to resolve issues and prevent problems promptly because projects are time-sensitive. The sponsor and the customer will support the unique needs of projects and work to make them successful. The whole organization, working through the project management office (for project management) or process owner (for product or service development), will identify and resolve issues, remove technical barriers that impede project success, and actively work to reduce challenges for future projects by refining the processes they follow or are exempted from following, as needed.

Targeted Areas for Improvement

One way that management can support a better project environment is by sponsoring improvement projects in targeted areas that can be implemented successfully. A model such as OPM3—or other, more specific management improvement models—is first used to identify areas that already support project success and to verify their effectiveness. The model is then used to compare what exists against chains of dependent processes and to target needed improvements in areas where necessary elements are missing. Some improvements can be made without projects to implement them. Others are more complex and require a full planning effort.

Some models are based on the stages of process improvement or on specific technical areas. OPM3 is based on project management, using examples of best practices in existing organizations worldwide to create an assessment database. Its best practices already have been shown to be effective.

Documenting Existing Processes

It is not enough to implement a model for organizational project management maturity, because a model is generic. It applies across organizations without regard to their type, size, economic environment, or unique purpose. The organization needs to integrate the processes already evolved for managing projects (the local process) with the best practices and standards derived from external organizations (the model).

To improve the project management environment, an organization first needs a documented project process to initiate, plan, execute, control, and close out projects. Benefits of documenting these processes include:

- Determining the common process underlying different projects
- Revealing the variations in performance from one group to the next in applying the process
- Identifying opportunities for improvement and making those improvements on a continuous basis
- Revealing best practices that, when repeated, can enhance project success in the future
- Identifying unique approaches to projects that are right for the organization

The key is to focus on project management practices that lend themselves to improved organizational performance—something organizations with low project management maturity tend not to do.[13]

Standardizing Common Processes

Once the different processes in the organization are identified and the common process across all projects is defined, the organization can create its standardized common process across projects. True, individual projects still will be adapting and tailoring that process to their own unique needs, but the common process across projects can be tracked, measured, refined, and improved.

The project management office (PMO) is the most likely place in an organization to place central responsibility for the common project management process. The PMO can range from weak to strong depending on the organization's level of maturity and need for central control. Some strong PMOs will:

- Be accountable for selecting which projects will receive scarce resources
- Have dedicated project management staff
- Manage key projects to completion
- Maintain documentation for projects and a database
- Approve changes to a project

A weak PMO often lacks management backing and considers itself lucky to have current project documents for records. It is called on to support projects with communications, administration, tool support, or record keeping rather than to provide guidance or leadership. The authority to decide on the process or to make changes resides with each project manager. The word *management* is left out of the title, so it is actually a "project office" rather than a "project management office." More mature project environments will ask the PMO to enforce established performance standards and measures, maintain best practice repositories, sponsor advisory groups, and conduct regular training programs to enhance the knowledge and practices of project management in the organization. The PMO will have stated management responsibilities. If projects are managed in groups with related outcomes and are accountable to management for results, the title may be "Program Management Office."

The most important element of success is to be sure that the authority given to the PMO matches the responsibility. The PMO must be able to carry out its assigned accountabilities.

As organizations become more aware of the strong link between projects and strategic goal achievement, improvements will be both top-down and bottom-up: Executive management will update its awareness of a key project's impact on the overall strategic goals of the organization and communicate priorities for project support back to the workforce. Through the PMO, the information gained from the project—and its benefit to the organization—will be fed back into the organization to make its management of comparable projects more effective and more efficient in the future.

In an ideal situation, the critical information the project manager and team need for making decisions will be available to them. Management will provide needed resources, and customer expectations will be managed to match the capabilities of evolving project processes. The people on the project will not have competing demands placed on them. The resources will be reasonably accurate for the duration of the project, and cash, materials, and expertise will be available when needed. Management will encourage and value properly planning projects before entering them into project scheduling software. Appropriate tools will be available to manage and track project progress and the detailed data from projects will not be inappropriately available, misinterpreted, or misused by stakeholders. The deadlines promised to the customer and the profitability expectations of the project will be reasonable, achievable, and responsive to the changes that occur normally when doing something for the first time. Areas of work too vague to be planned and estimated will be excluded from the project, since they cannot be effectively controlled without a plan. Managers who oversee projects under them will be discouraged from interfering with the work of the team and will be encouraged to provide necessary backing and support so the team can complete its work.

This environment sounds like a great place to manage projects. Most project management professionals, however, would not consider this ideal situation to be the norm in organizations today. It may be feasible in a few organizations that have practiced project management for a long time; those whose profits and business success are tied to projects come closest to the ideal. The rest of the organizations have some progress yet to make. But before real progress can be made, some type of objective means must be made available to raise awareness of current practices and their effect on project success. Once people are aware of the need for action, they are more willing to support needed change.

Continuous Improvement

Continuous improvement means using a process for applying the lessons of history to the creation of successful future projects. At the close of each project, the team captures "lessons learned" for use on future projects. Some of those improvements affect risk, or estimating, or control processes. Others affect the development stages of the project's final deliverable and technical processes. If the team's recommendations for improvement are routed to the process "owners" for each area and are referenced during the planning of subsequent projects, then continuous improvement can be made both to the project process and to the technical processes that produced the outcome and deliverable. As processes mature, the improvements are differentiated by what is most appropriate for a particular type of project and which are most common across projects.

Methodologies

Methodologies have a role in standardizing the way products are built so that novices, team members, and subcontractors all can do things the same way and create compatible outputs. Methodologies can provide a certain amount of value on projects that are repeated over and over in an organization by providing sequenced steps that together create a path for "stepping through" a project-related process. Typically a methodology depends on the definition of a high-level common process across projects, getting agreement on the process, and then specifying more detailed steps to complete. A fully developed methodology defines the roles that are to perform those process steps, the inputs needed to perform them, and the outputs that are expected after the process is complete.

Methodology is one way that organizations manage product life-cycle standardization. Methodologies are used in many organizations, including organizations that "manage by projects" in an operational mode. While such methodologies often are mistaken for project management tools, most are product-related or technical. To be effective, they need to be tailored to suit the project or nested within the project's core processes and phases: initiation, planning, execution, and closeout. If purchased externally, they need to be tailored to the organization's unique needs and project culture.

Operational quality principles contained in methodologies do not translate well to most projects because the deliverables produced by projects are by definition one of a kind. Process stability—that is, repetitive processes that produce deviations within an acceptable range—is an operations concept that many people apply to projects. However, the concept does not make sense using "first time" processes that one finds in a project's process environment. Even where processes are borrowed from operations, they are likely to be combined in new ways, making metric measurements of those processes less useful or reliable for decision purposes.

What does make sense is standardization and measurement of the project management process itself. As the process is documented, refined, built into software tools and methods, and reinforced by policy, the reliability of the process in delivering results can be monitored, tracked, and eventually managed with selected metrics. The metrics then can be used to make executive decisions regarding project delivery of strategic objectives. While many organizations have created their product development process, not as many have defined a common project management process. An organization capable of managing process variations within a Six Sigma range on their project management process would be a mature project management environment indeed!

A PROJECT'S BUSINESS AND WORK CONTEXT

The priorities of the business very likely will be the overt priorities that are reviewed, discussed, and monitored while the project is under way. They also will be used to evaluate the success of the project when it is over. These business priorities are a starting point for the initiation phase and are seen in the project's documented critical success factors. Similarly, the priorities of the functional area under which the project sits will determine what areas receive oversight and which elements are valued and encouraged.

- If the project is placed under executive management, it very likely will be evaluated in light of its contribution to strategic results and preparing for the future.
- If placed under financial management, the project is more likely to be monitored to see whether its numbers are accurate and whether the financial resources of the project are under control.
- If the project is placed under operating officers, it may be evaluated in terms of whether or not it is efficient in its resource utilization.
- If the project is placed under division managers, the focus of review likely will be on whether or not the project delivers on expectations.
- If the project is placed under a staff function or service manager, it may be reviewed in terms of compliance with organizational policy.

Earlier we pointed out that projects must decide what to do and what to ignore to be able to complete something new within defined time limits and resource constraints. It is easy to see that a project improperly positioned within the organization can be hindered in achieving its goals if the oversight it receives from management does not align with the project's purpose, managerial challenges, and design. As a general rule of thumb, the project should be placed high enough in the organization's hierarchy to have the authority to resolve any of the issues that arise within the course of its work. Ideally, to focus on the project outcome rather than procedures, the project manager should report to someone with a compatible managerial emphasis.

Some projects are formed in times of change and may reflect coming changes before those changes have been addressed formally in the business environment. Careful attention to such change effects—identification and documentation of those change effects in the project—can benefit their downstream application in the organization as a whole.

The business context in which the project is implemented, as well as alignment with legal and regulatory requirements, helps to manage the project's ultimate impact on customers and user communities and to ensure that the overall effort delivers the value management expects.

One of the benefits cited by management for using project management discipline is that the organization gains visibility into how results are achieved. The areas of application are evolving as the business environment evolves. Innovative areas of project management application include the development of new products, in military management, in public sector services, and in education. Some work contexts for project management application are surprising and quite innovative. The Chicagoland Executive Council (PMI Chapter) explored some of those applications in 2005, in 2008, and in 2010 by bringing together senior representatives from different industries in a major metropolitan area.[14] Participation over the years has crossed public and private sector entities, including military services, engineering and construction companies, marketing and public relations, health care and insurance providers, medical products, consulting, telecommunications, higher education, state government, city government, and the banking and finance sector.

As a result of forums, emerging trends are being identified in the executive-level application of project management. Most are in areas of high risk, potential high return on investment, or the need to leverage valuable resources. Some examples include:

- Military decision making, where decisions affect service member security
- Resource deployment, leveraging high-value limited resources by fast-tracking problem resolution
- Customer satisfaction, particularly where major contracts depend on long-term clients and client relationships must be managed as part of the project process
- State government services, defining leadership roles over projects and executive roles influencing multiple state agencies and their revenue streams
- City government administration and hazard management, systematically introducing computerized service response systems and handheld devices to dramatically shorten response time
- Higher education, where aligning project management methods across academic disciplines makes graduates more able to deploy learning on the job

Other areas are emerging as research continues to extend inquiry into the application of project management worldwide. Some of these innovations leverage the project's ability to use resources more flexibly, cross previously defined functional and organizational boundaries, and enable new leadership and managerial capabilities. The results enable the organization's executives to:

- Horizontally align new customer or operating relationships for the future
- Advance executive operating strategies such as lean manufacturing
- Create new strategic market positioning or enter new markets
- Develop fresh alliances with existing vendors and partners
- Leverage project-initiated contractual alliances on a global scale
- Improve revenue management via offshore component manufacturing
- Improve quality by automating information access and decision data
- Consolidate information systems and streamline services
- Place important customer (or patient) data in the hands of support personnel

Still others are using enterprise-wide management of projects to align results across multiple organizations and diverse groups. Project portfolio selection models are being used to reduce overall institutional risk—both cumulative enterprise-wide risk and the coincidence of multiple high-risk projects. Gaining new visibility through programs and portfolios into project dependencies helps executives:

- Identify, select, and sustain projects critical to strategic goal achievement
- Extend successful current methods to new areas of the global marketplace
- Test proposed models against market competition in new areas, such as environmental or "green" products
- Explore long-term profit potential of products via life-cycle market management
- Manage product life-cycle evolution to maximize product market upgrade strategy

Still others leverage the methods of effective enterprise-wide project management and best practices to:

- Implement systematic methods of portfolio governance across the enterprise
- Improve stakeholder involvement across multiple related projects
- Align projects over the entire product life cycle
- Involve customers in key decisions to improve performance and quality

From concept to design to implementation, as executive management links projects to strategy, the emphasis of the project management discipline shifts management's focus. The new focus on the potential opportunities and flexibility of projects enables more responsive organizational approaches in a changing business environment. Some of the benefits to executive management include:

- Leveraging the discussions during project initiation to advance strategy
- Tapping information from project planning and change management to more accurately predict trends in the workforce
- Focusing on causes of project problems to improve costly system-wide practices such as weaknesses in contract management
- Improving requirements and critical success factors to reduce costly rework
- Shifting emphasis from problem resolution during closeout to proactive communication of compliance with agreed-on project requirements.

As organizations become more mature in their management of projects, programs, and portfolios, they shift from reactive damage control to proactive design and effective plan execution. If organizations hope to stay ahead of the pace of change in the business and economic environment, that shift will be necessary.

And as the complexities of contracting with executives with differing cultural values puts increasingly greater attention on the needs of the customer rather than the producer, contracts will reap the benefits of added attention to gaining customer input at all stages of the product life cycle.[15]

Those organizations that easily respond to change are likely to leverage projects for strategic advantage. Those that are reluctant to change are less likely to benefit, either from the enterprise-wide alignment of project opportunities and benefits or from the best practices improvements that enhance the organization's agility, resource efficiency, and partnerships with organizations in decades to come.

LEVERAGING THE ORGANIZATION'S RESOURCES

Since projects are how organizations implement something new, and since the rapid rate of change in the business environment increases the proportion of overall resources that are allocated to projects rather than operations, executive management is paying more attention to projects than ever before. Financial backers want results for their investment. Money, time, and professional resources are expended on projects, and projects are less predictable in their return if they are unmanaged. Management wants to know what to expect and how to get more results for their investment in projects. Well-managed projects also bring credibility to their sponsors. Organizations that contract with management—or that provide services to projects—benefit from the added predictability that good project management brings to joint efforts.

Leveraging Financial Resources

Management is actively involved in assessing the effect of projects on enterprise resources and the effect of limits or available resources on projects. In profit-making organizations, projects are routinely assessed in terms of their consumption, use, leverage, or increase of revenue, some with financial formulas embedded in project initiation documents (net present value, internal rate of return, etc.).[16]

In many cases, individual projects do not deal with finance and return on investment unless the project itself is a cost-benefit analysis but focus rather on budgeting and managing costs of the project. The budget is a plan for allocating resources. Organizations budget financial resources across projects because there is a limited supply and many competing places that need the resource. Accurate budgets encourage accountability. Budgets with a reasonably accurate allocation of financial resources and material reduce waste by matching resources to effort, thus maximizing the financial return from the project.

Enterprise-wide project budgeting and management systems are one way for organizations to increase the visibility and responsiveness of project investments. When senior management approves a project, an estimated budget is allocated in a line item and is revised as more accurate estimates become available at the close of project planning. When management approves moving ahead with the project at the beginning of project execution, that budget is committed to underwrite the work of the team. In exchange for that allocation of budget, the organization expects the planned results from the project.

When detailed planning is complete, the project is ready to deliver those results and the authority to make resource decisions within the project is delegated to the project manager and team. If management expects the product or service to deliver benefits, those results are also evaluated after the project is complete. It makes sense, then, to place real executive attention on improving the accuracy of estimates, the predictability of applied best practices, and the timely delivery of product outcomes.

Project teams benefit when the enterprise-wide budgeting and financial systems link with project financial management updates, so both senior management and project management have access to current financial data.

Managing Project Management Professionals in the Organizational Structure

Professionals are an organizational resource. Organizations with a long history of project management typically define and acknowledge the senior status of experienced project managers by placing their job roles in the organization's job classification system and PMO. They give them more decision authority to make budget decisions without higher approval. Some organizations tie decision authority to credentials or being certified as a project management professional, in addition to the level of the role they hold. Organizations that do not have mature project management career tracks often put project coordinators in a support role because it is more difficult to determine accurately their level of competence, define their value contribution to the organization, or gain team support for their decision authority without a defined job hierarchy.

Leveraging the Project Management Professional's Role

Some European, African, and Australian organizations have defined the job hierarchy explicitly and have standards for staffing and promoting project professionals that apply across organizations. Some tie the project manager role to education systems and government job classification systems. Their standards have been adopted in a number of countries worldwide. Pacific Rim countries make extensive use of professional societies to strengthen the project manager's position and influence in key industries. As job standards and classifications are standardized across industries, recruitment of the right talent for the right job improves as well.

DETERMINING THE ORGANIZATION'S PROJECT MANAGEMENT MATURITY

An organization's project management maturity is the degree to which it is capable of continuously accomplishing what it sets out to accomplish to the degree and quality it intended. Maturity implies not only increased capability but also an increased awareness of the strengths and limitations of that capability.

Organizations use projects as the primary means for accomplishing strategic objectives. Maturity is not a point in time but a continuum. Just as individuals progress in maturity from a state of dependence to independence and then to full interdependence with others in a social community, organizations move from dependence on individuals to an ability to perform self-sufficiently and eventually toward full integration and alignment with their partners and customers in a business and economic context. Project management maturity implies maturity in systems, structures, processes, policy, and training in all the key knowledge areas and critical success factors for projects. Time, cost, quality, procurement, human resources, and risk management are part of that continuum. So are communications, scope management, and project integration within the larger organization's goals and strategies.

Organizations that are actively striving to improve their project management maturity evaluate where they are on that continuum, decide where they would like to be on that continuum to best serve the organization's mission and vision, and put conscious initiatives in place to improve their capacity to deliver results. Using project management to make those improvements allows the organization to target desired benefits, control the scope of the effort, and selectively deploy scarce resources to where they will have maximum impact on project delivery and strategic goal achievement. The individual project benefits by increased organizational project management maturity, but it takes years to implement improvements. Movement from one level to another in each of the nine areas identified as critical to effective project management relies on all dependent capabilities being in place. The more maturity an organization enjoys, the stronger relationship there is between improvements and financial return.

Project support offices, project offices, project management offices, program management offices, and project-friendly budgeting and management systems are some of the ways that management improves project control while maturity develops over time.

As an organization moves up the continuum of organizational project management maturity, the processes, systems, and support provided to individual projects increase until the environment not only becomes conducive to project success but also produces a cyclic process of continuous improvement over time. Projects are managed more smoothly and deliver results with a greater predictive accuracy.

Managing well in any organization requires a number of basic elements. To deliver strategic results effectively, the organization (single project or project office) needs:

- Executive leadership and direction in a coordinated context of resources and support
- Clearly defined goals, including a clear mission and vision that are aligned with the market and the economic sector
- Full information regarding its own resources—physical, human, and financial—and ways to determine what is immediately available for goal achievement
- A method for diagnosing what exists and what is missing in an integrated project management system
- A plan updated to reflect changes in the internal and external environment
- A means to assess its own success in reaching its strategic goals, with external opinion to make sure that it is accurately reflecting its real status when it does
- Data from monitoring and control processes to give management information to decide on next steps
- Infrastructure that supports the processes the organization performs to get results

Surprisingly enough, the elements that organizations need to perform effectively on a large scale are much the same as the elements required to manage projects. You could say that organizations simply are bigger, less structured, and more complex than projects and thus do not lend themselves to the application of project management principles. Yet some projects are bigger and more complex than the average organization. The processes are a lot alike, simply stated.

A Standard for Organizational Project Management Maturity

A framework of policy, standards, training, and tools allows organizations to mature. The standard for organizational project management maturity has been developed only recently. After a review of almost two dozen maturity models, the Project Management Institute determined that none of them adequately addressed the domain of projects. The development of OPM3 focused on management maturity of projects, separate from operations. It used volunteers who were senior practitioners in project management. Their work products integrated the elements of project management maturity from organizations all over the world, grouped them into best practices and capabilities, identified indicators that could be assessed if those capabilities were in place, and created pathways for progressive maturity. The pathways covered all the areas of project management knowledge already identified for projects.

Although the OPM3 model is complex enough to accommodate even the largest global organizations, an organizational maturity assessment need not be complex. The approach can be tailored to suit the size, complexity, and maturity of the organization. Often simple assessments can help determine needed improvements and gain quick support. (For an example, see the "Organizational Assessment" in Appendix C.)

Project Management Maturity Support Systems

A project will occur with or without external support. However, it is pretty much understood that the more external support that is given to the project, the less time and effort need to be expended on creating a success environment from the outset. If time and results are valued, achieving results in a timely manner becomes an overt goal on projects. It makes sense, then, for the organization to provide as much support as it can to achieve the goals of the project.

Project management support systems can differ significantly in the various contexts in which a project manager must operate to deliver a project result. The things a project needs that do not exist already must become part of the project scope and be added to the deliverables of the project. Ideally, the project can take advantage of prior successes to implement best practices. It can avoid problems by consulting the lessons learned from similar projects in the past. However, if the organization sets a goal to improve how projects are managed, it also will provide the means for best practices to be available to all projects and for improvements identified in lessons learned to be applied across the enterprise. At key points in the project process, the organization also will need to have clear and detailed procedures for making sure that lessons are captured, that improvements are identified, and that resources are acquired and deployed to implement those improvements. If an organization does not yet have a system for capturing and applying lessons learned from projects, it can form a project to create one.

It is clear that some of the success of a well-executed project can be attributed to:

- The sponsoring organization's readiness to support projects to their successful conclusion
- The options the project team has for creating any support systems within the project that are missing externally
- The knowledge, talent, and ingenuity of the project's leadership
- The willingness of the leaders to learn from the past and seek ideas for the future

While some organizations simply cancel projects that are not proceeding as planned, the wasted resources and lost motivation within the team are high prices to pay for poor planning. If more organizations approached success as the goal—and worked to create an environment for success—the burden for "reinventing the wheel" on every project would be reduced significantly.

The Team's Work Environment

The team's experience on a project can differ significantly depending on whether the organization's environment is supportive of the unique needs of projects. Contrast the following two scenarios.

In a nonsupportive environment, little base information is provided to the team regarding the current state of the organization and the project assumptions made by its creators. The team is left to discuss among themselves the potential authorities and constraints the team may have. Team members must try to determine the full implications of the requirements they are given on their own using static descriptions with little guidance about how the end deliverable will be used. They are given no information on how similar projects have been done in the past or how the organization judges a project to be successful. They are uninformed about any other projects that relate to what they are doing. They are not given permission or authority to meet with representatives of other parts of the organization to seek the information they need to plan the project properly. If they receive direction from upper management, it is usually peremptory and uninformed about the real conditions under which the project is operating.

As issues arise, the team either is left without a means to resolve them or else experiences long delays in getting resolution. As changes are made, those changes are not communicated well and reach only some of the team members. Individuals have different versions of the information. If they have a schedule available, it is not current. There is no interaction with management. The tools available to the team are the same as for other teams and may or may not be appropriate to the type of project they are undertaking.

They only get status information on the project periodically, but it does not have a level of detail that affects their work. They are informed only of the negative consequences of failure, not the potential for positive impact on the goals of the organization.

In a supportive environment, the team is briefed on the project's goals, vision, management expectations, critical success factors, constraints, and risks. The state of the organization and the potential effect of the project are explained. Each person is briefed on his role and how it relates to other roles and other projects. Use of the project's deliverable is described in performance terms, and the requirements are linked to specific job tasks and team members. Team members receive an orientation to the project, as well as training in special aspects of the project that may differ from their experience. The project plan and its updates are posted for ready reference at all hours, and updates are always distributed within the team. Management's support for the project and its outcome is visible, and the impact of the project's success on the organization is described. Tools available are explained in their use, including features that are to be used and those that are not to be used for the specific project. Systems and opportunities for team status updates and interpersonal communication are provided, along with training on their use. Checklists are made available to ensure no important steps are left out.

Figure 12-2 illustrates a force-field analysis of a project environment. It is not so important whether the team's project environment is fully automated in a modern office complex or provided with bulletin boards and boxes of files in a remote location. The functionality of the environment and its support of team job performance are the key. An organization and its lead-

FIGURE 12-2 Force-field analysis of a project environment. Factors in a project's environment can support or hinder the project's success.

Environmental Factors Supporting the Project's Success	Environmental Factors Hindering the Project's Success
Politics	Politics
Reward systems aligned with project and organizational strategic goals	Personal hidden agendas
	Competing demands on resources
Enough resources because projects are prioritized	Rewarding individual performance at the expense of the whole
Cooperation	No systems tools exist

ership, understanding the importance of project team support, can create a positive environment practically anywhere using solid project understanding and modern technology.

TECHNOLOGY TO ENHANCE ORGANIZATIONAL PROJECT MANAGEMENT MATURITY

When a team works within an organization that has achieved project management maturity, the environment is much more supportive from the beginning. Their office complex provides telephones, meeting rooms, structured workday schedules, support personnel, policies, and training and tools. More than likely team members share a common business culture and educational background, with knowledge and understanding of the rules, purposes, and potentials of the project and its support systems. Information for daily decisions is provided on handheld personal digital assistants (PDAs) and perhaps even at home through secure Internet services 24 hours a day. A central information location is established for those who are new to the organization or contracted from outside to support the project. Sponsor support, resource availability, tools and methods, training, policy support, and formal processes are identified.

Software to Support Management Decisions

Forms, tools, and methods are introduced as ways to create consistency in internal project systems. These are some of the types of support systems that would make the project manager role easier and those that, if missing, would make success difficult:

• Computerized systems to run project scheduling software and report status to the entire team anywhere they are located
• Systems that report project charges and expenditures, providing timely updates on the project status
• Time-reporting systems that track effort of team members on tasks in the project plan and reflect upcoming tasks for each team member

Additional systems and tools that could increase the rate of progress along the line of project management maturity include:

• Estimating tools that capture and record the estimates and actual numbers (effort and dollars) on current projects for more accurate prediction of resource needs in future

- Tools that aggregate metrics from multiple projects and present trends
- Systems that support the collection and sharing of closeout reports and provide a "keyword" searchable database for use by management and project planning teams
- Reference files on best practices from prior projects and benchmarks from similar organizations to adapt and improve project management practices over time

Systems to Maximize Performance

A number of systems support team effectiveness and improve individual performance:

- Staffing deployment systems that align skills with positions on active projects
- Online collaboration spaces for project teams to develop their deliverables
- Communications technology to gather information, share it, report changes, check status, and communicate new information to the team
- Information- and knowledge-sharing infrastructure so that the team has the reference material it needs and access to best practices and lessons learned

Workforce Development

It is not a big leap to extrapolate the need for creating a total environment to the need for acquiring and deploying specialized knowledge, skill, and ability on the project team. The people who have special knowledge of the critical success factors in each unique project environment must be identified, recruited, secured, and retained not only for project success but also for improving the project management environment across projects. The availability of knowledgeable project professionals improves decisions and speeds desired improvement.

As a general rule, the team should bring in the base technical knowledge and experience needed to deliver project outcomes. If the organization has all the technical experience it needs to perform the work, the project leadership's challenge will be to bring them into the project and protect them from being transferred back to other work priorities once the project is in progress. Teams will receive training to bring prior experience in line with the needs of each particular project, maximizing individual performance. Individuals hired from outside the organization will be briefed on the differences between the type of organization they worked for last and the new project culture. The right expertise will be placed on the right project team so that the organization gets the most from its staff dollars.

Strengthening the enterprise-wide project management culture helps retain quality professionals. Some organizations have made significant progress in putting in a supportive culture for managing projects. Once people have access to the tools and capabilities of a more mature project management environment, they do not want to give them up. Many will not accept a transfer out of the group with a more mature project environment to a less mature division of the company. Others hired from a more mature project environment outside the organization will simply leave within the first month on the job. As the implications of working in a less mature setting become clear, more sophisticated team members simply are not interested in going back to what they perceive as the chaos of the prior environment.

Multiple teams that are expected to work together toward a common result need more sophisticated coordination so that they do not undercut each other's success or work at cross-purposes. The reason the federal government documented and codified the project management process and methods used in NASA projects during the 1950s (see Chapter 1) was to establish systematic control over projects too complex to manage informally.

One of the effects of downsizing and cost cutting during lean economic periods is the replacement of senior personnel with cheaper labor. An unfortunate side effect of such staff cuts is the loss of experience and knowledge, both to the organization's workforce in general and to the mentoring of junior staff. Organizations that have come to recognize the critical importance of project management to their implementation of strategic goals will devote special attention to recruiting, retaining, and leveraging professional-level skill and talent in the project management community. While the benefits of effective project management are difficult to quantify, the losses attributable to poor project management are easier to see.

Senior management will typically take a results-oriented look at project management and work to achieve:

- Alignment of projects with strategy and business need
- Quality and value delivery for project sponsors and customers
- Appropriate project structure and team capability
- Active process frameworks for projects, including policy, standards, training, and tools that support a common project management process across divisions
- Technical architecture and governance to support advances in organizational project management maturity over time

Viewing project management as a professional discipline instead of a job role to be assigned to a team member implies seeking out and tapping into the knowledge, skill, capability, and experience of the project management professional. Organizations are not likely to quickly replace a senior physician with a medical intern or a senior lawyer with a junior staff attorney. They should be just as cautious in replacing senior project management professionals with talented junior staff. The risk to the organization as a whole is easy to underestimate if the organization has not achieved a basic level of organizational project management maturity.

Using Maturity Models for Improvement

When an organization makes a conscious decision to improve its organizational project management maturity, it helps to have a model or guide to work from. Maturity models have been created to guide organizations along the process maturity continuum. Many of them are derived from process management and quality movements over the past three decades. With the advent of OPM3, a model is now available that specifically addresses the enterprise-wide management of projects. A growing cadre of professional consultants is now available to assist an organization in making assessment-based improvements. Many of them have paid to receive formal training from PMI for the role. And PMI supports them with updated information and formal periodic training programs.

The organizational units most likely to be able to lead implementation of a model for improving project management maturity within an organization are those that have been successful in managing projects effectively in the past and are aware of project management best practices generally. The best practices contained in the OPM3 best practices database already have been established and tested by other organizations. It helps to remember that maturity models are designed for the analyst, not for the average worker. If the models are not aligned, a good analyst can position them, determine their overlap or missing coverage, and develop a construct for how they relate to each other. Tables of terms can be aligned so that the meanings are conveyed by a single set of definitions and terms. A baseline can be established and progress targeted by a certain date, with progress made on more than one continuum—just as is done in other programs. A plan can be developed to gradually implement needed change that supports existing efforts and integrates new ones. If using a model such as OPM3, an OPM3 specialist can serve as a mentor and help to align the processes and models that exist. She can create an improvement plan for the organization and provide training on how to apply the model.

Management can use oversight reviews to reinforce levels of maturity so the organization does not regress to a prior level. The review can be focused on different areas as the organization gradually advances in overall project management maturity. Although some organizations will try to jump right to the highest level of maturity in reviews without going through the platform development process at the lower levels, improvements made without a solid platform of established practices will not endure. Levels are sequential. Organizations that skip lower level milestones of maturity will find their employees operating at a prior level when they bring in an outside assessor to verify their "maturity level." Assessors look for artifacts that result from more mature practices. If those artifacts are missing, the organization is considered to be operating at the prior level of maturity.

At low levels of project management maturity, oversight should confirm:

- Projects are defined as *separate from operations.*
- Every project has an *assigned project manager.*
- Project managers are properly selected and *trained* in project management.
- Projects undergo formal *planning by the team.*
- Project plans are *approved* by management before the project work begins.

At midlevels of project management maturity, oversight can confirm:

- *Best practices* are used by individual projects.
- Defined *standards and methods* are used across projects.
- *Oversight* is conducted project by project.
- *Team members get training* in project management, not just the project manager.
- Projects can utilize a *Project Office* (PMO) for advice and guidance.

At higher levels of project management maturity, oversight can confirm:

- The integrated project *life-cycle methodology* is used by teams and by contractors.
- Standards are *similar across projects so they align in handoff of deliverables.*
- Projects are *reviewed* against the strategic plan before they are approved to begin.

- Project *benefits are tracked* at the program level and captured at project closure.
- A governance process provides management support, decisions, and direction across projects and programs.

At the highest levels of maturity, oversight confirms:

- A process to *improve project performance* is in place supported by management.
- Best practices are applied *across projects (enterprise-wide or in functional groups).*
- There is *continuous improvement* of processes practiced by teams and programs.
- Projects reuse *"lessons learned"* via a process and a common repository.
- The methodology is appropriate to the types of projects the organization does on a repeat basis, and the methodology is maintained and improved over time.

If more than one area of improvement is identified or more than one model is being used in different areas, for the sake of simplicity, work on one model should be pursued to a plateau and then work on another begun. As the models begin to reach a common level of advancement, the overlap will become clear. Until then, any progress helps.

THE PROJECT MANAGEMENT OFFICE OR PROGRAM MANAGEMENT OFFICE (PMO)

Progress in improving organizational project management maturity can be enhanced by establishing an organizational function devoted specifically to supporting projects. Organizations name their offices based on their understanding of their function. The responsibilities, organization, and terminology of these organizational units will vary considerably from one enterprise to another. Following are a few of the most common (see Figure 12-3):

   • *Project support office (PSO) or project office.* Organizations that are less mature probably will have independent projects scattered throughout the organization, but they will be managed independently, with little central direction or guidance. For those organizations, a centralized office that provides project support for individual projects may be a big step forward. Specialized staff can be assigned to help individual project managers work more effectively, plan their projects, estimate effort and resources, use software, identify best practices, resolve issues, streamline project results, and leverage individual knowledge and skills.

  • *Project management office (PMO).* Organizations that are standardizing and strengthening project management use a PMO to centralize data on multiple projects, disseminate information, advise on processes, advance best practices, search out benchmark information, draw in expertise in specialized areas, sponsor seminars, and perhaps monitor the impact of a particular project on a program or portfolio.

  • *Program management office (PMO).* Programs focus more effort on stakeholder management and delivery of project benefits and work to put a governance infrastructure in place for enterprise-wide management of projects. A program management office can provide policy, methods, tools, templates, and training for the management of projects, as well as:

  • Product management and testing information
  • Ratios of levels of effort per development stage and planning heuristics
  • Projected changes in the organization's established methods or policies
  • Current performance measures being used by management
  • Methods for developing and tracking requirements and improving compliance

FIGURE 12-3   Elements of project support offices. The support provided to projects by a PSO can vary significantly based on whether it is weak or strong.

Area	Weak	Strong
Standards methodology	May or may not exist	Documented
Forms templates	May or may not exist	Complete set of project templates
Human resources	No staff volunteers or shared resources	Projects are staffed by PSO employees
Compliance with methodology and templates	Optional	Mandatory
Project records	Collected and filed (document repository)	Created by PSO
Continuous improvement	Ad hoc	Automatic

A program management office can also provide:

- Advice on potential negative impact or demand while planning projects
- Updates on the organization's strategic initiatives and budget
- Sources of external expertise and information on the Internet

Once project managers have a common understanding of what the organization considers fundamental to a successful project and have aligned their processes and tools, integrating projects across groups can become the focus of program improvement. Policies that unite efforts toward strategic objectives, initiatives that leverage gains already made, and systems that deploy talent and resources to those initiatives are most likely to benefit the organization as a whole. Many times the PMO will help individual projects align with organizational policies, processes, and standards and also provide training on basic and specialized aspects of project and program management.

Other improvement approaches can be taken, including establishing centers of excellence (an environment for peer development and best practices) and communities of practice (peer networks in common areas of interest without reference to organizational or department lines). Not all approaches to organizational maturity promote project management, yet all advance some aspect of the project management maturity of the organization.

Implementing a PMO

If an organization does not have an organizational unit devoted to improving project management, it can put a project in place to create a PMO. If the organization attempted to create a PMO in the past but it was unsuccessful, it can use project management and change management to design a better fit and transition to the new model. Organizations do not change easily. Transition time is needed to move from tried-and-true methods to a more responsive approach. A team can develop the concept and tailor it to the organization's needs. A few opinion leaders probably will advocate change before the rest of the organization is ready, and early adopters will be identified to try the methods and make sure they work before the majority is willing or able to use the new options. Putting a spotlight on these efforts and sharing their experiences eases acceptance. Even with management support for the change effort, it is not easy. When a PMO is introduced for the first time, these are requirements for successful implementation:

1. *A supportive organizational culture.* Implementing a PMO will take longer if the organization has a top-down authoritative culture with "silos" of management territory under competing leadership. Project management requires open communications and cross-sharing of information and talent, assuming that the benefits of the project to the organization outweigh the individual benefits to a single division or department.

2. *Readiness to implement a PMO.* Individuals and groups may be loyal to different methodologies or views of project management and resist giving up their success to accept a central approach or version. A PMO works to achieve standardization across projects and across groups, allowing tailoring of those common approaches to individual project needs. However, full freedom to manage a project without direction from the organization does diminish. For better success, provide executive support publicly.

3. *Tolerance for paperwork/overhead.* Documenting processes, recording decisions, and communicating progress centrally can add to the workload of an already busy team. The benefits of documentation are not intuitively obvious and may need to be "sold." After transition, things get much simpler.

The strategic role of the PMO is to implement project management processes, policies, standards, and tools across the organization. Therefore—unless you redefine roles—you can expect resistance from dominant sectors that stand to lose power and influence. There may be political battles among groups that had top billing for their previous achievements or obstruction from those who have used individual influence to shape the views of management. To minimize these negative influences, adjust the performance recognition and reward system to shift management's support to the desired new behaviors and make the new rules visible through executive support, meetings, and publications.

Using a PMO for Improving Organizational Project Management Maturity

A PMO should increase organizational project management maturity by continuous improvement. There are many detailed improvements that are made by a PMO but are not visible to the organization. To enhance the status and leadership profile of the PMO, it helps to pick some visible ways to show the PMO's capability to excel and gain the confidence of the organization. Here are two:

• *Strategic projects.* Strategic projects provide project management guidance and leadership to a visible project with far-reaching results. The improvement will be both noted and discussed in conjunction with the PMO's work and role.
• *External benchmark projects.* Determine how the organization's progress in implementing a PMO compares with comparable organizations external to the improvement effort and publicize favorable findings.

The PMO may be brought into an advisory capacity to top management and asked to look at each project to ensure that:

• Each project is aligned with specific business goals for that quarter or year
• Each project is meeting management's targets, contributing outcomes that advance key process metrics, and conforming to top management policy on strategic use of resources
• Budget and resources are spent on the right project and acknowledge dependencies
• Senior management processes are included in the standard process model

Project managers will not be supportive automatically. Following a defined process can be perceived to undercut the creativity and satisfaction many project managers and leaders derive from running projects independently. Their freedom is somewhat diminished when a standard process is adopted. Those who already have their own style of managing may find the standard process is in conflict with approaches they have used in the past. Recognition systems can help reward those who use the standard process effectively, as well as those who submit "best practice" examples for tailoring the standard process to an individual project's unique needs. Valued individuals whose methods of management no longer align with the new approach can be transferred to other positions where their contributions will still support the organization's goals.

Early in the transition, it is prudent to solicit vendor alignment with the improved project management approach. The process needs to be "owned" by all the suppliers, as well as by all the departments, and such alignments take time. If a PMO is to provide value to them, they need to be involved in defining how that value will be observed and which areas of change have the greatest priority in their area. People are less threatened by change if they have a part in making change happen. The PMO leadership should take responsibility for:

- Managing their perceptions
- Developing an enterprise-wide change strategy
- Communicating it across business processes
- Giving senior management assignments and making them show up

Senior management cannot delegate its role in this to the project manager. Senior management must handle these aspects:

- Formal authorization of the program/project
- Formal delegation of responsibility to the project manager
- Senior designer authority "anointed by senior management"
- Use of project management metrics in the defined management objectives and performance measures

There should be a set number of performance measures that work throughout the enterprise, not just in one program or functional area. Periodically, a status review should be done to determine whether the organization has made progress against the continuum of organizational project management maturity and whether earlier gains have been sustained or lost. If progress is to be shared with managers outside the analyst group, a benign reporting method should be used so as to depoliticize the results. Some organizations use an anonymous spreadsheet that codes groups by letter or number. They do not report the status of any group for which there are fewer than three participating units. Color codes sometimes are used as well: green for goal achieved, yellow for works in progress, and gray (not red) for those not yet begun. If loss of progress is noted, some effort should be put into determining the systemic causes and putting corrective systems in place. People should not be held accountable for progress, because only the lowest levels of maturity rely on individuals to make their organization qualify as mature.

Selling the PSO or PMO to the Organization

One of the first tasks to address when implementing a change in the organization is what the functional groups will perceive to be of value. Do some research on the current status of projects in each area and clearly identify the desired results management wants to realize after a PMO is in place.

Use data to make the business case. Find out which projects are being managed successfully and why. Quantify what percent of projects are not being completed on time and on budget and why. Compare the amount of effort spent properly planning a project with its successful and timely execution. Quantify what percent of projects are getting done on time and on budget by collecting start and finish data. Track the range of deviation across projects by project type. Use proposals and actual finished-project closeout information to reduce data distortion in active projects. Using numbers from closed projects helps to avoid sensitivity to data gathering.

Use lists of "frequently asked questions" (FAQs) with their answers to respond to common concerns. Anticipate objections and have responses to those objections built into the initial presentations on the proposed PMO. Document results and communicate them broadly. Then set up the PMO office to help the projects or support the programs. Provide visible public support for the PMO leadership. Perhaps use a "test area" to show the potential for success. Post successes on public walls or in "war rooms." Eventually the PMO's success will proliferate to successes in other areas.

To smooth the transition to the new way of managing projects, involve management visibly and get project teams that are likely to be successful supporters actively involved with the PMO. Handle problems quickly and remove identified barriers promptly. Build rewards into the process.

Capstone Project Management Programs

When multiple strategic projects are being implemented across organizational lines, there can be whole areas of management concern that do not fall formally under any one organization's hegemony yet are crucial to overall success of the joint effort. Capstone project management programs may be necessary to align multiple projects into a single approach. Examples include many high-technology companies aligning to create a new technological market for their country, cooperative projects that cut across geographic boundaries, collaborative efforts across separate enterprises to manufacture a new product to meet a market need, alignment of government agencies providing disaster relief to a gulf community, and coordination of several military groups cooperating in a single defense initiative. Without a capstone program, the separate authorities may lack coordination. Without a capstone program, different configuration management practices and lexicons in use by each of the separate organizations can lead to multiple systems using different terminology, delivering project outcomes that generate confusion and cannot be integrated. Overlapping implementation schedules and conflicting decision methods may result in projects that not only crowd out each other's impact but also appear ineffective because the success criteria for the separate projects are so different. In other words, the diversity of approaches across projects can threaten the success of the overall initiative. A capstone project management system creates a separate project to integrate and align the organizational structures, training, risks, standards, and terminology across projects so that they make sense to those who will be using them to produce the intended result.

STANDARD PROCESSES TO IMPROVE PROJECT MANAGEMENT

The process used for managing projects in one enterprise group may vary from that used in another enterprise group, but the common process can be distilled from both and used across departmental boundaries. Once a common process is adopted across the enterprise and conforms to standards in the profession, it can be tailored to the specific needs of each group and project. Metrics can be selected to monitor and track common project elements across departments as stable project management processes are used repeatedly over time.

STANDARD METRICS

Trained metrics specialists can select strategic areas for tracking purposes that will produce useful decision data and benchmark those data against similar organizational data in the marketplace. Useful metrics on maturity include the percent of projects with accurate estimates, ranges of variations by type of project, correlation of planned start and finish with actual start and finish by planning method, patterns of resource use by phase across projects, resource-consumption curves across all projects by type, correlation of proposed benefits with realized benefits by type of project, accuracy and effectiveness of risk mitigation and loss reduction by risk management method, and comparisons of project performance with project manager experience level and training. Capturing different metrics can be useful:

- Planning metrics capture historical data from phase estimates at the project level and at phase gate reviews across projects at the program level; resulting ratios of resource use by phase and type of project can be used to create models for budget allocation.
- Value metrics can provide insight into the organization's ability to leverage resources to achieve strategic goals. Metrics on the expenditure of resources by type of project can be useful in predicting costs by total project

or by phase. The expenditure of resources against value produced at a specific point in the project can be measured on individual projects when data are reliable (see Chapter 11).

• Risk metrics are useful in managing portfolios and programs for visibility into sources and types of organizational risk across multiple projects. (The project sponsor determines the risk threshold for individual projects with the project manager and team. Top management determines the acceptable risk threshold for the organization's entire project portfolio and across multiple projects tied to strategic goals.)

As the processes are repeated, the metrics become more reliable. While these metrics are outside the project's control, the project does have control over the quality of metrics contributed to the management database. Senior project managers can often recommend which project data are adequately stable and reliable for inclusion in metrics-based decisions.

Metrics for use across projects are established by developing and using a stable process over an extended period of time. In organizations where a standard project management process has evolved and has been used for at least a year across projects, metrics can be developed across projects to predict trends related to projects. To create a risk metric for multiple projects, for example, a five-point scale can be established for a given risk event, with two columns for impact level and impact value. Together they generate a project risk score (sum of the highest 20 project risks). Using an aggregate of individual project risk ratings, the organization can create its own risk threshold to be applied across multiple projects and use it in project oversight. For example, when any single project's risk score trends toward exceeding the threshold, the executive responsible for oversight can begin to evaluate whether to extend it and increase cost or cancel it and absorb the loss of what has already been expended in the business context of the organization's strategic goals. As a precaution, collect metrics for an extended time before using them for decisions.[17]

Organizations have been striving for decades to find ways to stabilize the numbing effects of unrelenting change on their business environment. A number of approaches have proliferated across industries and within functional areas. None of them has been effective in addressing how organizations can improve their organizational project management maturity. One model, OPM3, provides surveys to identify current practices, dependent processes, and indicators of existing elements of project management maturity. Additional methods may need to be devised to improve the organization's status on the maturity continuum, particularly target areas where improvements will pay off. The receptiveness to such efforts will vary, depending on the organization. The solution, of course, depends not only on the environment of the organization undertaking its own improvement but also on management's view of the areas most likely to demonstrate success.

One of the most common units for hosting such efforts is the PMO, which can be strong or weak. Whether the PMO leads the effort or follows management's lead, the most important focus is to choose the best way to prepare the organization for change and to give the PMO adequate authority to do its job. Whether PMO stands for a project support office, a standardized central function to align projects, or a programmatic arm of senior management to implement change, a strategy and plan are needed to accomplish desired results. Whenever something completely new is implemented for the first time, the organization should launch the first effort as a project, applying project management processes to control goal achievement in an unpredictable confluence of variables. Once the initial effort has stabilized a platform for continued operations, the new function can be turned over to a manager and run as part of operations. Once the new operation is in place, it can be improved gradually over time. Ultimately, the entire infrastructure should be refined for an integrated supportive project management environment, including policy, standards, training, tools, and refined processes that support not only the creation and management of projects but also each of the project management knowledge areas.

CONCLUSION

The strategic context for project management is shifting. Many books written about project management in the past were created for industries, government, and contractors that had already adopted project management processes and practices in the mid–twentieth century. This book takes a twenty-first-century perspective. It interprets the basic concepts and practices of project management for those who manage projects in a professional context, positions them for technological and economic changes, and recommends strategies for improvement into the future.

The proportion of projects in organizations is increasing simply because the pace of change is increasing. Projects are how organizations launch new products, create new services, and achieve desired results in a different way from what worked in the past.

• In prior decades—particularly after World War II—organizations focused on operations. The challenge to management was controlling growth and stabilizing and controlling variability. Projects were seen as simply "nonstandard" operations, doing something different and often proving profitable as a result.

- Today projects comprise an increasingly larger share of the organizational budget. Project management is being recognized as a core business process, as necessary but different from operations. Organizations that wish to deliver on their strategic objectives with predictable results are focusing more attention on projects and project management. They are improving their project management environment, culture, methods, processes, and resources. Project management is designed to manage change, and change is the order of the day.

Today, project management as a distinct discipline has spread to many types of organizations and to countries around the globe. The people who use project management include managers, technical professionals, business analysts, product developers, consultants, researchers, and change agents. Higher education and even the lower grades are incorporating project management into their preparation of workers for the business world of the future.

Analysts predict an even greater demand for project managers in decades to come. The complexity of managing initiatives that cut across organizational and cultural boundaries requires professional skills and capability. Those who have decided to pursue a career in project management need a solid foundation on how project management applies in a professional work setting. They need a process for planning and executing projects and a good grasp of methods and practices that endure over time.

In earlier chapters we provided a definition of project management and why it requires different management approaches. Through examples and project management concepts, we presented the fundamentals of project phases for planning and management of the project, as well as how aligning the project boundaries with product life-cycle stages creates different types of projects.

The characteristics of the project management leader stand out from those of other types of management leaders. Project management leaders use different styles, views, and problem-solving approaches to create project solutions from those used by operations managers.

The process of managing projects is described and diagrammed—a simple but profoundly useful series of process steps that, if followed rigorously, result in a well-defined plan that maximizes resources and minimizes barriers. (A basic project process model is provided in Appendix A.) The resulting plan is entered into a scheduling tool, and progress is tracked as the team carries out the tasks in the plan. Only when a project is fully planned does the triple constraint apply, allowing the team to make trade-offs among the competing requirements and constraints, ultimately delivering quality performance on time and on budget. Some of the planning concepts that underlie this deceptively simple approach to projects include not only the development of a project plan, but also the project manager's role, character traits, autonomy, authority, and accountability, as well as her freedom to manage creatively the many challenges that projects encounter.

The process is described in detail over several chapters. Initiation is the process group that defines the boundaries, requirements, and constraints the project must honor, as well as the mission, vision, and critical success factors for the project itself. In high-level planning, the strategic elements of the project are defined and verified, and project success criteria, product or service requirements, and a work breakdown structure (WBS) are established for the project's approach. The team then undertakes detailed planning for execution of the plan. Incorporating prior project history, formulas, skills, and team contributions, the plan begins to take shape. Top-down estimates of management are integrated with bottom-up estimates of the team members who will do the work. Eventually an agreed-on plan is ready for management approval. The approaches to start-up are also created, preparing the team and the project site for effective work. The project manager integrates the tasks of the high-level and detailed plans, resolving issues, adding controls, and readjusting estimates of the effort and time needed to complete the project.

Then the project manager begins building and developing a team for project plan execution. Team methods and techniques are used to forge a working group focused on quality and results. The collaboration and cooperation of multiple viewpoints from stakeholders and customers are used to improve the quality of the plan and anticipate and mitigate risks. Management's support and involvement are solicited and engaged to give the project the organizational and political support it needs to succeed.

When the project shifts from planning to actually doing the work, facilitating project execution requires the use of the knowledge areas standard to the project management profession. All of the functional areas of knowledge and skill required to manage an enterprise are re-created on a limited scale as they apply to projects: project integration management, project scope management, project time management, project cost management, project quality management, project human resource management, project communications management, project risk management, and project procurement management are put in place to ensure the project successfully reaches its conclusion, delivering a quality product or service on time and on budget, to get management's desired results. Some processes apply throughout, others at key stages of the project.

There are core processes that advance the work of the project and facilitating processes that help to ensure success. While the stages of the deliverable may vary, the processes are common across projects. The project team applies relevant "best practices" and record lessons learned for the benefit of organizational improvement and successful future projects. Finally, at close-out, the project work and the administrative aspects of the team are finished, and the team disbands.

One area that is harder to create is a quality context for project management. By staying close to the issues of the project environment, using experts, tracking variables that affect the work, and using a professional information management and decision process, project managers and teams can help to ensure that the value of their work endures beyond the close of the project itself.

Controlling project work is an area that has been given a lot of attention in prior years. The tools and infrastructure of the work setting may change with technology, but they establish a means of testing the accuracy of assumptions and estimates, anticipating trends, accentuating positive influences, and reducing negative effects from unforeseen sources. (Some of the more common templates for consolidating the information needed for effective project planning and control are provided in Appendix B.) Controlling work has been an important function in the past due to the chaos created by rapid growth and large organizational structures. But market forces and global competitive environments have reduced both the number and size of organizations, and control is no longer more important than flexible responses to change.

The new focus in organizations is on diagnosing and improving how the organization as a whole manages its projects. Called *organizational project management maturity*, this new focus has been enhanced by a model for enterprise-wide use known as *OPM3*. As this and other models are applied, the ability of organizations to repeat project strategic delivery over and over again will improve and the financial return on the project investment will become clear. Individual project teams can use simpler guides such as the one provided in Appendix C to assess the elements needed for their success.

This book puts project management in context, explaining through examples and analogies not only what is needed to deliver successful projects but also why projects are managed differently from day-to-day operations. It emphasizes the interests of professionals working in today's global organizations and acknowledges today's changing infrastructure, shifting technology, and business context. It also provides pointers to additional sources of information.

As an added bonus, this book assembles a set of basic reference materials a project manager or project professional can use to structure and manage a project, to train the team, to generate discussion, or to review the organization's support across projects. The book's Appendixes include useful examples, case studies, and models.

A **Project Management Process Model** is included in **Appendix A**. The reader can use it as a road map for initiating, planning, executing (and updating) the plan, and closing out a project. It diagrams the basic managerial process steps a project must move through as it drives toward completion. A process model can be used to guide discussion as the team begins planning. It also can be used for discussing the project's management process with the project sponsor, the customer, the project team, and any contractors or subproject teams. It uses common terms that apply in most contexts. It also can serve as the enterprise-wide common process across projects because it is based on the consensus of professionals from different industries creating project management standards that apply globally.

The **Templates** provided in **Appendix B** are primarily tools for capturing and rounding out necessary information needed to manage the project process. These templates can be used to:

- Identify and collect the planning information needed to shape a project and get charter approval, such as the deliverable product's life-cycle stages to be included in the project scope, any organization processes affected, or the names of other projects that affect the project or will depend on its outputs
- Complete and refine existing formats the organization already uses, such as status reports or staff effort estimates
- Capture information that will become parts of the project's overall plan, such as customer requirements, deliverables acceptance criteria, issues, or risks
- Analyze the effects of changes on the plan, staffing, risk, schedule, or budget

Once the critical information is captured in one central location, the project team can tailor it to the unique needs of each project or use the completed templates as a basic resource to align information across projects. Some of the information such as team member names, the work breakdown structure, milestone schedules, and delivery dates—will be entered into scheduling software the team will use for tracking progress. Still others—

such as the project change request log—will be maintained in the team data files, continuously updated as the planning and management of the project progresses.

Template information is intended for use by the project manager and team to communicate with each other, with sponsors and stakeholders, and to manage the team planning process.

Other information in the back of the book, such as the **Organizational Assessment** in **Appendix C**, is useful in gauging whether the organization as a whole has the appropriate infrastructure and management practices to support project success. A survey like this one can be distributed manually to senior professionals and project managers and tallied offline for a confidential view of how the organization infrastructure and managerial practices stack up against best practices in other organizations. If improvement projects are under way, the results of such a survey may help determine change management strategy or flesh out the risk plan.

The **Case Study** in **Appendix D** and the **Deliverables' Life Cycles** in **Appendix E** are useful for training, college seminars, and project management discussion groups. Trainees can identify the phases of the project or the development stages of the project's deliverable, or they can select which stage(s) of the product life cycle will be included in project scope before the project is planned, improving management of stakeholder and customer expectations and budget justification.

The **Answer Key** to review questions and the **Final Examination** (both available online at mhprofessional.com) allow the reader to conduct structured self-study, a model encouraged by PMI when submitting PDU credits for maintaining the PMP credential (Professional Development Units = PDUs).

Regardless of the value contributed by process models, templates, procedures, software, and tools, it is still the project management professional who delivers the value on projects.

Those who are building a career in project management will find it useful to build on existing knowledge, test their knowledge and experience against others in the field, and contribute their advancements to the profession as a whole. Taking the test provided with this book can help build a foundation for further learning. Joining others in a professional society that operates globally not only will provide access to information in this advancing profession but also will prepare today's project management professional for job challenges in the future. Applying for and completing a project management certification can communicate your knowledge to others and help in setting goals for further career development.

KEY CONCEPTS TO REMEMBER

If you walk away from this book with nothing more than these, here are the key concepts worth remembering.

Projects are created to manage the creation of products, services, or plans that cannot be produced through normal operations. Projects are how organizations implement change. Many of the changes relate directly to the organization's strategic goals. Organizations that are effective at delivering strategic objectives are also good at projects.

Because of the risks inherent in doing anything for the first time, the project management knowledge and processes are designed to identify, manage, and mitigate risk. An organization's day-to-day operations address risk incrementally over a longer period of time. Management and customers need to acknowledge the risk aspects of projects and allow for variances.

Projects are created to structure work so that it can be accomplished successfully. Each project phase builds the necessary foundation for the next phase. Initiation, planning, execution, and closeout all have their management deliverables, enabling conduct of the next phase. Aligning the phases of a project with the stage of the product's life cycle determines the type of project.

You cannot manage what you cannot control, and you cannot control what you have not planned. If inadequate information exists to plan the project, a project must be formed to define the requirements of the project and create a plan. The triple constraint, often referred to as producing a final deliverable "on time and on budget" is a meaningless concept if the effort has not been properly planned and estimated and the estimate ranges have not been approved as reasonable and achievable by the project sponsor, customer, and team.

Even with effective processes, knowledge, skills, techniques, and tools, the project manager and team have a lot to manage. Projects are fraught with risk and unknowns. The project manager and team need the authority, decision autonomy, and discretion to decide what is important to the project and to ignore the rest. And they need the backing of management to do things differently within the project. Project management professionals are not just another manager with a different name. They are leaders whose job is to anticipate and manage potential future events. Teamwork, integrity, trust, and ethical professional conduct are fundamental to the profession and to earning and keeping the autonomy a project requires.

Planning is fundamental. People must perform it. Planning cannot be carried out by either a process or a tool. Quality planning enables quality projects. Quality planning requires team and stakeholder participation and good decision methods. Once a plan is developed, parts of it can be entered into a scheduling tool and status can be tracked against what the team agreed was reasonable. Plans, however, are never final. They are simply a means to effective project management. The only final numbers in a project are those at closeout.

Projects throughout history have been planned and managed with great success. Human analytical methods and manual tools have been around for centuries. But the ability to leverage technology in managing projects is a recent development. Since U.S. government and NASA projects in the 1950s were the first to codify project management processes and methods, and the early adopters were government contractors, many of the early tools and models in our technology today reflect the needs and interests of those organizations. New tools and methods are emerging to manage multiple projects across the enterprise and apply telecommunications, the Internet, and digital technology. Some are capable of managing at more advanced levels of project management maturity, enabling collaboration, customer involvement, and alignment of projects and subprojects across continents and time zones. But not every collaborative tool has sophisticated project management capability. Selecting the right tools and methods for different types of projects is one way the project professional shapes a project's approach to deliver results.

Just as management actually delegates aspects of the management job to professionals in functional and staff departments, management also delegates the management of projects to the project management office (PMO) and project professionals. These professionals differ sufficiently in their skill sets and values to warrant being called a separate profession. While not every project is large or complex enough to require a project management professional, every project needs a designated project manager.

Project management professionals are expected to comply with laws, practice ethically, continue their professional education, seek appropriate credentials or certification, and contribute to the common knowledge as in any other profession. When they undertake a project, they are expected to assess the complexity of the project and the adequacy of their own capability and knowledge. They should stay abreast of emerging technologies and trends to ensure their career futures and to help their own organizations advance in their project management maturity. Best practices and lessons learned are of value and should be part of every project.

The process of project management is common across all types of projects but tailored to the unique needs of each. Different industries may adopt a process tailored to their industry. A project management maturity model can help management put the process support and infrastructure in place to deliver repeated successes in a predictable manner and to improve how reliably the organization's management achieves its strategic objectives. While metrics are useful for supporting management decisions, only stable processes can be used to create metrics. While most processes in projects are too new to be useful in metrics management, a standardized common project management process across the enterprise can be. Data collected at transition points in the process model, collected in the same manner and refined over time, can create reliable project management metrics useful for decision purposes.

The scheduling software, templates, techniques, and heuristics of project management are simply job aids. The project professional holds the key to project success, working closely with the sponsor, customer, and other stakeholders to shape the project and deliver on its promises. Just as a physician uses years of practice to augment the knowledge gained in medical school to make an appropriate diagnosis of a patient's illness, and just as an attorney uses arguing before the bar plus mastery of case law and structured analysis to back up a professional courtroom strategy, the project management professional taps lots of hands-on project experience together with the PMBOK and management best practices to navigate the rough waters of the project environment. Project management is not just a role. It is not just a skill. It takes a lot of professional wisdom and creative problem solving to bring a project to a successful conclusion.

ADVANCING BOTH THE PROJECT AND THE PROFESSION

People who have chosen project management as their career can enjoy the benefits of advancements being made today in organizational project management maturity. Each project professional can contribute to a common understanding and promote recognition of the project management profession by becoming a practicing certified professional. Through PMI and other project management associations around the world, certifications and professional practice designations are available for professionals in project management worldwide.

Although many organizations have mature project management environments, many others do not fully understand the roles and rules associated with project management. As a result, they underestimate its professional complexity.

Individuals who are building careers in project management can do a great deal to establish credibility for project management through their actions. Using available avenues of education, peer networks, research, tools, professional certification, and common standards, each individual not only can benefit his own project but also can advance the profession. As the positions in project management mature and organizations integrate project management roles and positions into their career paths, the global network for career advancement also will stabilize and grow.

As project management professionals contribute to the organizational project management maturity of their employers and clients, others will be more likely to recognize the capabilities required for project success. More formal positions are likely to be established, allowing lifelong career advancement for those who choose project management as their career. If maturity keeps up with growth in the field, everyone will benefit.

As the pace of change increases in our society, the proportion of organizational resources devoted to projects will increase. Executives are putting more focus on projects to protect their investment and ensure their organization's goal achievement. Poorly managed projects can pose a threat to an organization's reputation, profitability, and even viability in a changing business future. As organizations advance their project management maturity, the improvements made to the project process will be reflected in increased revenue, better control over strategic initiatives, and more satisfied clients.

REVIEW QUESTIONS

1. In selling a PSO or PMO to your organization, one of the first tasks to address is what the functional groups will perceive to be its:
   a. cost
   b. value
   c. urgency
   d. importance
2. OPM3 is PMI's:
   a. open project management method and model
   b. organizational project management maturity model
   c. criteria for the certification of a project management professional
   d. none of the above
3. Strong project management offices will:
   a. be accountable for selecting which projects will receive scarce resources
   b. have a dedicated project management staff

      c.   manage key projects to completion

      d.   maintain documentation for all projects

      e.   approve changes to a project

      f.   all of the above

      g.   *a, b,* and *c* but not *d* and not *e*

4. **When applying process improvement concepts to project management, one of the several areas that process maturity must address is:**

      a.   the processes that the organization uses to support the unique functions of projects, most of which are somewhat different from those of operations

      b.   the unique processes by which products are created

      c.   *a* and *b*

      d.   none of the above

5. **Improvements in the organization's project processes will be made:**

      a.   bottom up

      b.   top down

      c.   within the projects

      d.   *a* and *b*

6. **Project management maturity implies maturity in:**

      a.   standards and policies

      b.   structures and systems

      c.   training in all key project management knowledge areas

      d.   training in all critical success factors for projects

      e.   all of the above

      f.   none of the above

      g.   *a, b,* and *c* only

7. **In a mature project environment, the host organization need not be supportive of projects.**

      a.   true

      b.   false

8. **Is project management increasingly recognized as a core business function?**

      a.   yes

      b.   no

9. **It is clear that some of the success of a well-executed project can be attributed to:**

      a.   the sponsoring organization's readiness to support projects to their successful conclusion

      b.   the options the project team has for creating any support systems within the project that are missing externally

      c.   the knowledge, talent, and ingenuity of the project leadership

      d.   the risk profile of the project and its costs

     e.   *a, b,* and *c*

     f.   *a* and *b* only

10. Using an aggregate of individual project risk ratings, the organization can create its own risk threshold to be applied across multiple projects.

     a.   true

     b.   false

A

PROCESS MODEL

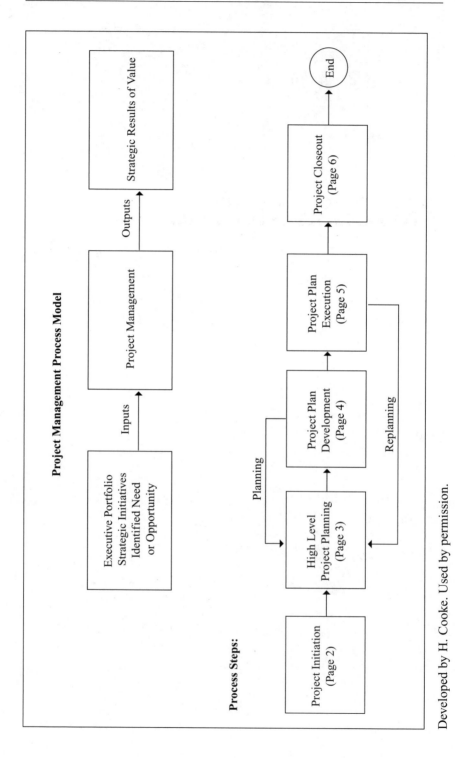

Developed by H. Cooke. Used by permission.

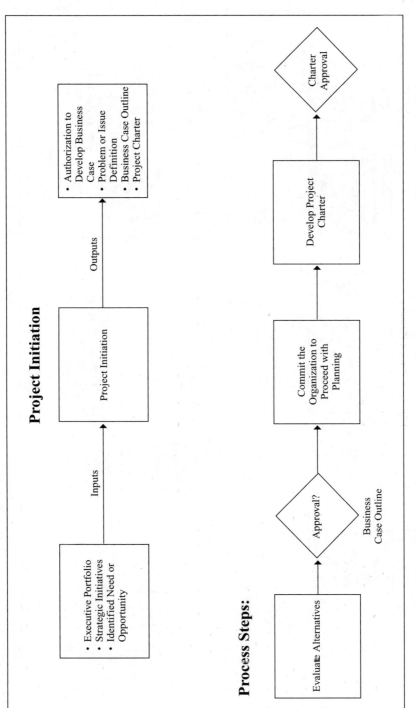

Project Initiation

Inputs → Project Initiation → Outputs

- Executive Portfolio
- Strategic Initiatives
- Identified Need or Opportunity

- Authorization to Develop Business Case
- Problem or Issue Definition
- Business Case Outline
- Project Charter

Process Steps:

Evaluate Alternatives → Approval? → Commit the Organization to Proceed with Planning → Develop Project Charter → Charter Approval

Business Case Outline

Developed by H. Cooke. Used by permission.

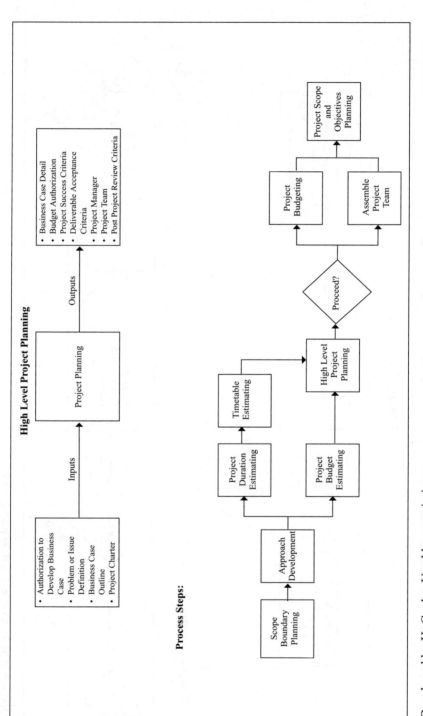

High Level Project Planning

Inputs:
- Authorization to Develop Business Case
- Problem or Issue Definition
- Business Case Outline
- Project Charter

Project Planning

Outputs:
- Business Case Detail
- Budget Authorization
- Project Success Criteria
- Deliverable Acceptance Criteria
- Project Manager
- Project Team
- Post Project Review Criteria

Process Steps:

Scope Boundary Planning → Approach Development → Project Duration Estimating → Timetable Estimating → High Level Project Planning

Project Budget Estimating → High Level Project Planning

High Level Project Planning → Proceed? → Project Budgeting → Project Scope and Objectives Planning

Proceed? → Assemble Project Team → Project Scope and Objectives Planning

Developed by H. Cooke. Used by permission.

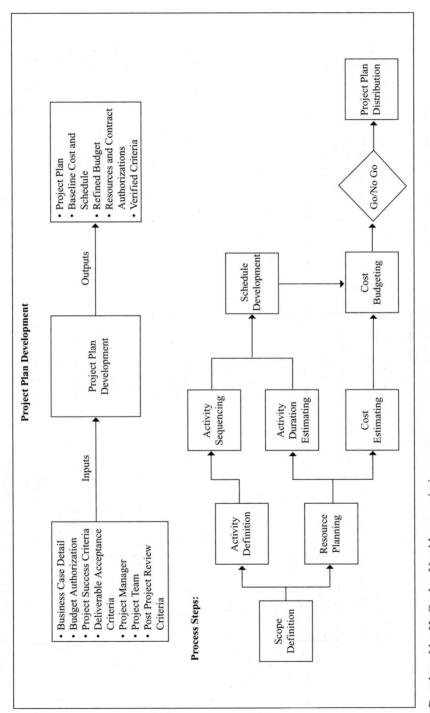

Project Plan Development

Inputs

- Business Case Detail
- Budget Authorization
- Project Success Criteria
- Deliverable Acceptance Criteria
- Project Manager
- Project Team
- Post Project Review Criteria

Project Plan Development

Outputs

- Project Plan
- Baseline Cost and Schedule
- Refined Budget
- Resources and Contract Authorizations
- Verified Criteria

Process Steps:

Scope Definition

Activity Definition

Resource Planning

Activity Sequencing

Activity Duration Estimating

Cost Estimating

Schedule Development

Cost Budgeting

Go/No Go

Project Plan Distribution

Developed by H. Cooke. Used by permission.

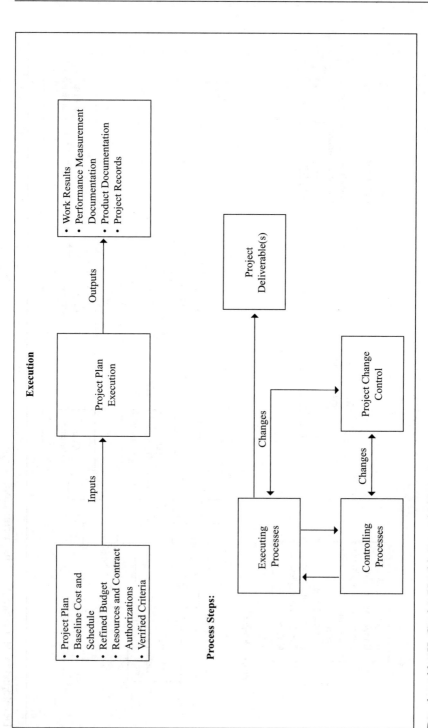

Execution

- Project Plan
- Baseline Cost and Schedule
- Refined Budget
- Resources and Contract Authorizations
- Verified Criteria

Inputs →

Project Plan Execution

Outputs →

- Work Results
- Performance Measurement Documentation
- Product Documentation
- Project Records

Process Steps:

Executing Processes

Controlling Processes

Project Change Control

Project Deliverable(s)

Changes

Changes

Developed by H. Cooke. Used by permission.

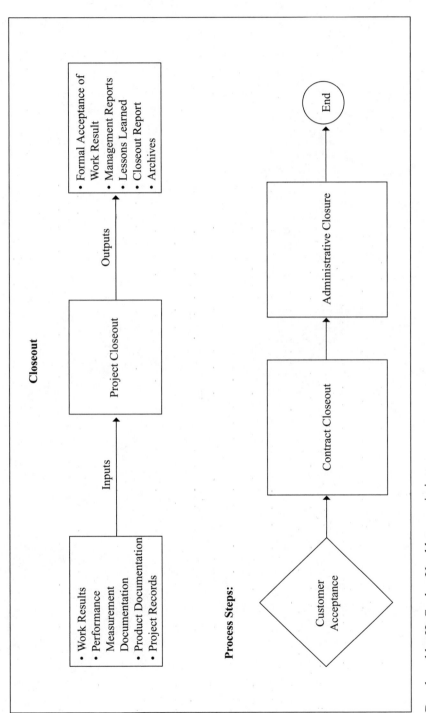

Closeout

Inputs
- Work Results
- Performance Measurement Documentation
- Product Documentation
- Project Records

Outputs
- Formal Acceptance of Work Result
- Management Reports
- Lessons Learned
- Closeout Report
- Archives

Project Closeout

Process Steps:

Customer Acceptance → Contract Closeout → Administrative Closure → End

Developed by H. Cooke. Used by permission.

APPENDIX

B

TEMPLATES

PROJECT CHARTER TEMPLATE

Prepared By:	
Date Issued:	
Project Name:	

Project Scope

Business Case	
Project Objectives	
Project Customers	
Customer Needs	
Final Deliverable(s)	
Customer Requirements	
Life-Cycle Stages	
Customer Acceptance Criteria	
Key Stakeholders	
Organizational Deliverables	
Organizational Acceptance Criteria	
Organizational Goals	

Project Assurance

Scope Risk Limit	
Reviews & Approvals Required	
Status Reports Required	

Project Resources

Team Assignments	
Deadlines	
Staff Effort Limit	
Spending Limit	
Organizational Constraints	
Project Priorities	

Used by permission. The Griffin Tate Group, Inc.

LIST OF DELIVERABLES

Deliverable	Customer Needs	Customer Requirements	Features/ Functions	Customer Acceptance Criteria

Used by permission. The Griffin Tate Group, Inc.

SCOPE BOUNDARIES TEMPLATE

Project Name:	Project Leader:

Deliverable Life-Cycle Stages Included	Why?

Processes Included	Why?

Processes That Are Not Included	Why?

Processes Affected	Why?

Projects Affected	Why?

Used by permission. The Griffin Tate Group, Inc.

INTERIM DELIVERABLES

Project Name:	Project Leader:	
Interim Deliverable	Internal Customer Acceptance Criteria	Measures

Used by permission. The Griffin Tate Group, Inc.

WORK BREAKDOWN STRUCTURE

Project Name: _____   Project Leader: _____

Project Name	Subproject Name/ Person Accountable	Final Deliverable(s)	Interim Deliverables

Used by permission. The Griffin Tate Group, Inc.

PROJECT ISSUES LIST

Date Issued:

Project Name:

Issue #	Description of Issue	Person Who Needs Resolution	Person Responsible to Resolve	Date Resolution Needed	Date Resolved	How Resolved
1						
2						
3						
4						
5						
6						
7						
8						
9						
10						
11						
12						
13						
14						
15						

Used by permission. The Griffin Tate Group, Inc.

SCOPE RISK ANALYSIS TEMPLATE

Deliverable	Risk Limit	Risks	Risk Rating	Countermeasures	Included?	Person Accountable to Implement Countermeasure

Used by permission. The Griffin Tate Group, Inc.

REVIEWS & APPROVALS TEMPLATE

Project Name:

Project Sponsor:

Deliverable	Person Accountable	Purpose of Review	Reviewers	Approvals? (Yes/No) Who?	Review Start Date	Review End Date	Person to Coordinate Comments

STATUS REPORTS PLAN TEMPLATE

Project Name: _____   Project Sponsor: _____

Report Name	Frequency or Due Date	Person Accountable	Content	Distribution

TEAM COMPOSITION ANALYSIS TEMPLATE

Project Name:	Project Leader:

CORE SKILLS REQUIRED

Skills Required	Team Representative	Team Status	Department Represented

STAKEHOLDER INTERESTS REPRESENTED

Processes Included	Team Representative	Team Status	Team Member Liaison

Processes or Projects Affected	Team Representative	Team Status	Team Member Liaison

Used by permission. The Griffin Tate Group, Inc.

MILESTONE SCHEDULE TEMPLATE		
Project Name:		**Project Leader:**

Phase	Date	Milestone
Planning		Project Start
		Project Plan Approved
Execution		
		Final Deliverable(s) Accepted
Closeout		Closeout Report Complete

Used by permission. The Griffin Tate Group, Inc.

DELIVERABLES SCHEDULE INPUT TEMPLATE

Project Name:

Project Sponsor:

No.	Subproject or Deliverable Name	Duration	Start Date	Delivery Date	Predecessors	Successors	Person Accountable
1							
2							
3							
4							
5							
6							
7							
8							
9							
10							
11							
12							
13							
14							
15							
16							
17							
18							
19							
20							

Used by permission. The Griffin Tate Group, Inc.

SCHEDULE RISK ANALYSIS

Project Name:

Project Sponsor:

Deliverable	Deadline	Risk Rating	Risk	Countermeasures	Included?	Person Accountable

Used by permission. The Griffin Tate Group, Inc.

STAFF EFFORT ESTIMATE TEMPLATE

Project Name: Project Sponsor:

Staff Effort				Staff Cost***		
Team Member or Subproject Name	Project Mgmt. Work Effort*	Deliverables Work Effort**	Total Staff Effort	Cost per Staff Unit	Total Cost
TOTALS:					
ACCURACY RATING:					
RANGE:					
STAFF LIMIT:					

Reason for Accuracy Rating of Staff Effort Estimate:

Used by permission. The Griffin Tate Group, Inc.

SPENDING ESTIMATE TEMPLATE	
Project Sponsor:	

Type of Expense	Cost
Internal Costs	
SUBTOTAL:	
ACCURACY RATING*:	
RANGE:	
INTERNAL COST SPENDING LIMIT:	
External Costs	
SUBTOTAL:	
ACCURACY RATING*:	
RANGE:	
EXTERNAL COST SPENDING LIMIT:	
INTERNAL & EXTERNAL TOTAL:	
ACCURACY RATING*:	
RANGE:	
TOTAL COST SPENDING LIMIT:	

Used by permission. The Griffin Tate Group, Inc.

PROJECT CHANGE REQUEST TEMPLATE

Project Name:	Project Sponsor:

Urgency:

	Change Request #:	Originator:	Change Requested By:	Date Requested:

Justification

Description of Change Requested:

Reason for Change:

Proposed Approach to Resolve:

Impact

Project Plan Area	Impact of Proposed Change(s)
Impact on Scope	
Impact on Scope Risk	
Impact on Schedule	
Impact on Staffing Effort	
Impact on Spending	
Other	

Approvals to Proceed:

Originator/ Date	Project Leader/Date	Sponsor/Date	Customer/Date

Used by permission. The Griffin Tate Group, Inc.

PROJECT CHANGE REQUEST LOG TEMPLATE

Project Name:

Project Sponsor:

Change Request #	Originator	Description of Change	Date	Scope Risk Impact	Schedule Impact	Staffing Impact	Spending Impact	Change Approved? Yes/No
1								
2								
3								
4								
5								
6								
7								
8								
9								
10								
11								
12								
13								
14								
15								

Used by permission. The Griffin Tate Group, Inc.

PROJECT STATUS REPORT TEMPLATE

Project Name:	Project Sponsor:

Reporting Period:	From:	To:

Changes to Plan:

Description of Change	Date	Change Approved?	Revision to Plan

Scope Status:

Deliverable	Internal Customer Acceptance Criteria Met?	Explanation/ Plan of Action

Schedule Status:

Milestone/ Deliverable	Planned Date	Actual Date	Projected Date

	Amount Approved	Actual Spent to Date	Forecast to Completion	Projected Total at Completion	Accuracy Rating of Amount Remaining	Range (Low– High)
Staffing						
Spending						

Overall Scope Quality:	____ Exceeds	____ On	____ Below	____ In Jeopardy
Overall Project Schedule:	____ Exceeds	____ On	____ Below	____ In Jeopardy
Overall Staffing Status:	____ Behind	____ On	____ Over	____ In Jeopardy
Overall Spending Status:	____ Behind	____ On	____ Over	____ In Jeopardy

Issues:

Issue	Action Taken	Action Required	Person Accountable	Required Date

Used by permission. The Griffin Tate Group, Inc.

CUSTOMER/SPONSOR
SATISFACTION FEEDBACK SURVEY

Project Name: | Project Sponsor:

Project Results	Strongly Disagree				Strongly Agree
1. Final deliverable met my acceptance criteria.	1	2	3	4	5
2. Delivery dates met my needs.	1	2	3	4	5
3. Final cost was acceptable.	1	2	3	4	5
4. Organizational deliverable met acceptance criteria.	1	2	3	4	5

Comments:

Project Process	Strongly Disagree				Strongly Agree
1. Project Plan was complete and worked.	1	2	3	4	5
2. Management/sponsor supported the project.	1	2	3	4	5
3. The change management process was effective.	1	2	3	4	5
4. Status reports were clear and complete.	1	2	3	4	5
5. Customer review meetings were effective.	1	2	3	4	5
6. Project team kept the sponsor/ customer informed.	1	2	3	4	5

Comments:

Suggestions for Improvement:

Used by permission. The Griffin Tate Group, Inc.

LESSONS LEARNED RECOMMENDATIONS

Project Name:		Project Sponsor:

PROJECT RESULTS	Went Well	Needs to Change
Scope/Deliverables		
Team Composition		
Schedule		
Staffing		
Spending		
Risks		
PROJECT PROCESS		
Teamwork		
Project Initiation		
Project Plan		
Project Execution		
Project Closeout		

Recommendations:

Used by permission. The Griffin Tate Group, Inc.

APPENDIX

C

A P P E N D I X

ORGANIZATIONAL ASSESSMENT

While there are many factors involved in an organization's project management maturity that do not involve the project team, individuals within the organization can apply their knowledge, skills, tools, and techniques to organizational and project activities to achieve the aims of an organization through projects.

It is in the best interest of the sponsoring organization, its customers, and its project teams to apply best practices and manage its projects, programs, and portfolios in alignment with the achievement of strategic goals.

Use the checklist below to confirm those elements of organizational project management maturity that are involved in your project(s).

Each statement describes a condition of an organization's ability to create successful projects. Circle the number on the scale from 1 to 5 that you think most accurately describes things as they actually are in your organization. Use your assessment to determine the areas you think your organization could improve.

Scale Guidelines

1. Absolutely does not describe our organization
2. Barely describes our organization
3. Moderately describes our organization
4. Adequately describes our organization
5. Absolutely describes our organization

Management Commitment	
Statements	**Scale**
1. Management accepts accountability for the outcome of projects in their areas and in the organization in general, including any project problems caused by an ineffective system.	1 2 3 4 5
2. Project management is seen as a core competency for managers, leaders, and individual contributors.	1 2 3 4 5
3. Managers, leaders, and individual contributors have been trained in core project management skills.	1 2 3 4 5
4. The senior management team accepts accountability for the entire project management system.	1 2 3 4 5

Project Management Method

Statements	Scale
5. The project management method chosen by the organization is consistent with and supports other leadership and business initiatives such as total quality management, team participation, customer focus, etc.	1 2 3 4 5
6. Everyone working on a project is required to use a standard project management method.	1 2 3 4 5
7. Management requires standard status reports from every project team.	1 2 3 4 5
8. Management requires a standard project plan from every project team.	1 2 3 4 5
9. The project management method maximizes the contributions of everyone on the project team.	1 2 3 4 5
10. Management fully supports the project management method chosen by the organization.	1 2 3 4 5

Project Steering

Statements	Scale
11. There are project steering councils in place to select and oversee projects.	1 2 3 4 5
12. All projects are reviewed for strategic fit by the project steering group before they are chartered.	1 2 3 4 5
13. *All* projects are prioritized by a project steering group and resources are allocated by priority.	1 2 3 4 5
14. No more than 100 percent of available resources are allocated to projects.	1 2 3 4 5
15. Key indicators of project progress are reviewed periodically by a project steering group.	1 2 3 4 5

Project Sponsorship

Statements	Scale
16. There is a sponsor for every project team.	1 2 3 4 5
17. All sponsors complete charters as part of project initiation.	1 2 3 4 5
18. Sponsors ensure that project teams have the resources they need to complete the project.	1 2 3 4 5
19. Sponsors champion projects and provide support to project leaders.	1 2 3 4 5
20. Sponsors own the recommendations for improvement generated by the team and ensure that the recommendations are acted on by the management team.	1 2 3 4 5

Deliverables Process Optimization

Statements	Scale
21. Business processes used by projects have been mapped.	1 2 3 4 5
22. Business process templates have been created for the deliverables processes commonly used by project teams.	1 2 3 4 5
23. All key deliverables processes used by project teams (i.e., the software development process or new product introduction process) have been optimized.	1 2 3 4 5
24. Process measures have been identified for all key deliverables processes.	1 2 3 4 5
25. Management ensures that the deliverables processes used by project teams are improved continuously or, when required, reengineered.	1 2 3 4 5

Align Horizontally	
Statements	**Scale**
26. Goals are set for cross-functional processes and projects first, and then functional goals are set so that they align with cross-functional goals.	1 2 3 4 5
27. The reward and recognition systems reward teams as well as individuals.	1 2 3 4 5
28. Functional resource managers work collaboratively in self-directed management teams.	1 2 3 4 5
29. Management has been trained to work horizontally as well as vertically.	1 2 3 4 5
30. Managers walk the talk.	1 2 3 4 5

Accountability	
Statements	**Scale**
31. Each manager is held accountable for the success of the projects of which his or her area is a part.	1 2 3 4 5
32. Sponsors are held accountable for the success of the project leader.	1 2 3 4 5
33. Functional managers are held accountable for contributing to the success of the whole project.	1 2 3 4 5
34. Project leaders are held accountable for the success of the whole project.	1 2 3 4 5
35. Project team members are held accountable for the results of the whole project in addition to their individual results.	1 2 3 4 5
36. Accountability is unconditional.	1 2 3 4 5

D

CASE STUDY

THE WRIGHT BROTHERS' RECORDS
OF THE ACTUAL FLIGHT

Orville wrote:

> Before leaving camp [Kitty Hawk] in 1902 we were already at work on the general design of a new machine which we proposed to propel with a motor.
>
> [*Flight testing*] We left Dayton, September 23, and arrived at our camp at Kill Devil Hill on Friday the 25th. We found there provisions and tools, which had been shipped by freight several weeks in advance. The building, erected in 1901 and enlarged in 1902, was found to have been blown by a storm from its foundation posts a few months previously. While we were awaiting the arrival of the shipment of machinery and parts from Dayton, we were busy putting the old building in repair, and erecting a new building to serve as workshop for assembling and housing the new machine.
>
> [*Risks realized, schedule delays*] Just as the building was being completed, the parts and material for the machines arrived simultaneously with one of the worst storms that had visited Kitty Hawk in years. The storm came on suddenly, blowing 30 to 40 miles an hour. It increased during the night, and the next day was blowing over 75 miles an hour. In order to save the tar-paper roof, we decided it would be necessary to get out in this wind and nail down more securely certain parts that were especially exposed. When I ascended the ladder and reached the edge of the roof, the wind caught under my large coat, blew it up around my head and bound my arms till I was perfectly helpless. Wilbur came to my assistance and held down my coat while I tried to drive the nails. But the wind was so strong I could not guide the hammer and succeeded in striking my fingers as often as the nails.
>
> [*Execution resumes with flight training*] The next three weeks were spent in setting the motor-machine together. On days with more favorable winds we gained additional experience in handling a flyer by gliding with the 1902 machine, which we had found in pretty fair condition in the old building, where we had left it the year before.
>
> [*Use of outside experts*] Mr. Chanute and Dr. Spratt, who had been guests in our camp in 1901 and 1902, spent some time with us, but neither one was able to remain to see the test of the motor-machine, on account of the delays caused by trouble which developed in the propeller shafts. While Mr. Chanute was with us, a good deal of time was spent in discussion of the mathematical calculations upon which we had based our machine. He informed us that, in designing machinery, about 20 percent was usually allowed for the loss in the transmission of power. As we had allowed only 5 percent, a figure we had arrived at by some crude measurements of the friction of one of the chains when carrying only a very light load, we were much alarmed. More than the whole surplus in power allowed in our calculations would, accord[ing] to Mr. Chanute's estimate, be consumed in friction in the

driving chains. After Mr. Chanute's departure we suspended one of the drive chains over a sprocket, hanging bags of sand on either side of sprocket of a weight approximately equal to the pull that would be exerted on the chains when driving the propellers. By measuring the extra amount of weight needed on one side to lift the weight [on] the other, we calculated the loss in transmission. This indicated that the loss of power from this source would be only 5 percent, as we originally estimated.

Equipment problems and workarounds: Unnerved by the correction and an inability to test it, they found two more problems:

The first run of the motor on the machine developed a flaw in one of the propeller shafts which had not been discovered in Dayton. [Two weeks were required to send for a new tube shaft and make the repair.]

A new trouble developed. The sprockets which were screwed on the shafts, and locked with nuts of opposite thread, persisted in coming loose. After many futile attempts to get them fast, we had to give it up and went to bed much discouraged. [Solution: "If tire cement was good for fastening the hands on a stop watch, why should it not be good for fastening the sprockets on the propeller of a flying machine? . . . The trouble was over. The sprockets stayed fast."]

[*Risks realized*] More weather delays, wind, rain and snow. A wind of 25 to 30 miles (per hour) blew for several days from the north.

[*Metrics and an alternative path*] While we were being delayed by the weather we arranged a mechanism to measure automatically the durations of a flight from the time the machine started to move forward to the time it stopped, the distance traveled through the air in that time, and the number of revolutions made by the motor and propeller. A stopwatch took the time; an anemometer measured the air traveled through; and a counter took the number of revolutions made by the propellers. The watch, anemometer, and revolution counter were all automatically started and stopped simultaneously. From data thus obtained we expected to prove or disprove the accuracy of our propeller calculations.

More delays, too little wind: Additional mechanical problems surfaced:

On November 28, while giving the motor a run indoors, we . . . discovered that one of the tubular shafts had cracked. [Two weeks to replace.] I did not get back until Friday, the 11th of December. Saturday afternoon the machine was again ready for trial, but the wind was so light, a start could not have been made from level ground with the run of only 60 feet permitted by our monorail track.

Monday, December 14th, was a beautiful day, but there was not enough wind to enable a start to be made from the level ground about camp. We

therefore decided to attempt a flight from the side of the big Kill Devil Hill.
. . . [He names his team: Daniels, Westcott, Beacham, Dough, and O'Neal,
who helped him get the machine to the hill, a quarter mile away.] We laid the
track 150 feet up the side of the hill on a nine-degree slope. With the slope
of the track, the thrust of the propellers, and the machine starting directly into
the wind, we did not anticipate any trouble in getting up flying speed on the
60-foot monorail track. But we did not feel certain the operator could keep
the machine balanced on the track.

    We tossed a coin to decide who should have the first trial. Wilbur won.
I took a position at one of the wings. . . . After a 35 to 40 foot run, it lifted
from the rail. But it was allowed to turn up too much. It climbed a few feet,
stalled, and then settled to the ground near the foot of the hill, 105 feet below.
My stopwatch showed that it had been in the air just 3½ seconds. In landing
the left wing touched first. The machine swung around, dug the skids into the
sand and broke one of them. Several other parts were also broken, but the
damage to the machine was not serious. While the test had shown nothing as
to whether the power of the motor was sufficient to keep the machine up,
since the landing was made many feet below the starting point . . . on the
whole, we were much pleased.

    Two days were consumed in making repairs. . . . When we arose on the
morning of the 17th, the puddles of water, which had been standing about the
camp since the recent rains, were covered with ice. The wind had a velocity
of 10 to 12 meters per second [22 to 27 miles per hour]. We thought it would
die down before long, and so remained indoors the early part of the morning.
But when ten o'clock arrived, and the wind was as brisk as ever, we decided
that we had better get the machine out and attempt a flight. We hung out the
signal for the men of the life saving station. . . . We realized the difficulties
of flying in so high a wind, but estimated that the added dangers in flight
would be partly compensated for by the slower speed in landing.

    They laid the track about 100 feet north of the new building, went in
to warm from the biting wind, and were joined by their "team" of Daniels,
Dough, Etheridge, Brinkley, and Moore. They measured the wind several
times just before the flight and just after. "The records from the
Government Weather Bureau at Kitty Hawk gave the velocity of the wind
between the hours of 10:30 and 12 o'clock, the time during which the four
flights were made, as averaging 27 miles at the time of the first flight and
24 miles at the time of the last." They checked their measurements against
a government standard of winds.

    [*Lessons learned: audacity and calculation*] With all the knowledge and skill
acquired in thousands of flights in the last ten years, I would hardly think
today of making my first flight on a strange machine in a twenty-seven mile
wind, even if I knew that the machine had already been flown and was safe.

After these years of experience I look with amazement upon our audacity in attempting flights with a new and untried machine under such circumstances. Yet faith in our calculations and the design of the first machine, based upon our tables of air pressures, secured by months of careful laboratory work, and confidence in our system of control developed by three years of actual experiences in balancing gliders in the air had convinced us that the machine was capable of lifting and maintaining itself in the air, and that, with a little practice, it would be safely flown.

[*Public relations*] One of the life saving men snapped the camera for us, taking a picture just as the machine had reached the end of the track and had risen to a height of about two feet. [Without that afterthought, today's museums would have little to display.]

[*Project closeout plus risk realized*] While we were standing about discussing this last flight, a sudden strong gust of wind struck the machine and began to turn it over. Everybody made a rush for it. Wilbur, who was at one end, seized it in front. Mr. Daniels and I, who were behind, tried to stop it by holding to the rear uprights. All our efforts were in vain. The machine rolled over and over. Daniels, who had retained his grip, was carried along with it, and was thrown about head over heels inside of the machine. Fortunately he was not seriously injured, though badly bruised in falling about against the motor, chain guides, etc. The ribs in the surface of the machine were broken, the motor injured and the chain guides badly bent, so that all possibility of further flights with it for that year were at an end.

Product disposition and maintenance: They shipped the aircraft back to Dayton, where years later it was caught in a flood and its box was covered with twelve feet of water. The remains were used to reconstruct the current aircraft, which was on display at Massachusetts Institute of Technology in 1916 and was returned to its hanger in 1924. It began an air tour to promote commercial aviation in 120 cities and towns. The tours introduced many people to aviation before being canceled because of the Great Depression. Henry and Edsel Ford decided to pave the runway—a first—in concrete. The flyer was placed in the science museum in London. When finally it returned to the United States, it was placed in the National Air and Space Museum in Washington, D.C.

Epilogue: The public only remembers the product, not the project: The first powered flight of human beings was truly a project. It used conceptual development, initiation, research, specialists, planning, quality standards, prior project experience with nonpowered flight, site selection, team selection, quality-based decision methods, and metrics to establish quality gates for project completion. Once in the execution phase, it used controls, measurements, problem resolution, communications, risk management, and team management. The life cycle of the "product"—the aircraft—did not end with the project. It made many more flights to promote aviation, and finally, retired, it provides history and inspiration to us today. The Wright Brothers National Monument at Kill Devil Hills, the "History of Flight" exhibits at the Chicago Museum of Science and Industry, and the display of the original refurbished craft at the National Air and Space Museum in Washington, D.C., continue to tell the story of this monumental achievement.

Darrell Collins, a seasonal ranger at the National Park Service and Wright Brothers National Memorial at Kill Devil Hills, North Carolina, acknowledges that a university (Wright State) and an air force base (Wright-Patterson) have been named for these heroes, but he still feels that the brothers have not yet had their due recognition. "Achieving the brothers' dream of the first successful powered flight has had tremendous consequences for the United States and the world," he says. "No major aeronautical research facility is named for the Wrights, and history books don't always give them their due. The fourth grade social studies text in North Carolina devotes less than a page to them," Collins notes, with chagrin. "But I'm hoping the anniversary of their flight really brings them the recognition that they deserve." Exhibits all over the world are honoring these aviators, project managers, and aeronautical engineers. Today they are considered breakthrough innovators. Douglas Gantenbein ("Celebrating Flight," *National Parks*, July–August 2003, p. 35) concludes: "True pioneers, the brothers possessed a combination of intellect, curiosity, and just plain gumption that exemplifies the best of the American Spirit."

The project customer in the first powered controlled flight was not the airline passenger. It was the scientific community and pilots. The brothers themselves, as pilots, had a life-and-death stake in a successful flight.

Risks	Possible (Guessing) Countermeasures
Loss of control (airplane flips over)	Hold wings steady—men
Loss of power/altitude (due to erroneous calculations)	Use subject matter expert (Chanute)
Uneven runway	Build monorail
Environmental conditions (No constant steady breeze)	Proper site selection/research
Equipment failure	Spare parts
Unanticipated problems with design	Testing unit parts, prototypes on gliders
Storm damages building	Repair it

DELIVERABLES' LIFE CYCLE

Projects exist to move a deliverable(s) through the deliverable's life-cycle stages. As illustrated in the following examples, different terminology is used to describe the life-cycle stages of some common products, services, or processes. The first example is for a product; the second is for an improvement in a product, process, or procedure; and the third is for a process—all of them different deliverables in similar projects. [Deliverables may be a product, service, or process.]

Life-Cycle Stage	Type of Deliverable Is a Product
Concept/Define	Definition of features/function
Design	Detail of product features
Build	Build prototype Test prototype
Start-up	Inspect, test, trial run
Delivery	Turn over to owner (End of project)
Operate/Maintain	Use product
Retire	Retire product

Life-Cycle Stage	Type of Deliverable Is a Six Sigma–Improved Process or Procedure or Product
Concept/Define	Define
Design	Measure
Build	Analyze
Start-up	Implement
Operate/Maintain	Control
Retire	Six Sigma projects are over at the end of control stage (End of project)

Life-Cycle Stage	Type of Deliverable Is a Process or Procedure
Concept/Define	Process/define inputs, outputs, equipment
Design	Process steps designed
Build	Test/train
Start-up	Start-up process
Delivery	Turn over to owner (End of project)
Operate/Maintain	Use process
Retire	Retire or replace process

Tip: When defining the scope of a project, determine whether the project's end deliverable will be a product (as in the first example on the prior page); a Six Sigma-improved process or procedure or product (as in the second example on the prior page); or a process or procedure (as in the above example).

List which of the first four or five life-cycle stages your team will accept responsibility for and are in the project's budget and time frame (concept through design, concept through start-up, concept through delivery, or retire product). Remember that operating and maintaining the deliverable is usually the responsibility of the operations group that will accept delivery and generate the intended benefits—unless the project's outcome is a service. Include the corresponding steps from the right side of the example in your project plan.

NOTES

CHAPTER 1

1. Jack R. Meredith and Samuel J. Mantel, Jr., *Project Management: A Managerial Approach*, 3rd ed. New York: Wiley, 1995, Chap. 1, p. 1. Used by permission of John Wiley & Sons, Inc.
2. Founders James R. Snyder, Eric Jenett, Susan Gallagher, Ned Engman, and J. Gordon Davis, cited in PMI's thirty-fifth-year celebration, 2004.
3. Author Helen Cooke, as PMI's member-elected chief financial officer, signed the check for new PMI property in Newtown Square, PA. PMI was growing so quickly that an adjoining lot was purchased for the Knowledge and Wisdom Center before the construction team had even completed the main building for the new headquarters.
4. Author Helen Cooke, a member of the Standards Committee, was a strong advocate for keeping the *PMBOK* common across industries. She added the word *Guide* to its title, reflecting a growing understanding that no single document could contain the common knowledge across the profession.
5. *A Guide to the Project Management Body of Knowledge* (*PMBOK Guide*). Newtown Square, PA: PMI, 1996.
6. *A Guide to the Project Management Body of Knowledge* (*PMBOK Guide*). Newtown Square, PA: PMI, 2004, Sec. 1.2, p. 4.
7. International Project Management Association (IPMA) and Australian Institute of Project Management (AIPM) efforts, as well as other professional associations listed in Appendix E at the end of the *PMBOK Guide*, 3rd ed., and the *PMI Project Management Fact Book*.
8. *A Guide to the Project Management Body of Knowledge* (*PMBOK Guide*). Newtown Square, PA: PMI, 2000, p. 6. The 2008 edition of the *PMBOK Guide* moves process information to a glossary.
9. A Standish Group survey reported a 20 percent success rate for information system/information technology (IS/IT) projects.
10. PMI membership data, 2010.
11. PMI Fellow and PMP David Pells, as an elected officer responsible for public relations, launched PMI's overt visibility in executive magazines, further fueling

the exponential growth of the Institute's membership and certification program in the early 1990s.

12. William Ibbs and Justin Reginato, *Quantifying the Value of Project Management*. Newtown Square, PA: PMI, 2002, p. 21.

13. Software Engineering Institute, Carnegie Mellon University, Pittsburgh, PA.

14. Author Helen Cooke was one of the guidance team members leading the OPM3 project; she managed synthesis of the model 1999–2002.

15. "People can work in detail on the same initiative and not recognize they are all part of the same effort because they cannot step back far enough to see the total picture. They are like people weaving different corners of the same tapestry." R. H. Cooke, lecture, Argonne National Laboratory, Argonne, IL, 1999.

16. *A Guide to the Project Management Body of Knowledge* (*PMBOK Guide*). Newtown Square, PA: PMI, 2000, p. 20.

17. An analogy is the difference between playing the tune "Chopsticks" on a piano, which is quite simple to execute, and playing it on a guitar, which is very complex. Demonstration by musician B. J. Pouttu, Laramie, Wyoming, 1970.

18. The PMI Standard for Program Management, a PMI Global Standard (Newtown Square, PA: PMI, 2006), specifies that the program manager must delegate decision authority to the project manager.

19. Compare with the management by objectives (MBO) approach of the 1970s, affecting top management, middle management, and first-line management. See George L. Morrissey, *Management by Objectives and Results*. Reading, MA: Addison-Wesley, 1970.

20. An example of a single person project is Beryl Markham's 1936 flight from England to North America (New York). As the first person to fly west across the Atlantic from England, she was doing something unique for the first time, different from her normal operations of scouting big game on the African plain. Beryl Markham, *West With the Night*, New York: North Point Press, 1942.

21. From the Chunnel Project linking England to the mainland of Europe, 1986–1991. "These largest undersea caverns in the world measure 527 feet long by 60 feet wide and 35 feet high, a distance spanned by trains moving 100 miles per hour in about 35 minutes." *PM Network*, July 1992.

22. Author Helen Cooke was one of the consultants doing preliminary visits to state planning agencies.

23. BRP Partners, First African Regional Conference, PMISA, Gauteng, South Africa, 1997.

24. The United States, Australia, South Africa, Finland, and Japan show how government and business can work together on community and world initiatives. See also Chapters 7 and 12.

25. William Ibbs and Justin Reginato, *Quantifying the Value of Project Management*. Newtown Square, PA: PMI, 2002.

26. Ibid., p. 21.

27. For survey results: Ibid., pp. 21–25.

28. BP Amoco stock dropped to nearly half its value in six weeks following the explosion on the deepwater horizon platform and the subsequent release of crude oil into the Gulf of Mexico on April 22, 2010.

CHAPTER 2

1. The de facto standard on project management, *A Guide to the Project Management Body of Knowledge*, states, "a project is a temporary endeavor undertaken to create a unique product or service." See *A Guide to the Project Management Body of Knowledge* (*PMBOK Guide*). Newtown Square, PA: PMI, 2008, Sec. 1.2, p. 5.

2. A .35-micron microchip processor would be an example of a deliverable consisting of the outputs of multiple projects. Each high-tech project creates a sophisticated technology that produces only a part of the final chip.

3. Revised estimates were that the time required to build a pyramid was 20 years, not 30, as Herodotus had estimated, according to Craig Smith, engineering consultant, WTTW, Chicago, November 7, 2003. Even these revised estimates compare with 400,000 effort-years on the project.

4. Ken Burns, producer of *The American Experience*, film on Public Television, 2003.

5. Senate hearings on the Gulf oil spill and newspaper coverage reveal a complex interaction of isolated risk management decisions affecting such areas as cement quality, testing cycles to evaluate gas pressure in the oil flow, and reliance on commonly used wellhead blowout preventers in deep water. See "BP Cites Crucial Mistake," *Wall Street Journal*, Vol. CCLV, No. 122, May 26, 2010, and "Safety and Cost Drives Clashed as CEO Hayward Remade BP," *Wall Street Journal*, Vol. CCLV, No. 151, June 30, 2010.

6. The "Process Diagram" in Appendix A shows the phases as processes that flow through the project life cycle. Subsequent pages contain second-level processes below the first diagram-supporting processes for each phase. Third-level processes are not shown but are related to the facilitating processes described in Chapter 9. The term *facilitating processes* was coined by William Duncan, PM Partners, Lexington, MA.

7. Paula Martin and Karen Tate, *Project Management Memory Jogger*. Salem, NH: GOAL/QPC, 1997, p. 57.

8. One expectation of a project manager who is a professional is not to take on the management of a project she is not confident she can deliver. Planning helps define what is achievable. After detailed planning reveals what is achievable within the time, scope, and resources allowed, and the project manager is unable to negotiate acceptable refinements, if expectations still remain unreasonable, the project manager may choose to put the discrepancy in the risk plan for management approval or step down and recommend another take her place.

9. See Helen Cooke, "Project Replanning: Points in a Process Model," PMI Seminars and Symposium, Advanced Track, Chicago, 1997. For natural replanning points, see also the arrows that point back to prior phases of the project in the process model in Appendix A. Source reference: *PMBOK Guide* 1996, pp. 11, 38.

10. U.S. Defense Secretary Donald Rumsfeld on Iraq postwar planning effort. Public Television news broadcast, 2003.

11. A project manager's performance on a complex project can be compared with an attorney's performance in court. When embarking on a complex legal challenge in court, a manager can decide to hire an experienced attorney with a credible

track record in similar cases or a general attorney. The outcome of the case often
rests on the professional knowledge, skills, and court methods of the attorney
and lessons learned from handling prior cases.

12. IIT Design Institute, Chicago, IL, 1994.

13. In his book, former White House speech writer Daniel Pink says design now
reigns even in ordinary elements of our lives such as cleaning brushes and
wastebaskets. Daniel H. Pink, *A Whole New Mind: Why Right-Brainers Will
Rule the Future.* New York, NY: Riverhead Books, 2005. p. 34.

14. Many automated software packages in the twentieth century were developed
originally for the construction industry and focused on control.

15. When the *PMBOK Guide* was developed as a standard for project professionals,
some industries issued a certificate of added qualifications to tailor the standard
to the unique needs of their industry.

CHAPTER 3

1. Tom Ingram, *Managing IT Projects for Strategic Advantage.* Sylva, NC: PMI
Communications, 1998, p. 38.

2. Corporate executives in Frank Toney's "Executive Forum Report" (draft, Capetown, South Africa, 1997) flagged "honesty."

3. William Ibbs, *Quantifying the Value of Project Management.* Newtown Square,
PA: PMI, 2002, p. 21.

4. Frank Toney, "Executive Forum Report," draft, Capetown, South Africa,
1997.

5. John P. Kotter, *Power and Influence Beyond Formal Authority.* New York: Free
Press, 1985, p. 173.

6. Ibid., p. 172.

7. Example cited in James S. Pennypacker, and Jeannette Cabanis-Brewin, eds.,
What Makes a Good Project Manager. Havertown, PA: Center for Business
Practices, 2003, p. 35.

8. Robert W. Galvin, *The Idea of Ideas.* Schaumburg, IL: Motorola University
Press, 1991, pp. 84–85.

9. Frank Toney, *The Superior Project Manager.* New York: Marcel Dekker,
2002.

10. Deborah Bigelow, "Project Management Best Practices Report," in James S.
Pennypacker and Jeannette Cabanis-Brewin, eds., *What Makes a Good Project
Manager.* Havertown, PA: Center for Business Practices, 2003.

11. Daniel H. Pink. *A Whole New Mind: Why Right-Brainers Will Rule the Future.*
New York, NY: Riverhead Books, 2006, pp. 29, 39.

12. James S. Pennypacker and Jeannette Cabanis-Brewin, eds., *What Makes a
Good Project Manager.* Havertown, PA: Center for Business Practices, 2003,
pp. 7–8.

13. Ibid., p. 8.

14. *A Guide to the Project Management Body of Knowledge (PMBOK Guide).* Newtown Square, PA: PMI, 2008.

15. J. R. Meredith and S. J. Mantel, *Project Management: A Managerial Approach.*
New York: Wiley, 1995, p. 129.

16. Ibid.

17. Deborah Bigelow, *What Makes a Good Project Manager.* Havertown, PA: Center for Business Practices, 2003, p. 9; and *PM Network*, April 2000.
18. Professor Brander Matthews of Columbia University, quoted in Tweed Roosevelt, *Theodore Roosevelt: A Brief Biography*, theodoreroosevelt.org/life/biotr.htm.
19. Viscount Lee of Fareham, English statesman, in Tweed Roosevelt, *Theodore Roosevelt: A Brief Biography*, theodoreroosevelt.org/life/biotr.htm.
20. J. Bushini, "The Panama Canal." Lawrence, MA: Small Planet Communications, 2000. smplanet.com/imperialism/joining.html.
21. As a teen, author Helen Cooke's paternal grandfather walked across the Isthmus of Panama with his brother in transit from Finland to San Francisco while her spouse's paternal grandfather was a civil engineer building the canal.
22. Author Helen Cooke, who is 100 percent Finnish, exhibits this style of leadership.
23. Author Tate exemplifies these characteristics, necessary in volatile or sensitive projects but not common to all project leaders.

CHAPTER 4
1. *A Guide to the Project Management Body of Knowledge (PMBOK Guide)*, 4th ed. Newtown Square, PA: PMI, 2008, Section 1.3.

CHAPTER 5
1. Helen Cooke, *Financial Aspects of Product Launch: Clarifying Project Value.* PM forum.com/viewpoints/index.htm. Dec. 2009.
2. *A Guide to the Project Management Body of Knowledge (PMBOK Guide)*. Newtown Square, PA: PMI, 2008, p. 118.
3. For mapping of project management processes to the process groups and knowledge areas, see Figure 3-9 in the *PMBOK Guide* (2000).

CHAPTER 6
1. Figure 6-1 shows reasons for projects in the private sector. This manufacturer is a customer of author Karen Tate.
2. This risk analysis table is for a single project. For multiple projects, risks can be grouped by type of risk—such as organizational risk or technical risk—rather than by deliverable. Then the score presents a total risk rating for each project in that risk category. The organization can gain insight into common risks by tracking types of risks across projects and implement enterprise-wide risk management strategies.
3. This woman was a project sponsor on one of Helen Cooke's projects.

CHAPTER 7
1. Developing an aluminum plant in a jungle will incur different nuances of cost from developing an oil field or gas plant in a desert, and experienced estimators may be needed. Author Cooke's father-in-law was an expert estimator in global oil field development. His father in turn was an engineer on the Panama Canal.

2. The *PMBOK Guide*, 4th edition 3.7.1 lists "Close Project or Phase" as "the process of finalizing all activities across all of the management Process Groups to formally complete the project or phase." Inputs are the project management plan, accepted deliverables, and organizational process assets. The process outputs are a final product, service, or result transition and organizational process assets updates. This is a process point for Project Integration Management, a key knowledge area of the *PMBOK Guide*.

3. Helen Cooke, "Financial Aspects of Project Launch: Clarifying Project Value," *PM World Today,* December 2009. See PM Forum Viewpoint Articles, pmforum.com/viewpoints/index.htm.

4. Author Helen Cooke worked on a project that kept its records in a storage trunk in the basement of a military arsenal. The team had complete access, and the system worked well.

5. These phases may be managed within a single project rather than in a program, as cited in the *PMBOK Guide*, 4th edition, Chapter 3. Upon exit of a design phase (of a product or service or result), which requires customer acceptance of the design document, the design document provides the product description for the *PMBOK Guide's* Planning and Executing Process Groups in one or more subsequent phases. In multiphase projects, processes are repeated within each phase until the criteria for phase completion have been satisfied (41). Project management processes ensure the effective flow of the project throughout its existence. Product-oriented processes specify and create the project's product. Product-oriented processes are typically defined by the project life cycle and vary by application area (37).

6. *A Guide to the Project Management Body of Knowledge (PMBOK Guide)*, 4th ed., Newtown Square, PA: PMI, 2008, Chapter 8, p. 189.

CHAPTER 8

1. Leadership is a whole-brain activity, according to Dr. Katherine Benziger, author of *Thriving in Mind: The Art and Science of Using Your Whole Brain*, Carbondale, IL: KBA LLC Publishing, 2003, pp. 118–120. She says, "What is distinctive about leadership is that because of the range of tasks a leader needs to be able to do themselves, as well as the range and variety of people with whom the leader must be able to connect and build trust, more than most jobs it requires someone who has developed all four modes." She continues: "There are very few people who have actually developed their natural lead, i.e., their preference and both its auxiliaries . . . even those who have developed their natural lead and its auxiliaries are weak in understanding the needs and challenges presented by their weaknesses. Thus, if the job of leadership is truly whole-brained, then the best solution is to use a team to fill that job."

2. Ned Herrmann, *Applied Creative Thinking.* Charlotte, NC: Herrmann International, 1986.

3. Daniel Goleman, *Emotional Intelligence.* New York: Bantam Books, 1997, p. 34.

4. Ibid., p. 43.

5. Beryl Markham, *West with the Night.* New York: North Point Press, 1983, pp. 285–86.

6. Consensus does not necessarily mean agreement; it means that those who may not agree nevertheless can "go along with" the group or "live with" the result.

7. Bruce W. Tuckman and Mary Ann Jensen, *Stages of Group Development*. NJ: chimaeraconsulting.com/tuckman.htm, 1977.

8. Values in Cross-Cultural Contexts, International Project Management Association, Helsinki, Finland, June 2009.

9. As organizations emerged from one of the most challenging economic environments in decades, automation was one of the healthy sectors for profitability and growth. "Radical shifts take hold in manufacturing," Marketplace Section, *Wall Street Journal*, Vol. CCLV, No. 46, February 3, 2010.

10. "Digital Nation," *Frontline*, Public Broadcasting System, February 2, 2010.

11. Ibid.

CHAPTER 9

1. The public understanding of the role of the project management professional is evolving. The *PMBOK Guide,* 3rd edition, *2004*, in Figure 4-1, p. 79 "Project Integration Management Overview," shows the inputs and outputs to processes citing the use of methodologies, information systems, and expert judgment that the project manager and key team members use to create the key project management deliverables that result from initiating the project and planning it: the project charter, scope statement, and project management plan. Figure 4-1 also shows high-level processes the project manager and team use to direct and manage project execution, monitor and control project work, perform change control, and close the project. Figure 4-2 of the 3rd edition sequences these processes with reference to preparing other elements of the plan besides the schedule, and linking with certain organizational procedures such as contract and administrative closure or contract documentation procedures at closeout (Figure 4-2, Project Integration Management Processes Flow Diagram). By 2008, these integration processes are flagged as being the result of expert judgment rather than the result of methodologies and information systems as in 2004. By 2008, information systems are applied only in 4-3 "Direct and Manage Project Execution."

2. Investigations into causes of the BP oil spill, with work subcontracted to Transocean Ltd., the rig's owner, focus on "whether better coordination between the two companies might have prevented the disaster" in the Gulf of Mexico in April 2010. "Rig's Final Hours Probed," *Wall Street Journal*, Vol. CCLVI, No. 15, July 19, 2010.

3. *PMBOK Guide*, 2004, 2008

4. Points for integration are at key transition points in the "Project Management Process Model," Appendix A, presented by Helen S. Cooke, "Project Re-Planning: Points in a Process Model," PMI 1997 Seminar/Symposium, Chicago, Advanced Track, 1997. Large and complex projects including many government projects put significant attention to development of not only requirements but also specifications for the end product during project initiation that must be met for product acceptance by the customer. Project Integration Management was added as a ninth Knowledge Area in Chapter 4 of the 1996 *PMBOK Guide*.

5. Science: "Behavioral Economics," Jerry Adler. *Newsweek*, Vol. CXLIV, No. 1, July 5, 2004.
6. See *A Guide to the Project Management Body of Knowledge* (*PMBOK Guide*). Newtown Square, PA: PMI, 2000, Section 1.2.3, p. 5.

CHAPTER 10

1. Mihaly Csikszentmihalyi, *Beyond Boredom and Anxiety*. San Francisco: Jossey-Bass, 1975.
2. Project Manager, Chunnel Project, England. *PM Network*, PMI, 1992.
3. Reprinted from David A. Garvin and Michael A. Roberto, "What You Don't Know About Making Decisions," *Harvard Business Review*, No. 108–110, reprint R0108G, Sept. 2001: Copyright © 2001 by Harvard Business School Publishing Corporation; all rights reserved.
4. Ibid.
5. Museum of Science and Industry Exhibit, Chicago, December 2003. Amelia Earhart would later be the first person to fly a helicopter across the United States.
6. Douglas Gatenbein, "Celebrating Flight," *National Parks*, July–August 2003, p. 35.
7. Ibid., p. 33.
8. Neil Armstrong, citing Tom Crouch in "Bishop's Boys" at the Air and Space Museum's *Countdown to Kitty Hawk: Celebrating a Century of Powered Flight and Half Century of EAA (Experimental Aircraft Association)*, a video produced by the EAA Aviation Center, P.O. Box 3065, Oshkosh, WI.
9. Ibid.
10. Orville Wright, "How We Made the First Flight," *Flying*, December 1913, and *The Aero Club of American Bulletin*, 1913. Entire account was reprinted in 2003 (the 100th anniversary of controlled flight) on the Federal Aviation Administration (FAA) Aviation Education website, faa.gov/education/wright/wright.htm.
11. Douglas Gatenbein, "Celebrating Flight," *National Parks*, July–August 2003, p. 32.
12. Orville Wright, "How We Made the First Flight," *Flying*, December 1913, and *The Aero Club of American Bulletin*, 1913. Website referenced in note 10.
13. Douglas Gatenbein, "Celebrating Flight," *National Parks*, July–August 2003, p. 35.

CHAPTER 11

1. *A Guide to the Project Management Body of Knowledge* (*PMBOK Guide*). Newtown Square, PA: PMI, 2000, p. 36.
2. Albert Einstein quoted in TrueVue public relations campaign poster, 2004.
3. *PMBOK Guide* 2008, section 3.6.4.
4. *PMBOK Guide* 2008, section 3.6.5.
5. Frank King, project manager of the Calgary Olympics event, in a keynote address to the PMI Seminar/Symposium, Calgary AB, Canada, 1990.
6. *PMBOK Guide* 2008, section 3.6.6.

7. Helen Cooke, "Project Replanning: Points in a Process Model," PMI Seminar/ Symposium, Chicago, IL, 1997.
8. *PMBOK Guide* 2008, section 3.6.7.
9. Discussions by author Cooke with a program manager at Nokia in Finland, November 2008.
10. Author Helen Cooke's experience at McDonald's corporate headquarters in Illinois.
11. *Combining Earned Value Management and Risk Management: A Practical Synergy.* David Hillson. Presentation, PMI Global Congress, Advanced Track PMP. Anaheim, CA, October 25, 2004.
12. *A Guide to the Project Management Body of Knowledge* (*PMBOK Guide*). Newtown Square, PA: PMI, 2008, p. 368. As detailed in item 6, preventive actions were added to the earned value section in the 2000 edition of the *PMBOK Guide*.

CHAPTER 12

1. Author Karen Tate provides examples of project-specific management tools in her handbook written with Paula Martin, *The Project Management Memory Jogger*, 2nd ed., Salem, NH: GOAL/QPC, 2010.
2. Dr. David I. Cleland, Ph.D., and Bopaya Bidanda, Ph.D., at the University of Pittsburgh, published an ambitious anthology of viewpoints from leading project management professionals around the globe on the likely state of project management in 2025. They addressed how the discipline will be used to manage the future tactical and strategic changes that will impact products, services, and organizational processes. *Project Management Circa 2025*, Cleland and Bidanda, editors. Newtown Square, PA: PMI, 2009.
3. William Ibbs and Justin Reginato, *Quantifying the Value of Project Management*, doctoral research later published by PMI. Newtown Square, PA: PMI, 2002, p. 21.
4. James S. Pennypacker, ed., *What Makes a Good Project Manager.* Havertown, PA: Center for Business Practices, 2005.
5. *A Guide to the Project Management Body of Knowledge (PMBOK Guide),* 4th edition, Newtown Square, PA: PMI 2008, 1.5, p. 14 cites OPM3 for enterprise project management process capabilities, and on page 191 lists OPM3 as a process improvement model along with Malcolm Baldridge and the information systems Capability Maturity Model Integrated (CMMI), categorizing them under the project quality management section as quality improvement initiatives. OPM3, initiated in 1996 and launched in 2003, is distinguished from the other initiatives as being a maturity model that addresses project management as distinct from operations, and the organization's ability to effectively manage all types of projects enterprise wide regardless of the product or service.
6. *OPM3 Knowledge Foundation.* Newtown Square, PA: PMI, 2003, p. xiii. The OPM3 model provides a way for organizations to understand organizational project management and to measure their maturity against a comprehensive and broad-based set of organizational project management best practices and plan for improvement. Author Helen Cooke helped PM John Schlichter gain CEO and

board support for funding OPM3 in 1996 and was project manager for synthesis of the OPM3 model 2000–2001.

7. Ibid., Section 1.3, p. 5.

8. Ibid., Section 1.2, p. 4.

9. Ibid.

10. Ibid., Section 1.3, p. 5.

11. Ibid., Section 1.2, p. 4. and *The Standard for Program Management.* Newtown Square, PA: PMI, 2006, p. 4.

12. Sarbanes-Oxley Act in the United States holds senior officials explicitly accountable for the organization's resources. Companies that leverage their PMO for this effort will have a significant advantage in maintaining accountability for those resources allocated to projects.

13. William Ibbs and Justin Reginato, *Quantifying the Value of Project Management.* Newtown Square, PA: PMI, 2002, p. 37. The authors caution that not investing in improvements or investing without regard to the contribution of those improvements to the achievement of strategic goals weaken the organization's ability to deliver results.

14. Author Helen Cooke as vice president of the Chicagoland Chapter of PMI, founded the PMI Chicagoland Executive Council as an independent organizational unit associated with the Chapter's Outreach Program. The initial "Executive Forum on the Strategic Value of Project Management" was held at the Chicago Palmer Hilton on April 14, 2005, with PMI CEO Gregory Balestrero as keynote speaker. Its goal was to support the PMI global policy to make project management viewed as indispensable to business success at the executive levels of management, to encourage executive interaction, to explore the benefits of enterprise-wide project management at higher levels of the organization, and to provide a forum for exchange at top levels of management. The first meeting pooled enterprise examples of the strategic value or project management from corporations, construction, the military, transportation, marketing, consulting, higher education, government, and metropolitan school districts. The resulting report was made available to Executive Council participants.

15. The focus on the customer is a growing trend. Dr. John W. Danford, in *Roots of Freedom*, points out that in the mercantile system the interest of the consumer is almost constantly sacrificed to that of the producer, and it seems to consider production, and not consumption, as the ultimate end and object of all industry and commerce (Adam Smith, *The Wealth of Nations*). John W. Danford, *Roots of Freedom: A Primer on Modern Liberty.* Wilmington, DE: ISI Books, 2000, p. 141.

16. Helen Cooke, *Financial Aspects of Project Launch: Clarifying Project Value*, PMFORUM Viewpoints article, pmforum.com/viewpoints/index.htm, December 2009.

17. For more detailed instruction, see Robert W. Ferguson, "A Project Risk Metric." Unpublished paper, Software Engineering Institute, Carnegie Mellon University, Pittsburgh, October 2003.

INDEX

INSTRUCTIONS FOR ACCESSING ONLINE FINAL EXAM AND CHAPTER QUIZ ANSWERS

I f you have completed your study of *The McGraw-Hill 36-Hour Course: Project Management,* you should be prepared to take the online final examination. It is a comprehensive test, consisting of 73 multiple-choice questions. You may treat this test as an "open book" exam by consulting this book and any other resources. Answers to both the online exam and the chapter-ending quizzes can be found on The McGraw-Hill 36-Hour Course Information Center landing site for each book (please see the instructions below for accessing the site).

Instructions for Accessing Online Final Exam
1. Go to www.36hourbooks.com.
2. Once you arrive on the home page, scroll down until you find The McGraw-Hill 36-Hour Course: Project Management and click the

link "Test your skills here." At this point you will be redirected to The McGraw-Hill 36-Hour Course Information Center landing site for the book.
3. Click the "Click Here to Begin" button in the center of the landing site. You will be brought to a page containing detailed instructions for taking the final exam and obtaining your Certificate of Achievement.
4. Click on "Self-Assessment Quiz" in the left-hand navigation bar to begin the exam.

Instructions for Accessing Answers to Chapter-Ending Quizzes
1. Follow Steps 1 and 2 above.
2. Click "Chapter-Ending Quiz Answers" in the left-hand navigation bar.

ABOUT THE AUTHORS

Helen S. Cooke, M.A., PMP, and Fellow of the Project Management Institute, is a 25-year veteran of project management. She has managed more than 50 projects and has worked on five continents. A keynote speaker at industry events worldwide, she teaches for DePaul University's Management Development Center in Chicago and leads a consulting practice advancing the project management maturity of organizations. Prior to cofounding OPM Mentors, she held management positions with United Airlines, McDonald's Corporation, AMS, Deloitte, and Northwestern University. She headed a PM Center of Excellence and a PMO, and was a mid-level manager in the U.S. government. Active for 23 years in the Project Management Institute, Helen was elected vice president and served on PMI's Global Board of Directors for six years. She chaired the Council of Chapter Presidents, was an elected officer of the PMI Educational Foundation, a reviewer for the *PM Journal*, and developer of the *PMBOK* and OPM3. She is a past president of the Chicagoland Chapter and founded the chapter's executive council.

Karen Tate, M.B.A., PMP, is founder and president of The Griffin Tate Group, Inc., a Cincinnati, Ohio–based project management training and consulting firm. She has worked with projects and project teams for more than 25 years and now trains and consults with corporate, nonprofit, and government organizations globally, in Asia, Europe, South America, and North America. Karen held positions with General Electric, Bechtel Corporation, and Kentucky Fried Chicken Corporation. She served six years on the Global Board of Directors of the Project Management Institute, and was designated a Fellow of the Project Management Institute for her sustained service and significant contributions to PMI and the project management community. This is PMI's highest and most prestigious award that is presented to an individual.